Islam:
The Fear and the Hope

Habib Boularès

Zed Books Ltd
London and New Jersey

hed in French
France by
s, in 1983.

ated edition
on N1 9BU, UK
and 171 First Avenue, Atlantic Highlands, New Jersey 07716, USA,
in 1990.

Copyright © Habib Boularès 1990
Translation copyright © Lewis Ware 1990

Cover designed by Andrew Corbett
Typeset by EMS Photosetters, Rochford, Essex
Printed and bound in the United Kingdom
by Billing & Sons Ltd, Worcester

British Library Cataloguing in Publication Data
Boularès, Habib

Islam.
1. Islam
I. Title. II. Islam. *English*
297

ISBN 0-86232-944-2
ISBN 0-86232-945-0 pbk

US CIP data is available from the Library of Congress

Contents

Translator's Preface

In this admirable book the former Tunisian Minister of Culture and Information, Habib Boularès, inquires into the nature of Islamism and in tracing its contemporary development demonstrates the degree to which the rise of Islamist religion has occasioned an assault on traditional Islamic moral values. Yet while it is true, the author counsels, that Islamism has shown its most radical aspect to the world, the Islamic faith which such radicalism claims to represent in its most pristine form need not inspire fear.

Boularès admonishes us that on no account are we to confuse faith with political religion. If like all great religions Islam is fundamentalist in the sense that its doctrines refer to immutable truths whose revelation has led to the founding of a great moral culture, then Islamism exposes the darker side of belief where men pervert truth in order to shape it to the cause of expediency. For Islamism is politicised truth: it thrives on the militancy of the ignorant; popular religious commentary nourishes the mindless zeal of its followers, ignites the fire of their fervour, and sets them on a collision course with secular authority against which the newly born Islamist opposes a rigid, banal moralism and a freshly traditionalised concept of the body of believers.

Thus the book is both an analysis and an appeal. In clear and unequivocal language Boularès analyses the Islamist world view and demystifies the Islamist mission; he exposes to the full light of reason the problematic Islamist concept of holy war; he warns that when Islamists exemplify their own behaviour as right and just they weaken the force of a faith that for more than a millennium has bound Muslims together in a flexible global society; he asserts vigorously that allegiance to a territorial state, a concept towards which the Islamist directs his hostility, does not necessarily contradict the Islamic requirement of transcendental loyalty to a greater religious community. The author sees the antidote to Islamism in a reconfirmation of historical Islamic values. His essay appeals to the believer's sense of continuity with the past upon whose oft forgotten humane and humanistic credo he/she is asked to construct a new spiritual order relevant for modern times and for the future. Because Islam is as capable today of integrating humankind with the universe as it was in the past, despair is condemned and hope is exalted. This constitutes the true message of the Prophet; and it is the message Habib Boularès reaffirms on every page of this volume.

For the Islamic spirit to triumph over the distortions of Islamism every Muslim must shoulder personal responsibility for his/her moral, social, economic and political renewal and regeneration. By the same token, we in the West, by virtue of the ties that attach our history inextricably to that of the East, must assist this undertaking by showing an exemplary tolerance of the dilemmas that the Muslim world is undergoing in its adjustment to the demands of modernity. Towards the rebuilding of the Abode of Peace, *Islam: The Fear and The Hope* has made an important contribution.

LBW
Montgomery, Alabama
July 1990

Introduction

The famous choreographer Maurice Béjart, a convert to Islam, was interviewed by journalists at the time when summary executions were being carried out in Iran. To a representative of French television, who asked him if he was not somewhat embarrassed to profess a religion in the name of which so much blood was being spilled, the imperturbable artist replied – and I quote from memory: 'Why? I hold to a vision of the world, to an ethic and not to the acts of men in power.' Nothing can sum up the problem better than this.

On the other hand, an orientalist of renown, who had devoted his life to making Islamic civilisation comprehensible to the European public, told me of his great disappointment: 'Do not speak to me any more of Islam. I see in Islam a daily tragedy. Each time I begin to explain to my students the human import of this religion, I give the impression of nonsense.' In his own way, he was describing the trauma lived by millions of Muslims.

In 1979, I myself reacted sharply to the claim by the new courts established in Iran that the butchery in which they engaged was Islamic justice. At that time, I wrote an article denouncing such imposture and all attempts to support it. The tendency, at that time, in many sympathetic circles in the world was to justify the excesses of the new Iranian regime by the horrors committed under the reign of the Shah. There were nevertheless many who found in this Islamic justice a reason for their unspoken hatred of Islam or for the Iranians who they confused, in general, with the Arabs. My references to the Quran and to the Muslim traditions got no reaction. When I was elected to the Tunisian National Assembly in 1981, I introduced a bill of amnesty for all political prisoners, including the Islamic militants jailed only a few months before. Those of my friends who read the bill in question were astonished by it. Was not the liberation of the admirers of an Iranian-style regime an occasion for their taking up arms again? My opponents fell, without realising it, into the same odd way of thinking as the Teheran lawyers. They judged people not according to their deeds but by virtue of their belonging to a school of thought, a class, or a system.

Today, it is true, Islam is very frightening. That cannot be denied. One can find the reasons for this in the revolting images broadcast in the last three years by the world's television networks. But must this necessarily be so? Must Islam necessarily frighten the world?

Many books have been written on the Iranian revolution, the sudden changes in the Middle East, the quarrels of the Egyptian regime with its opponents, the Afghan resistance, the insurrection of Filipino Muslims, the strife of Black Muslims in the United States . . . Why not add one more to these? Such a study would have little justification if it were simply a question of relating the facts or of analysing the tumultuous relations of Islamic movements with governments in power. It would be better justified if the study tended to cover all the Muslim countries so as to bring to light what is truly the actual situation throughout the world of Islam. An undertaking of this sort has its merits without a doubt, if only for the totality of information it puts at the disposal of the public. Such an undertaking risks, nonetheless, leaving basic questions unanswered.

So it is necessary to go beyond events with a view to the discovery of the mechanisms of thought and of action which determine in these countries the relationships between the individual and his society, between the rulers and the ruled, between dissenters and power, and what leads to progress or to disaster. These mechanisms exist and one is struck by their permanence and their capacity of resistance to cultural diversity. Moreover, when one asks oneself about the chances the Iranian example might have to spread, what is one expressing if not the vague impression that the evolution of the Muslim nations could be similar everywhere while at the same time one admits that these nations are not all identical.

This book is both a report of actual events and an essay. Islam is its subject and Islamism its province. Islamism is used in the precise sense of an action carried out by militant Muslims so that their concept of religion penetrates the state and society. It is preferable to the words *revivalism* and *fundamentalism*, which do not take into consideration all its possible contexts. Revivalists exist in Islamic countries as do fundamentalists, and one must not fail to point out what makes them different. Nevertheless, those among them who have a certain familiarity with European languages and call themselves 'Islamists' indicate by this that the objective, with few exceptions, is the same for all.

The debate they carry on is not new. The conditions under which they act are those of the present. The ideas they profess are those of the past. The profound drama that Muslim societies are undergoing, for which Islamism is a catalyst, merits a better approach than that dictated by passionate reaction. For Muslims it is a question now of the destiny of their fourteen-centuries-old faith, and for them, as well as for the rest of the world, a question of the future for close to a billion human beings. At a time when economic as well as cultural relations are taking on a global dimension, no one can be unconcerned with the future of the Muslim world, nor with the relationships it has with the international community.

To understand this, a number of important points must be made. Without attempting to do a systematic historical study one can nevertheless investigate a past, sometimes recent, sometimes remote, with a view to placing an event in its proper context or to measuring the extent of its influence.

In analysing Islamism one is struck by the ability of its actors and sometimes even of its observers to abolish time; they may quote in this context an author of the ninth century as if he were speaking today; they may make an abstraction of the moment in which he lived; they may forget that scholars of religion were in their own times sometimes the partisans of established power and sometimes its opponents. Yet the actors who appear today on the Muslim scene are themselves also caught up by the question of power in varying circumstances. They live in the present and use all the material means of Western civilisation. But they reject the socio-economic structures into which they were born and oppose to these a concept of the communal life tied to a pastoral, nomadic, agrarian and ultimately a commercial environment. They make an abstraction of what has led the Muslim world to be what it is today and reason as if they were at the dawn of Islamic history about to ask themselves how to organise the new society.

With this manipulation of history by the Islamists, the present undergoes the perverse effects of the amplification and the distortion of facts by a flow of information so rapid that it leaves little time for reflection and still less for the serene contemplation of phenomena. Thus, international public opinion shows a veritable fixation on the Ayatollah Khomeini without realizing that this Iranian patriarch in the last analysis offers only his practical success as a theme for the meditation of militants in other Muslim countries. In truth, these people have been more seduced by the ideas of the Pakistani Mawdudi or the Egyptian Sayyid al-Qutb. If tomorrow Islamism were to triumph in other regions of the world it would not be a victory for Khomeinism but rather for the theories of these two thinkers who today are known throughout the Islamic world. The most active Islamic movements claim one or the other as master or try to synthesise the ideas of both. As for the success of this activism, however relative, how can one understand its reasons without first considering the challenge that must come from the countries which are all located in what is called the Third World and which are all involved, for better or for worse, in the search for a means of rapid development?

It is surely right to say that these difficulties are not unique to Muslim countries. Why then should Islamism seem to be alone in reflecting the promises of a new spring? Some blame the impasse toward which the classical means of Western development appear to have led. Others ask themselves if there is not ultimately a fundamental incompatibility between the Islamic and Western worlds which cannot be breached no matter how much they desire it. Islamic society is indeed stirring. Its most active elements do not find an ideology for struggle except in Islam. Other doctrines mobilise militants who do not always disdain the recourse to violence. If Islamism succeeds in bringing men together, its success has reasons which ought to be recognised; and the radical aspect which it most often assumes should not mask the existence concomitantly of pacifistic, modern, reforming ideas. The problem faced by the Muslims is not simple. To the well-known difficulties of development is added the weight of tradition and the intervention of religion in everyday life. To overcome or bypass these obstacles, many formulas have been advanced or tried. Some take it for an axiom that the world of Islam is closed. Others imply that man is undergoing an unbearable process of cultural uprooting. The greatness of the struggle led by those who refuse to choose sides is precisely in their effort to realise, for more than a century, a modernisation that does not separate man from his roots and does not create a gulf between him and his fellows.

If today Islam is ready to give itself new meaning, what can this new meaning be if not to establish the greatest possible communication among men. Every true Muslim believes, in fact, that his religion addresses itself to all men and that it is valid for all time and all places. The challenge that the modern world hurls before Islam is quite simply for Islam to prove it.

1. The Sword and Destiny

The year 1979 will remain in the annals of Islam as the year of the awakening. It began well for the Islamist movements. On 16 January, Muhammad Reza Pahlavi, the Shah of Iran, left Teheran with his family. Information gathered later would intimate that he did not really believe that this was the end not only of his regime but also of one of the world's oldest monarchies. On 2 February, the Ayatollah Ruhollah Moussavi Khomeini returned to his country after sixteen years of exile. More than the departure of the Shah, it was the return of Khomeini which sealed the victory of the revolution against the imperial regime. A delirious people celebrated its deliverance and proceeded to avenge its dead, whose number during the preceding year had grown daily at each successive confrontation with armed forces reputed to be the best in the region. Nevertheless, it was an ambiguous victory. Was it a victory for Islam, that is, for the faith, that galvanised the masses in Teheran, Qum, Isfahan, and Mashad? Was it a victory for a multifaceted organisation, the only one which the Shah's police, the sinister SAVAK, could not bring to heel? Was it a victory for a man, for Khomeini, who refusing all negotiations and compromises obliged all public forces, all clandestine organisations, all elites to make a simple choice for or against the Shah? But for the time being, and not only in Iran, people celebrate their victory of a nation, hardly concerned for what might come next. With some exceptions, no one in the world felt the need to feel sorry for the Shah, nor, in the beginning, for the deaths of so many of his functionaries. The delegations which followed one after the other to Teheran were going to a party in order to present their best wishes to the new people in power. Witness the accolade given by Khomeini to Yassir Arafat, President of the Palestine Liberation Organisation. Other Arab delegations were sent to Iran from North Yemen, Algeria, Syria, Libya, and from certain Gulf states. Even the Americans thought that there were some grounds for an understanding with the new masters.

Very quickly, however, questions began to surface. Heads rolled at a dizzy pace. A so-called Islamic justice offered to the world the spectacle of unleashed barbarism. The justifications became more and more byzantine. On the outside, among the ranks of the most fervent defenders of the revolution, uneasiness was evident: was this Islam?

On 16 June 1979, Captain Yusuf Ibrahim, an instructor at the artillery school in Aleppo, the second largest city in Syria, led the attack against the entire class of student officers. What were the results of this action? Between thirty and eighty-two were killed, according to some sources. The government in Damascus immediately held the Muslim Brethren responsible for the massacre. At that time I was in Amman, in Jordan, and the local association of the Brethren assured me that their Syrian colleagues were not to blame. Several days later, the Syrian association issued a communiqué through the Jordanian Brethren placing the responsibility on the sectarian policies of President Hafiz al-Assad. One is playing here with words. Whether or not the Muslim Brethren did indeed commit this crime, the bloodletting in Aleppo can be seen as a settling of scores between the regime and its opposition in which the Islamists were more determined and better armed.

A month and a half later, it was Latakia's turn, still in Syria, to become, between 30 August and 4 September, the scene of clashes between religious factions. The results were 10 dead and numerous wounded. Following on the heels of the events in Damascus and Homs, the Latakia clash succeeded in giving militant Islamism the image of a bloodthirsty movement.

It was not until the end of 1979 that the world understood the extent of veneration that Muslims could hold for the place chosen as the next target of the revolution. On 20 November, 222 assailants, according to official statistics, invaded the Haram al-Sharif (the holy sanctuary) of the Kaaba in Mecca and proclaimed as Mahdi – that is, considered by a portion of the faithful to be the Rightly Guided One – one of their own, a certain Muhammad Ibn Abdallah al-Qahtani. The Saudi authorities reacted vigorously and evacuated the holy places. But the well-armed insurgents took as hostages those present and began to resist.

The world was shocked. Even before Islam the Kaaba and its surroundings had been considered inviolable. That, in fact, is the meaning of the word *harem*. Anybody under threat of persecution has the right to seek protection there and thus to obtain a guarantee of security. But to barricade oneself behind its walls with arms is to violate a law which Islam has perpetuated throughout the centuries. The Prophet Muhammad himself, when he conquered Mecca in 630, reminded believers that the right to use force in the Holy Sanctuary had been permitted by God on a day and at an hour of His choosing. Moreover, he counselled his followers, and in this was obeyed, not to resort to arms except when absolutely necessary. The action of the insurgents in 1979 was thus a sacrilege in the eyes of Muslims.

Was it necessary, however, to dislodge them by force of arms? The Saudi authorities hesitated several days. They tried to convince the insurgents to surrender. Shots were exchanged from the walls of the sanctuary between lookouts and the troops who were besieging them. Finally, on 25 November, five days after the start of the insurrection, a council of Muslim theologians issued a *fatwa* (juridical consultation) authorising the forces of order to assault the holy enclosure and make use of their arms to dislodge the insurgents.

Still the military hesitated. The government declared that it wanted to spare the lives of the hostages. It was later revealed that they had appealed to specialists from the French police for help. Within a few days an assault was mounted and on 4 December the affair came to an end. The casualties were heavy. One hundred and seventeen insurgents died and probably as many hostages. One hundred and twenty-seven military were killed and there were 451 wounded altogether. Five days later, sixty-three prisoners were executed after a summary trial.

The affair was even more serious since it had taken place in a country that was thought to be immune from this kind of uprising because it is known for the religious rigorousness of its state philosophy, Wahhabism. What the insurgents had been denouncing was the conduct, contrary to religious laws, of the rulers, their corruption, and the laxity of their morals. Their group was not composed only of Saudis. It has not been established exactly how many nationalities were represented among them, but among the prisoners who were executed on 9 January 1980 there were 41 Saudis, 10 Egyptians, 6 South Yemenis, 1 North Yemeni, 3 Kuwaitis, 1 Iraqi, and 1 Sudanese. Among the rebels there were, it seems, several Moroccans, and it was from Beirut that an obscure 'Islamic Revolutionary Movement of the Arabian Peninsula' had claimed, on 26 November, responsibility for organizing the seizure of the Kaaba.

This was a curious insurrection which aimed at the proclamation of a new religious truth in the person of an inspired zealot, supported by initiates from many nationalities and which, at the same time, took part in a larger, perhaps purely Saudi, peninsular political movement. This zealot – the Mahdi – was called, like the Prophet, Muhammad Ibn Abdallah, and had in turn a southern ring to his surname, al-Qahtani. Legend states, in fact, that the Arabs come from two branches: that of Adnan in the north of the peninsula and that of Qahtan in the south. Moreover, the leader of the rebels, Juhaiman al-Otaiba, was not unknown and this was not his first try at troublemaking. He belonged to a tribe known in Saudi Arabia and the rivalries of the tribes could not help but reinforce his determination.

What the world would remember of this uprising was that the country most rigorous in its public application of religious law had been exposed, as much as others, to an Islamic militancy that did not refrain from using force and did not hesitate to violate the sacred character of the Holy Places. Three times in the same year, in Iran, Syria and Arabia, opposition had been raised against different regimes in the name of Islam and observers needed no more than that to conclude that Islamism would henceforth constitute a danger and that Khomeini's revolution was about to spread to Iran's neighbours.

Instead of leading to a better understanding of this phenomenon, the succession of events only made the picture more murky. The Aleppo massacre was only a curtain raiser. All the principal cities of Syria experienced clashes between Islamists and the forces of order which ended in February 1982 in Hama. The army and the special forces laid siege to the town and after three weeks of combat and massive destruction brought the insurgents to bay. Certain Western newspapers cited the fantastic figure of 20,000 dead. True or not, this gives an idea of the size of the battle.

In June 1980 incidents occurred in Morocco, which up to that time had been spared by the religious movements. In Fez, considered by many a holy city, the forces of order came up against the initiates of a new sect led by a certain Lahsen Zitouni. The results were three dead and ten wounded.

In December of the same year in Kano, in northwestern Nigeria, the police grappled with a sect stirred up by a zealot, al-Hadj Maroua Maitatsine. The clash left no less than 4,000 dead. Two years later, in the northeast of Nigeria, in Maiduguri to be exact, the same sect was heard from again. Nearly 450 dead were counted after two days of rioting.

In February 1981, Islamic militants occupied the science faculty of Tunis University and held its dean hostage. Held responsible by the government, the leaders of the MIT – the Movement of Islamic Tendency, unofficially recognised – denied any participation in the events on the university campus but did not condemn the student action. The authorities needed no more than this to decide precipitously, in July, to arrest the principal members of all Islamic organisations. Seven hundred militants were tried and many received stiff sentences.

Neither did Algeria escape this wave of violence and, although quickly contained, incidents in Annaba and Algiers in May 1981 between Islamic activists and left-wing students very nearly degenerated into riots. But twice in 1982, again in Algiers, clashes of the same kind left on the field, in January and in November, one dead and numerous wounded.

Then came the most spectacular event of all, the assassination on 6 October 1981 of Anwar Sadat during a grand parade that had been organised in a Cairo suburb to commemorate the 1973 war with Israel. Four commandos jumped down from a truck that was part of the military parade, opened fire on the reviewing stand and proceeded to carry out what can best be described as an execution.

As did the Iranian revolt, the Cairo event awakened the most violent passions. While Arabs of all political persuasions cheered, the Western world showed its confusion. The men in power in the Arab world seemed divided between a feeling of satisfaction that this 'traitor' to the cause of unity had received his just reward, and of embarrassment, even of fear, stirred up by the membership of his executioners in an extremist religious organisation. This feeling was further reinforced by the uprising in Assiut on 8 October, where clashes between police and Islamic militants caused the death of fifty-three persons, of whom forty-four were policemen. The Egyptian government reacted with vigour and before 1981 was out, about 2,500 'fundamentalists' were put behind bars whereas 66 officers and 104 NCOs were cashiered from the army. But what other proof is required to show the strength of Islamic organisations in their infiltration of the military?

Thus, from Iran to Morocco, by way of Bahrain (where a plot was frustrated in December 1981), Arabia, Syria, Egypt, Tunisia, Algeria and Nigeria, an intransigent Islamism proclaimed itself henceforth the enemy of the regimes in power. Is this to say that we are witnessing the first precursory signs of an impending Islamic revolution? And when Islam awakens, will the world be called upon to change its organisation, its systems, and its values? Is Islam a source of dread?

On Monday, 10 November 1980, Islam began its one thousand four hundred and first year. Fourteen centuries have passed since the Seal of the Prophets, Muhammad, son of Abdallah, of the Quraish tribe, abandoned Mecca to take refuge in the city of Yathrib (some hundreds of kilometres to the north, on the road to Jerusalem and Damascus) in AD 622, almost thirteen years after he began preaching the new faith.

Muhammad called upon his followers to believe in the one God of Abraham, whom the Arabs recognise as their ancestor, of Noah, of Jacob and of Joseph, of Moses and of Aaron, of John the Baptist and of Jesus. Muhammad's social environment was not prepared for this conversion although the references to the Prophet were not altogether unknown among the Arabs. Pagans and polytheists lived together with Jews, Christians, and Hanafists; that is, those who observed the monotheistic traditions of Abraham, at best without precise rules.

Mecca, then, was not only the place where the Kaaba stood, this temple whose foundation was attributed to the biblical patriarch. It was also the centre of a flourishing commerce for more than a century. Located halfway along the trade route from Yemen to Jerusalem and at the only junction between the Red Sea and the Arabian hinterland, it became a real marketplace. The Quraish tribe which dominated the town was thus both the necessary middleman for the caravans that plied the desert and the guardian of the Holy Places. The temptation to make of the Kaaba not only the temple of the God of Abraham but also the geometric centre of Arab beliefs was hard to resist. At the moment Muhammad took up his vocation, there were more than 300 idols in stone or in wood to which pilgrims from all the tribes of the peninsula came each year, in the last month of the lunar year, to render homage. To preach monotheism was not only to dismantle a sociocultural system; it was also to threaten powerful economic interests.

Consequently, the reaction of the Quraish gradually became more and more violent as the number of converts gradually increased. In 622, the persecuted Muslim community had only one remaining alternative: leave Mecca. At the request of some converts from Yathrib, they emigrated to that city where they were later joined by the Prophet. This emigration – *hijra* in Arabic, from which the English word 'hegira' is derived – was to change the fortunes of Islam radically. The successors to the Prophet understood this well when they chose this moment for the beginning of the Muslim calendar instead of the date of the Prophet's birth.

Apart from the call to submit to the One God (the meaning of the word Islam), the new faith was enriched by a legislation which would diversify and expand over the years. In that city of Yathrib, which would later be known as Madinat al-Rasul, city of the Messenger of God, or simply Medina, the City, it was necessary to arrange for the living together of the *Muhajirun*, the Emigrants, and the *Ansar*, the Helpers. Already a faith with a universal message, Islam also provided the raison d'être for a community where blood ties were replaced by the fraternity of faith. All Muslims are brothers and equals before God whatever their social origins, their tribal affiliations, or their economic means. And, in this respect, all brothers owe each other mutual assistance. Very quickly, the need for a common legal point of reference was felt in order to supplement tribal customs, to transform them, and tq integrate them into the new way of life. To the credo, to the cosmogony, to the ethos of the message of the Meccan period was added a *shari'a*, that is, a law which was permanently developing, whereas the rituals and the practices of the cult were already established. Medina became like the cities of ancient Greece, a city-state whose leader, the Prophet Muhammad, organised its internal life and its relations with the outside and principally with the city of Mecca, where the impious continued to bait the Muslim exiles and to persecute the converts who had not had the luck to leave in time.

As Medina was located on the road leading from Mecca to Palestine, war was inevitable between the two cities. Besides, how could one preach the faith of Abraham in One God, and abandon His temple to the pagans? Did not the Muslim state run the risk of being snuffed out by a boycott that could only grow in vigour? Medina became Sparta and the war against the Meccans ended finally after nine years, in 630, with the triumphant entry of the Muslims into the Kaaba. The idols were destroyed. And yet Muhammad did not transfer the capital to Mecca, and Medina was to remain the centre of Islam for thirty years after the death of the Prophet in 632. Within forty years, during which Medina played a preeminent role, the world was to be transformed. Even when Medina had ceased to be the centre of the empire, it continued to exert a profound influence on the evolution of ideas.

In the Quran – the word of God revealed to Muhammad and which every Muslim believes to be sacred and unalterable – one classifies the verses, *ayat*, and the chapters, *surat*, according to their Meccan or Medinan origins, the latter having to do more with the law. In addition to legislation, the Islam of Medina developed the concepts of nation and community, what one calls the *umma*; of the striving to extend the faith, the famous *jihad*; and of the rights of mankind, that is, the relations with non-Muslims. Later, Medina would contribute to the birth of political ideas concerning 'the commanding of the faithful' and the sacralisation of the *Sunna*, the traditions of the Prophet and his companions. That is why for fourteen centuries the faithful have maintained a great nostalgia for this early Islam, fraternal, communal, but also pure and puritanical where the strength of belief brought forth miracles. It was not only the Islam of a profound spiritual reformation, but was also the point of departure for a great social, economic and imperial transformation.

The fascination for this first epoch of Islam is still found in the ideologists of many Islamic movements today. Is not the most intransigent of present Egyptian organisations called Takfir wa Hijra, which can be translated both as 'expiation and emigration', with an explicit reference to Muhammad's *hijra*, and as 'excommunication and flight from the society of the impious'? How could believers, among whom the force of their faith always encourages exaltation and intolerance, not feel themselves moved by prodigious power to lead a nation gone astray back to the straight path?

The Arabs were a handful of tribes. Islam united them. In certain cases they formed themselves into city–states. Their faith led them to prodigious accomplishments. All of Arabia submitted to Islam after the conquest of Mecca (the Arabs say *fath* 'opening', for conquest, as if the cities or the countries not converted had been floundering in impiety). All the Middle East was 'opened' to Islam within a few years. Fifteen years after the death of the Prophet, Arab warriors invaded Ifriqiya, the Roman *Africa* which is the threshold to Europe. Within scarcely a century, the flag of Islam was carried to the centre of France and to the foothills of the Himalayas.

Islam not only made the Arabs a conquering nation. Its universal message was also received by other peoples of vastly different cultures. In the west, the Berbers and the Nilotic peoples picked up the baton in the race to propagate the faith. In the east, it was the Persians and the Turks of the steppes who accomplished the same mission. Later, it would be the turn of the black Africans, the Mongols under Tamerlane, the Ottoman Turks, the Hindus, and the Malays. A whole history has been written which instructs the successive generations that nothing can resist the force of faith provided it is pure.

The image of the fanatical Muslim throwing himself into a war for the triumph of God with no one to oppose him does not correspond in any way to the historical story. Islam itself has suffered devastating shocks: two centuries of Crusades, the tidal wave of the Mongols of Genghis Khan and his nephew Hulagu, the *Reconquista* of Spain, the loss of Sicily and the Balkans, and finally, the modern colonisation which spared hardly any Muslim countries, to say nothing of the countries of Central Asia absorbed today into the Soviet Empire. A simple calculation shows that in the past fourteen centuries Islam has been made war upon more than it has warred on others.

On that mediaeval image, too, of a Muslim on horseback brandishing his sword in the sunlight, the collective unconscious superimposes another: that of a man, downtrodden and humiliated, or a woman hidden from view, of a resigned humanity, under the spell of what one calls *mektoub*, that is, what fate decrees. It is not simply a question here of the haughty picture painted by the colonial West. There are many Muslims who, having been humiliated by the reality of these experiences, rose in revolt against it. That is why, since the eighth century in some countries and since the fifteenth in others, the retreat from progress has not ceased to plunge Muslims into a mortal lethargy. For more than a century the search has been for a way to release the Muslim world from this state of affairs. But there has been no proposal which has gained general agreement.

Present-day disorders have engendered either enthusiasm or fright, according to individual or national conditions. Taking Islam as their point of departure, rebels and dissidents have focused attention on religion. Thus Islam has brusquely frightened many, and not only non-Muslims. Which of the two images will impose itself on the world: that of the resigned fatalist or that of the Cairo commandos who executed Sadat?

When Islam awakens . . . but which Islam? Today almost one billion Muslims live on all the continents. The most credible statistics give the number of 950 million for 1979.[1] Forty-two countries called themselves Muslim and have joined the Organisation of Islamic States.[2] Of these, twenty-two are members of the Arab League, twelve are in Africa, seven in Asia and one in Europe (Turkey.)

To these countries one must add those which for reasons of internal stability avoid all references to the religion of their populations (like Nigeria, Liberia and Ethiopia); the physically divided countries, such as Cyprus, federal states that are part of the Soviet Union or of Yugoslavia but which do not have their own international existence; and finally nonautonomous communities such as those in the Philippines, or not recognised, such as those in China. Taking into consideration Muslim emigrants in Western Europe, Canada, the United States and South America, one can state that Islam is found in the four corners of the globe. So it is not just the religion of a single people: whites, blacks and Asiatic adhere to a faith whose universal character is self-evident to them. Neither is Islam a religion of a single culture. Various linguistic communities have absorbed Islam into their cultural environment, which it has in turn profoundly influenced.

In the Muslim world, the Asiatic element (Indonesia, India and Pakistan, for example) dominates whereas the Arabs represent only fifteen percent of the total! One must be precise here because it often happens that, in the West, Arabs and Muslims are confused. Certainly, Arabness and Islam are historically and culturally synonymous, but all Arabs are not Muslims and all Muslims do not speak Arabic. The Arab area stops where Iran, Turkey, and Saharan Africa begin. Is it Arab Islam that is necessarily on the rise? Apparently not! Iran is not Arab. And the success of the Islamic revolution in that country has reminded the world that it is in the name of Islam that the Afghan resistance is fighting the Soviet occupation and the Moro insurgency the Filippino government.

The Arab countries thus are not the only ones to have been touched by this tumult. These situations arise from causes specific to one or the other country. It is necessary to search for the answers, particularly in Iranian, Afghani and Filippino circumstances, as well as in the problems of Black Muslims in the United States. That would permit posing the problem on another level, that of a common denominator which might obscure the individual characteristics. A hasty conclusion might lead one to say then that such a common denominator is possible since Islam alone brings together all these diverse peoples and so one ought to search the religion itself for the causes of the disorder.

Let us observe rather that the Muslim countries are not all affected by the movement and let us ask ourselves about the reasons for the pacifism of Yugoslav, Indian or Kenyan Muslims. Let us note, despite all appearances, that dissident movements have, in general, hardly any ties with each other. What is more, they do not profess the same doctrines and do not belong to the same branches of Islam. Shi'ism, on which we will speak further, is in the majority only in Iran. But in this country, the Islamic revolution has brought together all tendencies and has aggregated to itself lay movements, down to and including the communists. In Bahrain the Shi'ites contest the power exercised by the Sunnis. In Syria, it is the opposite. It is the well-structured Sunni organisations that have taken up arms against the power monopolised by the Alawite minority, a dissident branch of Shi'ism. In Egypt, Tunisia, Algeria, and lately in the Sudan, where Sunnism is the only doctrine to which the population adheres and where Islam is, in principle, the state religion, spiritual homogeneity has hindered neither the appearance of opposition movements nor their growth, to say nothing of Saudi Arabia where fundamental Sunni Wahhabism has found a current of opposition more puritan than itself among the insurgents of Mecca who threw themselves into a lost battle.

More than simple nuances, it is doctrinal differences that distinguish Islamist movements from one country to another and sometimes within a single country. We see this in Afghanistan, Egypt, the Sudan and Tunisia. In the latter country, where Sunnism reigns, one has no difficulty paradoxically in admiring the Shi'ite Khomeini and Sunnite Pakistani Mawdudi. Yet one is sometimes opposed to the Sunni Organisation of Muslim Brethren in Egypt and in Syria. Disturbances are, hence, not affairs of sect, of doctrine, or of Islamic schools of law. Neither are they the result of entirely new phenomena.

When the revolution triumphed in Iran, Westerners asked in the press the following two questions: will Khomeinism spread, and where? The events of 1979 seemed to justify those who were waiting to see the conflagration kindled throughout the Muslim world. They forgot that all the movements which signalled their appearance with violent acts since 1979 are old and well known.

The Muslim Brethren, of which much has been said, were founded in Egypt in 1928 and in Syria around 1945. The Ansar of the Sudan have been active since the nineteenth century and their political party, the Umma, was created in 1945. The activities of Takfir wa Hijra signalled its presence in 1971 on the banks of the Nile. And it was at the beginning of the 1970s that most Islamist movements saw the light of day in Tunisia. No doubt all these movements felt encouraged by the Iranian revolution. No doubt some of them did not hesitate to request aid from foreigners whom they considered brothers in religion. But to believe from this in a destiny for the Islamic Internationale or in a Khomeinist Comintern organised for subversion is to jump to unwarranted conclusions.

The questions one must pose are quite different. Why do Muslim societies explode or foster such explosive potential? Why do these explosions occur here today, tomorrow elsewhere, while Islam has been in existence for fourteen centuries and has known a great period of expansion as well as a long regression? Do Muslims revolt against the past or for the past, and if so, what past? Mental laziness has found its expression in the word *revivalism* which one sticks like a label on the forehead of all Islamists. Besides its origin in a Catholic tradition, the word, as I have already pointed out, covers a multitude of views but does not explain reality. Anglo-Saxons prefer the word *fundamentalism* which renders better the Arabic word *usul*, principles, yet it cannot adequately explain the differences.

The Libyan leader Qadhdhafi considers that the principles are found only in the Quran. Others add to this the tradition or *Sunna* of the Prophet; that is, his words and deeds. Others extend the meaning of this word to the first four caliphs (successors) of Islam as do generally the Sunnites, or to the deeds of the fourth caliph Ali and his successors, as do the Shi'ites. Thus one sees that to be a fundamentalist signifies nothing precise. And what of the blatantly conservative or past-oriented movements in which tradition includes the founders of the four schools of law and sometimes, for the Wahhabism of Arabia, the doctrines of its disciples? Finally, what of those who project themselves into the future, who reject the accretions accumulated during the centuries and who call for true reform?

Evidently this is a serious problem for the Muslim world. In theory, this question is a challenge to thinkers, to religious hierarchies, to the guardians of the City of God, and to national leaders and to young people, thirsty for spirituality: how to live one's faith in this century? In practice, the same problem gives rise to a difficult debate concerning the mobilisation of humankind within a religious framework with all the moral risks it implies compared to the easy advantages it provides.

This problem is of interest not only to Muslims. The world has at its disposal two images of *homo islamicus*: the warrior and the fatalist. But the Muslim of today is not concerned about choosing one or the other. What one calls the acceleration of history is nothing but an extension, on the global scale, of meaningful human activities, amplified by the speed of the transmission of information. To push forward the limits of knowledge, microscopic and cosmic, has become a universal task. The methods used, requiring a permanent mastery, have inferred an economic organisation, a methodology for the communication of knowledge and of techniques. As a consequence, society finds itself profoundly changed. Even more, it finds itself in the midst of permanent transformation under our very eyes. And this being done, society produces values.

How does the Muslim understand his place in this environment? Does he seek to fall back on traditional ideas in a continually expanding universe or does he resolve to participate in his times? Is it possible for him to take part only as someone who is acted upon or as an agent of destruction?

It is to be noted that, despite all the talk condemning the West, its material civilisation and its morality, all Muslims are its clients. The Ayatollah Khomeini returned to Teheran in a jet plane and not on horseback. Muslim hospitals are equipped with ingenious devices, products of the latest technology. Petroleum is transported in giant tankers. Certain countries make use of communication satellites and everybody fights with recently manufactured weapons. Now all these tools are the products of a certain organisation of activity, of knowledge and of research, of certain economic relationships, and of a society in which man occupies a predominant place, thanks in great measure to his struggle for definition and the respect of his rights.

On 19 September 1981 the Islamic Council, a private organisation bringing together Muslims of various backgrounds and having its seat in London, made public in Paris the text of an Islamic Charter of the Rights of Man. A French journalist asked a pertinent question at that time. Why was an Islamic charter necessary when all that was required for Muslims was to rally behind the Universal Declaration of the Rights of Man? The answer to the question has two aspects. It is necessary for Muslims to adhere to the Universal Declaration of the Rights of Man because it represents an ideal common to all men. It is also necessary to remind all Muslims what religion teaches them about respect for mankind. So it is not a question here of opposing an Islamic charter to a universal charter but of saying to those who call all their actions Islamic, whether they belong to a sect, an organisation or a religious hierachy, that when one touches on the essential, on man, on life, or on death, faith is not in contradiction with the attainments on which all humanity agrees.

Notes

1. The statistics to which we refer are those of the Institute of Islamic Studies in Jidda, Saudi Arabia. The census takes into consideration the percentage of Muslims in the population of all nations of the world, including the small communities of immigrants in non-Muslim countries.
2. The countries of the OIS are Algeria, Saudi Arabia, Bahrain, Egypt, the United Arab Emirates, Iraq, Jordan, Kuwait, Lebanon, Libya, Morocco, Mauritania, Oman, Qatar, Somalia, The Sudan, Syria, Tunisia, North Yemen, South Yemen, Palestine, Afghanistan, Bangladesh, Indonesia, Iran, Malaysia, the Maldives, Pakistan, the Cameroons, the Comoros, Gabon, Zambia, Guinea, Guinea-Bissau, Burkina Faso, Mali, Niger, Uganda, Senegal, Chad and finally Turkey. Moreover, Nigeria and the Muslims of Cyprus and those of the Philippines as well have the rank of observers. On the other hand, those of India, China, the USSR, Bulgaria and Yugoslavia are not represented. With respect to this, see the dossier published by the review *Maghreb-Machrek*, no. 98, third quarter 1980, Fondation Nationale des Sciences Politiques, Paris.

2. The Conditions of Revolution

When an oil well catches fire, the world takes notice. The understanding of phenomena that appear on the surface of societies is often obscured by the intrusion of immediate events. So it is necessary to strip the event of its superficial meaning in order to measure its importance. One can weep over the man killed by a machine-gun bullet. Will we be able to prevent others from dying if we refuse to comprehend why the Iranian Revolutionary Guard has agreed to execute him, why a parody of justice has condemned him, and why a clergy has seized power in a country with the kind of Islam that rejects the existence of all clergymen?

The events of 1979 alarmed world opinion first, because they occurred in Iran and second, because they shook Saudi Arabia. As in all cases of this sort, multiple interests were at stake. In the same vein, the Iran–Iraq conflict, which broke out in September 1980, aroused considerable interest, whereas another conflict which has been going on in the Western Sahara since 1975 elicited much less passion. There is no hypocrisy implied here. One need only read random declarations and commentaries to realise that the threat against which the countries of the Gulf were attempting to protect themselves was not of the kind that would overthrow traditional societies but rather the kind which might hinder the supply of oil to the industrialised world. It is that interest, in the most economic sense of the word, which hid from the eyes of outside observers the realities of a prodigious fermentation within Muslim societies.

We must realise that when Muslims heard the news from Iran, Egypt or Syria, their reaction was to ask themselves: what if that happened here? Or, why could that not happen here? Inasmuch as Muslims live in symbiosis with the societies to which they belong, they know that Islamic reformism is not new, that the cease-fire line has been crossed many times in Muslim societies, and that a point of rupture can be attained very quickly in certain conditions. Stability is extremely precarious in societies in the process of awakening. The starving do not have the strength to revolt and the well fed think only of rest. It is the undernourished who rise in revolt with the greatest violence since they know that they can obtain better. The expressions 'third world' and 'countries in the process of development' do not take into consideration the infinite variety of social situations. It is not by chance that the most aggressive Islamist movements spring from traditionalist sources at moments when societies are undergoing profound changes. That is because during these critical phases man is constrained to seek a coherence, an equilibrium between life as he lives it and life as he perceives it, between the realisable and the desirable; and finally, between present and future existence.

Over the years, the Ayatollah Khomeini changed neither his attitude nor his way of thinking. From his places of exile he struggled sixteen years against the Shah. He never ceased to declare that the Shah's power was illegitimate and that it must be rejected. It was not Khomeini who adapted himself to the growing opposition, but the opposition which attached itself to him, a priestly figure whose inflexibility tolerated no subtleties. A superficial history might claim that the event that sparked the final explosion was the death of the demonstrators at the end of 1977 and the beginning of 1978. Further investigation, however, would show that the Shah had been the victim, without a doubt, of his own faults and his megalomania, and also of what he aspired to create during the last ten years of his reign. From 1963 to 1973 he attempted an agrarian reform – the White Revolution – that did not bring to the peasantry the lasting improvement in their way of life that they expected to obtain. Industrial culture flourished but the production of grain and meat did not meet the general need. It was not until 1966 that the exploitation of natural gas was undertaken and in the same year oil production took a great leap forward, amplified later by a tenfold rise in prices following the global oil crisis of 1973–4. It was during the 1970s that massive industrialisation began. The economic order took precedence. The social order was ignored. And in 1971 the King of Kings invited his people and the world to be spectators at unheard of festivities organised at Persepolis to celebrate the two thousand five hundreth anniversary of the monarchy. Was it surprising that the opposition chose to mark the occasion by distancing itself from the regime? The Shah's reaction was to outlaw all organisations opposed to him and to institute, after March 1975, a single party system so as to demonstrate the stupidity of all institutional challenges to his power. The divorce had been made final.

It was at the same time that Tunisian opposition movements increased and that tensions began to characterise the relations between the unions and the government supported by the single party system. The situation in Tunisia was different from that prevailing in Iran. But the general context was the same: a society in full transformation discovers the rupture between the economic and the social order. During the sixties, Tunisia experimented with a developmental system based on the cooperativisation of production and the commercialisation of agricultural products. The effort came to both an economic and political impasse. The government chose to change the economic orientation of the country while maintaining the political status quo. Cracks in what was called 'the national unity' ensued. The seventies inaugurated the era of private capitalism; flaws in the social fabric reappeared more and more, and frustrations multiplied. Certain classes and certain regions considered themselves left to their own devices. When one begins to ask oneself about the kind of society one wishes to live in, how can one deny to believers the right to propose their own model? All present-day Islamic movements in Tunisia use the 1970s as a point of reference for the period during which social as well as political tension began to be felt.

In this context one often thinks of the Muslim Brethren. Their organisation is not recent. It was in 1928 that the association was founded in Egypt by a young teacher, Hassan al-Banna (1906–49) in Ismailiyya. It was expanded considerably in 1936 with the intense struggle against the British occupiers. It became a national organisation with headquarters in Cairo and developed a network of cells in other Arab countries. Although a cultural association in the beginning, it took on a political face very quickly and militated for Arab unity and pan-Islamism. It aimed at reinstating a central belief of the faithful in a universal caliphate which Mustafa Kemal Ataturk, the father of modern Turkey, had outlawed in 1924.

The Brethren continued to develop during the Second World War, that period of historical hesitation which led many to believe that armed force could make anything possible. Egypt had served as a battlefield, and after the war many Egyptians worried about their fate. After 1946 the affair of Palestine would offer militant organisations the opportunity to make their vision of the Arab future clear. The Muslim Brethren could not avoid taking a part in that enterprise. Their bitterness was great when the Arabs suffered defeat in the first war with Israel in 1948. When the Egyptian Prime Minister, Nuqrashi Pasha, was assassinated, the responsibility was laid at the feet of the Muslim Brethren. And in the same year the Egyptian Secret Service carried out the murder of the imam and founder of the movement, al-Banna. His successor, al-Hudhaibi, brought the organisation to a new stage in its evolution and compelled it to reexamine its ideas.

The history of the Muslim Brethren continued, nonetheless, to be marked by successive phases of marriage and divorce with state power: an understanding with the 'free officers' led by Nasser in 1952; in 1954, an attempt to assassinate Nasser in Alexandria (he was accused of usurping power for his own profit and of putting Egypt on the socialist and nationalist path); repression and outlawing of the movement; creation of Syrian and Jordanian branches where Egyptian émigrés played an important role: dissolution of the Syrian association when Syria united with Egypt between 1958 and 1961 and Nasser decapitated the organisation by hanging its third leader, Sayyid al-Qutb, a prolific thinker and writer but a mediocre politician.

Since then, although the organisation continued to exist and to publish at the whim of the authorities its weekly *al-Dawa* (The Call), many other Islamic militants also began to think about the modes of action and the models of society they could propose to the people. And they were not alone, for in Egypt, as in all Muslim countries, power mixes with religion. Apart from the permanent control exercised on the prestigious mosque–university of al-Azhar, the most celebrated in the Islamic world – Anwar Sadat, who since his youth had associated with the Muslim Brethren, wanted to go one better. He wanted to direct the Islamist movement to his own advantage. In May 1971, after having eliminated the pro-Soviet group led by Nasser's former lieutenant, Ali Sabri, he created a Union of Religious Associations consisting of no less than 1,000 Islamic 'committees' to fight against, as he put it, the pernicious influence of 'atheistic Marxism'. The result was to give cause to anyone with Islamist notions.

Thus, Islamism entered a period of expansion which was to last for two and a-half years. After the October War of 1973, Sadat's acceptance of negotiations with Israel, through the intermediary Henry Kissinger, the American Secretary of State, so irritated his ally Qadhdhafi that the latter put an end to his honeymoon with Egypt. Qadhdhafi sought the aid of Egyptian Islamic militants or, to be more precise, the Islamists divided into pro-Sadat and pro-Qadhdhafi factions. One group remained faithful to the original association organised around Shaykh Umar Talamsani and the newspaper, *al-Dawa*. Another group took for its leader Said Ramadhan, who had for a time taken refuge in Saudi Arabia. These two men supported Sadat, and the latter succeeded even in having deputies elected to the parliament. A third faction fell back on cultural activities and grouped around the newspaper *al-Sharia* (The Law) but a fourth group, called derisively *al-Kaffaratiyya* (the Ex-communicators), went into hiding and resorted to terrorism.

It was this group that caught the public's attention. In 1971, several months after the death of Nasser, certain of its militants, not knowing what the future held, created Takfir wa Hijra. Both a political and religious organisation, the movement owed its first impetus to an engineer, Shukri Ahmad Mustafa. The members led a communal life, married among themselves according to traditions unsanctioned by the state, retired to the desert to pray and purify their souls, and indulged themselves in an indiscreet analysis of Egyptian society which merited, according to them, destruction because of its corruption and moral laxity. It mattered little whether it was a clandestine sect or a subversive movement; the government could not tolerate the underground activities of the Takfir wa Hijra. Numerous crimes were attributed to it, although the attack on the School of Military Engineering in Cairo, in April 1974, was the work of a certain 'Islamic Liberation Party' financed, it was said, by Colonel Qadhdhafi. In 1976, the police believed that they had dismantled the entire organisation whose membership they estimated at 2,000. But on 3 July 1977 the group surfaced again, kidnapping and then assassinating a 68-year-old cleric Shaykh Muhammad Hassan Zahabi, former minister of Waqf.[1] Five days later the founder of the sect was arrested along with 350 suspects including a number of military officers and NCOs. When the old man's murderer was finally caught, it turned out that he, Ahmad Tariq, was a former police officer. Obviously the Islamist movements did not recruit their members uniquely from among youth or the students.

It was not by chance that these events took place in 1977. That year was marked by disturbances in Cairo on 18 and 19 January which in August were to intensify the debate over the application of Islamic law and end in interconfessional riots. When one recalls that this was the year in which Sadat went to Jerusalem, one understands better the context in which Takfir wa Hijra was acting.

Another group, called Jihad, of which 300 members were brought to trial in

December 1982, had been noticed as early as 6 January 1980 when it attacked two Coptic churches in Alexandria. And when one counts the Islamic Vanguard, the Party of God, the Muslim Brethren who remained faithful to the teachings of al-Qutb after his death in 1966, and al-Jamaat al-Islamiyya of Hilmi al-Gazzar, one has given more or less the complete list of Islamist organisations. At the risk of repetition, it must be recalled that the assassination of President Sadat on 6 October 1981 did not come about out of the blue. The break with all the Islamists was definitely consummated at the time of his trip to Jerusalem in November 1977. The break was reinforced the following year by the Camp David Accords, and then, in 1979, by their logical conclusion in the peace treaty with Israel. And so Sadat lit the fuse when in September 1981 he arrested more than 1,500 Islamic militants including Umar Talamsani, alienated the Azhar University, and called down upon his head the anathema of its rector for having inferred that Shaykh Talamsani, who was trained there, was a dog, the supreme insult in Egypt. 'The Azhar' said the rector, 'trains scholars, not dogs.'

Even in Syria and surrounding countries, the Islamist movements have a long history. From 1940 Islamist activity in Palestine, Jordan, Lebanon, and Syria was evidenced. As in Egypt, it was the period of the struggle for Syrian independence; and, like what was happening along the banks of the Nile, conflict was perceived as an essential transitional phase. But, more than in Egypt, the vast majority of Syrians, who had never accepted the cutting up of historic Greater Syria into pieces after the First World War, were moved by the themes of Arab unity. At the time of the first Palestinian war of 1948, the Muslim Brethren also, united since the end of the First World War under the leadership of Mustafa al-Sibai, joined the 'Army of Salvation' (Jaysh al-Inqadh). The bitterness of the defeat led them to support the coup d'état of 1949 which overthrew the civilian regime and inaugurated a series of insurrections in Damascus. In 1954 they were represented in parliament, but not long afterwards they suffered a setback when the Egyptian–Syrian union of 1958–61 was proclaimed and Nasser forbade their activities. The collapse of that union did not benefit them as much as one might have expected, first, because it marked, despite everything, the disintegration of the unionist idea, and second, because it allowed the rise in Syria of the Baath party, which was socialist and secular. The leader of the Brethren, who succeeded al-Sibai in hiding, was exiled in 1964 after the outlawing of the movement.

The organisation splintered. Groups and subgroups were born: the Muhammad Youth in Damascus; the Phalange of Muhammad in Hama; the Mujahidin, etc. The struggle against the government knew no respite. Clashes occurred in Hama in April 1964; again in Hama and in Damascus in February 1965. The repression was brutal. Clandestine action was stepped up and in 1973 real riots broke out which threatened the existence of the Damascus regime. The leader of one of the most active branches, Marwan Hadid, died in prison in 1974. Individual acts of violence followed in a regular succession. From 1976 onwards, assassination became commonplace and culminated on June 1979 in Aleppo with the senseless massacre of an entire class of future military officers.

The instigators of these troubles belonged to groups of Muslim Brethren who probably no longer had any connection with the parent organisation. But how could the parent organisation avoid paying the price for these actions?

In 1980 Issam al-Attar passed the leadership to three men: Said Hawa, Adnan Saadeddine, and Muhammad Bayanuni, who were all three close to the Egyptian Brethren. The movement, nevertheless, did not reunite. The leadership of Hadid's branch, which called itself the Vanguard of the Muslim Brethren, fell to Adnan Oqla who maintained the radical orientation of his immediate predecessors, Abd al-Sattar Zaim, who died in 1979, and Hisham Jumbaz, who died in 1980.

Despite everything, it seems that Bayanuni succeeded in bringing together the factions temporarily on the occasion of the massive uprising in Hama in February 1982. The manifesto that carried his signature on 10 February was published in the name of the Syrian Islamic Front which seemed to group together the Mujahidin (Strugglers) of the Islamic Revolution, the Vanguard, the Phalange of Muhammad, and perhaps even the Islamic Revolutionary Movement of Aleppo.[2]

One can see that in Iran, Tunisia, Egypt, Syria, and Arabia all these movements were political. The officials of these states were not deceived. In Syria, for example, President Hafiz al-Assad called a meeting of the National Front on 26 September 1979 which was composed of the diverse political parties that underpinned his regime. In a well-structured speech he attempted to define the political and social nature of the troubles afflicting the country.

These problems were undeniably political. But were they first political and then religious? One might object that it was in the interests of the official leadership to portray the Islamist movements as political parties that used religion to exploit the credulity and the sensitivity of the masses. A reading of the Islamic manifestos left no doubt on this score. In Syria the words that appeared most often in the manifestos were repression, oppression, tyranny, despotism and terrorist state. In Egypt one read corruption, misery, alliance with Israel and despotism. Before the court that tried him in December 1981, the leader of the group that killed Sadat exclaimed, 'I killed the Pharaoh.' This epithet was evocative and ambiguous. In the Quran, Pharaoh indeed incarnated both religious imposture and despotism. In Iran it was illegitimacy and dictatorship that were first denounced. In Afghanistan both Marxism and the Soviet occupation were the targets of the rebellion. In Bahrain the opposition between Shi'ites and Sunnites was not the only antagonism encouraged by Iran. The opposition drew its virulence from more profound social antagonisms. Traditionally peasants and fishermen, the Shi'ites had emigrated more than others into the towns where they represented a proletariat so deprived that an American specialist did not hesitate to evoke the Irish predicament when he wrote: 'The Shi'ite–Sunnite dichotomy is transforming Bahrain into another Belfast!'[3]

The question whether these movements are primarily political or religious is really secondary. It is a fact that wherever these movements grow, society in its evolution shows signs of disarray and imbalance. It is also a fact that wherever these movements become radical and cross the line between non-violence and armed action, the regime in place has already demonstrated political intolerance and police brutality. Up until now one has been discussing those countries in which Islamist movements have been most prone to violence. But one can also point to the opposite in Jordan where the Muslim Brethren are men of position without, at the same time, giving umbrage to King Hussein. One can also point to Senegal where nothing of importance can be accomplished politically without the agreement of the Tijaniyya and Muridiyya brotherhoods. Moreover, Senegal is one of those Muslim countries where the brotherhoods, called in Arabic *turuq* – that is, paths to the understanding of God – still exist and play a role that is at once political, economic and, naturally, religious. Forgotten was the tumultuous period in the middle of the nineteenth century which saw the birth of al-Hadj Umar's Tijaniyya, under conditions which make one think of present-day Iran. Today like its cousin, the Muridiyya, it has become a hierarchical organisation of many branches, each one consisting, according to its leaders, of nearly one million members.[4]

The common denominator of all these warring Islamist movements is that they convey the idea of revolution. From the examples given, a theorem may be deduced: all situations of social crisis in Muslim countries are accompanied by religious movements of seditious character. A country shakes off its lethargy, often secular, and once the process of industrialisation, agricultural modernisation, capitalist or socialist fiscal accumulation, and urbanisation begins, the period of breakdown follows. If only to speed the process up, the leadership will feel more and more inclined to act despotically, deaf to the rumours in the city, blind to the movement of the sediment that is dredged from its bed and carried along by the current. The more they treat people harshly, the more the revolution swells to the point of explosion. The fate of landless peasants and the inhabitants of Brazilian favelas is to be pitied. Yet it is not clear what in Egypt or in Iran, to take only two of the most prominent examples, leads inexorably to a similar situation. In Brazil the Church defends the oppressed and the downtrodden. Why, in Muslim countries, does not what passes for a church do the same?

Here we are at the heart of a crucial question. Why seek refuge in religion? An uprising can be launched and even spark a revolution in the name of political, social, and humanitarian ideals! If one can understand that the founders of such movements, by personal conviction or by calculation, have recourse – and this is what we accuse them of – to religion in order to assemble their troops, one understands less well why the faithful respond to their call.

That the Muslim community in the Philippines considers itself bullied and revolts against central power, all the while relying on a common social base for the solidarity that binds together its members, seems completely natural. Apart from political considerations, the Irish are classified as either Catholic or Protestant. The Afghan case is still clearer. In a country which has remained inward looking for so long and where the structures of a mountain people are maintained intact, the means of recourse against the brutal incursion of the foreigner can only be traditional. It is equally logical that, in the Pakistan born of a rupture with the Indian community in the name of religion, Islam is the keystone of the state and that nationalism is identified with faith. And yet how can one explain the success of Islamist activism in Tunisia, Algeria, or in Egypt, in these homogeneous and open nations where a modernist social and political tradition has developed?

Spirituality is exercising a strong attraction on man at the end of the twentieth century and the Muslim world has not escaped its magnetism. One has only to make an inventory of the sects and the new 'religions' that have sprung up in order to state that man today is in search of safe anchorage. The time of Marxist or capitalist truths is over. Economism has endured a long while under the assaults of sociology and anthropology. Yet materialism can no longer explain everything. Social science theories have brought about a spectacular return to the idea of man. And this general tendency has been reinforced by the conversion of the industrialised countries which have abandoned the notion of national liberation or class struggle to concentrate henceforth on the emancipation of the individual. An abstraction concocted from his citizenship, his culture, and his colour, man has become a value in himself. The counterpart of this evolution is the individual who, left to his own devices, has found himself caught up in the tempest that has overtaken him. He wants to fly on his own wings and to pull free of earth's gravity but on the condition that the return to earth is guaranteed – a film such as *Space Odyssey* well illustrates this psychological drama. Man finds himself in the situation of a sailor who imagines he cannot live without the sea, provided that there exists somewhere a home port.

The sudden infatuation for religion is surely due, in this context, to a crisis of values provoked by the technological advances we are presently witnessing. The progress of nuclear physics, the discoveries of molecular biology, voyages in space, and the invasion of our lives by the media have created new conditions of existence and have assigned man an obsolete place with respect to matter. All value systems correspond to a technological state. Values have always been tied to concrete, material realities. When suddenly the ground slips from under his feet the human being vacillates. Curiously we have heard this explanation on many occasions in Tunisia from the mouths of university students, believers, and militant Marxists.

A Syrian journalist who was writing a doctoral thesis on the place of women in the Quran deplored the fate of her sisters in the Gulf nations. Broaching the question of the evolution of human intelligence, she assured us during a discussion in Paris that a prince whom she had interviewed not long before did not believe that man had even set foot on the moon. Not that he lacked information, it was just that he refused quite simply to believe it. Show this man that the feat had been accomplished and you shake his universe! And yet he still rules one of the oil rich principalities and has the ear of world leaders. What, then, can be said for the illiterate masses and the traditionalists of the various schools?

Let us be careful, however, not to fall into the trap of associating religion and ignorance. Pakistani physicist Muhammad Abd al-Salam, who received the Nobel Prize for Physics in 1979, did not hesitate to write in the *UNESCO Newsletter* of August/September 1981:

> I am personally involved, as a man of science, in the search for unity in the fundamental forces of nature, beyond their apparent disparity. That the basic unity and symmetry of nature must ultimately be uncovered, this is what we believe as physicists, *it is what I believe as a Muslim*.

> And in this respect it is worthwhile noting verses three and four of chapter 67 of the Quran entitled 'Dominion'.

> He who created the seven heavens one above the other: no want of proportion wilt thou see in the creation of God most gracious. So turn thy vision again. Seest thou any flaw? Again turn thy vision a second time: Thy vision will come back to thee dull and discomfited, in a state worn out.

> Such is the faith of all physicists, the faith that inspires and sustains us. The more our research is able to penetrate the secrets of the universe, the greater our marvelling, the greater our astonishment.

Abd al-Salam knew how to reconcile science with faith. The prince mentioned above did not have this pleasure. But many people other than the Pakistani Nobel laureate have devoted their energies to this question and not without mistakes. At any rate, it would be wrong to believe that the instigators of Islamist movements recruit their partisans from the illiterate masses alone. It has already been noted that the founder of the Egyptian Takfir wa Hijra was an engineer. In Tunisia, the sources of Islamism are found in the engineering schools, the faculties of medicine and science of the national university. The link between scientific progress and the return to spiritual values is not to be doubted. Even if, by virtue of their diversity and the difference in their national situations the totality of Islamist movements cannot be reduced to a civilisational phenomenon, it would nevertheless be true that the recourse to religion in order to substitute, in a revolt against the holders of state power, one model for another may be explained in part by the existential need to find stability in a troubled world. This need becomes all the more pressing as the old forms of life collapse and the failure of solutions hastily put into practice seems obvious. This failure is fourfold.

● Failure, first, to educate men. Inspired by the desire to catch up with the West, educational programs did not take into account the gap that existed for nearly eight centuries between the Islamic world and the countries that fostered scientific and technological progress. Either these programs ignored the gap and contented themselves with addressing young Muslims as if they were Americans or Germans, or else they compensated for this long decline by exalting the past as if the Golden Age of Islam had stopped with the coming of European colonisation. In both cases the result was a kind of schizophrenia. An Islamist university student summed it up well when he declared in the course of an interview: 'We have found our independence but not our identity.'

●   Failure next of the modes of development which succeeded nowhere in assuring full employment, nor in substantially reducing inequalities, whether they were social, regional, or between countries. The impasses that the capitalist or socialist orientations brought about were perhaps different but they made equally suspect all the models engendered, especially by the evolution of the European continent. It was not at all surprising in this regard to observe the proliferation of books, seminars, and congresses dealing with Islam, the economy, and society. The research that numerous politicians and university teachers insisted on carrying out on 'Islamic socialism' was born of this preoccupation.

●   Failure besides of the political system that claimed to have patched up the cracking social structures with a semblance of democracy, or that justified under the rubric of underdevelopment the monopolisation of power by one man, one oligarchy, one clan or one military junta.

●   Finally, a social failure, to the extent that the traditional relationships of family and tribal solidarity disappeared, victims of economic and urban constraints, without any new compensatory relationships being created in their place.

These failures, one suspects, are relative. The picture is not dark everywhere. It is necessary only for individuals or for groups to perceive these failures as a serious disease in order to justify the quest for a replacement model. One does not have to be a university graduate to feel involved in this quest. The need for roots is felt, however confusingly, by people belonging to all social classes. The theme of *asala*, which is translated generally as 'authenticity', has been inscribed in every program of every government and of every party in Islamic lands. Even the communist parties allow themselves to flow with the current sometimes, so great is the pressure to align with others and with one's own culture.

So, the return to Islam appears to be a panacea. Later in this book the question will be taken up of what those who devote themselves to the quest for a new model for existence believe they have found or ought to find in the Muslim faith. For the moment, suffice it to say that we are the witnesses to a resurgence of religiosity. The mosques are full and on certain days overflow with the faithful. Mosques are springing up everywhere. Private prayer rooms are making their appearance in factories and office buildings. In many countries students demand that lessons stop at the hours of prayer. Every year the number of pilgrims to Mecca increases.

This historical movement is not unique to Islam. At other times many people have known similar crises. Thinking globally, the English historian Arnold Toynbee said in the beginning of the fifth chapter of his monumental *Study of History*:

I have discovered that the process of disintegration apparently follows a common model in most cases. The masses distance themselves from their leaders who then try to hold on to their position with the use of force as a substitute for the power of attraction they have lost ... I have also discovered a psychological schism in the hearts of those born at this unfortunate time. Discordant psychic tendencies, which almost always exist in a latent state in human nature, are given free rein. Men lose their sense of direction, and rush forward into culs-de-sac in the hope of escape. Great souls withdraw from life; even greater souls strive to transform life into something higher than the simple life we know on earth and thus sow the seeds of new spiritual progress.[5]

This resurgence of religiosity has a double meaning which corresponds to a division of the faithful into two categories. The majority of those who are attending Friday prayer again are in fact people who have rediscovered faith and seek refuge in it, or seek that peace of mind to which the distortions of the century have driven them. This return to the mosque is the concrete manifestation of fundamental questions to which the Muslim of the end of the twentieth century has not always found an answer. Faith has always constituted the refuge of the hopeless everywhere regardless of their religion. The religious factor ought never to be eliminated from social analyses. In every man there exists what the mystics call the flicker of divine truth which gains in intensity under fixed conditions. In other words, one can say that before death, before a grave threat, or quite simply before the unknown, man instinctively seeks refuge in myth, in superstition, or, better yet, in faith.

The second meaning is more political. The faithful in question here are never less believing than those of the other category, but a certain undeniable political calculation plays a role in their behaviour; that is, that the regimes that take an unyieldingly despotic position permit dissidents no institutional outlet for expression. A repressive and unresponsive political system opens the way for a revolt of the believers.

It has been noted above that Iran, despite all its vicissitudes, had for a long time maintained a certain plural political, if not actually democratic, life and that, in 1975, it definitely closed all avenues of political expression in order to install a single-party system. This signified to the population that it could no longer expect from the regime anything that resembled the normal functioning of institutions. The people were condemned either to submit or to rebel; and, in the latter case, they took the path of illegality.

Likewise, it has already been stated that at the same time Tunisia was experiencing a proliferation of religious movements. But there the point of departure was different. The country had already been placed under the official tutelage of a single party in 1963. From one internal crisis to another, the 1970s saw the development of dissent and of repression. Little by little it became evident in the eyes of all of the opponents that there were only two paths open for political activity: that of the unions and that of the mosque. Moreover, these two solutions did not seem to be divergent on the surface but could even blend, if not mix completely one with the other, in certain regions or with respect to certain problems.

The common factor in all Muslim countries, as elsewhere in countries of different religious persuasions and a high proportion of believers (the Christians of Poland, for example), is that the political system does not dare attack religious practices. One can regulate the opening and care of mosques or increase their number so as to disperse the believers, but there are necessarily moments when places of worship are open and become the focal points for unauthorised meetings. Little by little the network of mosques becomes a network of resistance and the movements grows.

In Tunisia, after the bloody clashes between the armed forces and the workers which, on 26 January 1978, caused so many deaths, a communist said with bitterness:

> What can we do? If we meet in groups of more than 10, if we distribute pamphlets, we are liable to heavy prison sentences. The Islamists, on the other hand, have the mosques at their disposal as locales and the *minbars*, the pulpits, as places from which to harangue the crowds without it costing them a penny since religious buildings are maintained by the state. How can you expect Islamic activism not to flourish?

The same phenomenon took place in Egypt, in Syria, and in Turkey. It is happening on a large scale today in Algeria. The more one bolts the doors of legal dissent, institutional and organised, the more the religious road, which has obligatorily remained open, appears as the only direction to take.

Yet Islamist activism is still small, even if its violent outbreaks often shake worm-eaten systems. Once again, this activism is political in its immediate motivation and in the tension that characterises it. Now it is not because people feel the existential need to find their roots that they discover in themselves the heart of a guerrilla. In 1975, in Tunis, on the occasion of the night of 27 Ramadan (the Night of Destiny celebrated throughout the Muslim world), a young university student, Hind Chelbi, was entrusted with the traditional address before the President of the Republic, Habib Bourguiba. It was the first time that a woman undertook this role. Her talk caused a sensation. Before the president, who struggled for women's rights and did everything possible so that women might abandon the veil, she wore a costume similar to what people throughout the world call the chador, a long opaque veil covering the head and neck and falling straight to the ground from the shoulders. This gesture rapidly took on symbolic value, and very soon one saw this costume on the streets of the capital. Nonetheless, Hind Chelbi refused all offers of membership in Islamist organisations that were immediately proffered.

One should not forget, however, that the focus of attention on the Islamic phenomenon has left in the shadows other manifestations of rebellion common to countries that have known serious tensions. On the political scene Islamism is not alone. The violence that has exploded in the Muslim world – which is an integral part of the Third World and suffering from all its woes – is the bitter fruit of underdevelopment, of dictatorship, and of depersonalisation. The ideologies that have rooted there nourished those fruits and ultimately outstripped them, and, far from being limited to Islamism, find their source in a very large spectrum of social and cultural ideas.

In a situation of tension, where multiple elements compete to ripen the fruit of revolt, unresponsive systems invite a show of force. The result is either the military *pronunciamiento* or the popular uprising.

Certain regimes, careful to conciliate the religious sentiments of the popular masses, have at least once encouraged Islamism to play dirty tricks on the Marxists, the latter having been up to this point the only effective recourse for the masses. Egypt attempted to do just this when in 1971 President Sadat made the decision to create 1,000 religious committees. Tunisia, which between 1968 and 1976 had reserved its jails for leftists, tried it too. As for Qadhdhafi, he took charge of Muslim reformism in his own country. All the apprentice sorcerers ended up by finding the mosques (or what the mosques symbolise) closed to them. Evidently Machiavelli has never got along with God.

Notes

1. *Waqf*, plural *awqaf*, is property held in trust. In Muslim tradition it refers to gifts of land made by landowners to religious or charitable institutions. Also called *hubus* or *habus*, plural *ahbas*.
2. See the articles of Elizabeth Picard in *Maghreb-Machrek*, Fondation Nationale des Sciences Politiques, Paris, and, in particular, no. 87 first quarter 1980.
3. See John Duke Anthony, 'Arab States of the Lower Gulf,' quoted in *Maghreb-Machrek*, Paris, 1977, no. 77.
4. On African religious organisations, consult Vincent Monteil, *L'Islam noir*, third edn (Paris: Editions du Seuil, 1980).
5. See Arnold Toynbee, *l'Histoire*, French translation (Paris-Brussels: Editions Elsever-Sequoia, 1975), p.303.

3. The Fear of Islamism

The intervention of religion in the realm of politics generally annoys those who call themselves rationalists. They do not hesitate on occasion to make that known, forgetting most often that Israel is founded also on its religion. Let us look for a moment at the sects and other religious parties that claim the right to govern the life of Jews living in Palestine. The fundamental justification of the creation of a state open to the Jews of the world in a country that was not empty has its referent in the Mosaic Law and in Scripture. Only an interpretation of the Bible permits the Israelis to claim, whether they are practising Jews or not, that this land has been promised by God to the Chosen People of Jacob's stock. If the Jews had lived there in great numbers continuously from time immemorial, the recourse to tradition might have served as a justification. But to increase from some tens of thousands at the beginning of the century to several million citizens thanks to a systematic policy of immigration and of the expulsion of Palestinians who themselves had never left the region was one of the most stupefying acts of the twentieth century. And it was the West, champion of the separation of Church and State, cradle of secularism, that helped in the creation of this state founded on the idea of a return to the Promised Land. The intrusion of religion into political decisionmaking did not bother the European socialists, nor the American technocrats. Neither did it bother the atheists of Moscow who were the first to recognise the state of Israel.

Consequently, the Arabs have the right to say that the Crusades are not over. Was it not, at least outwardly, in order to free the Holy Sepulchre from the domination of the Muslims that for two centuries European armies followed one after the other on the battlefields of the Middle East? The argument, if not the objective, was religious. It is the same in the case of Israel.

In Northern Ireland, the civil war that has been going on for decades opposes Catholics and Protestants. In the West one closes one's eyes to this fact, pretending to see there only a conflict between two classes, the dominant and the dominated. And yet this domination is based on religious affiliation, and the Irishman who decides to choose sides does so acording to his faith and not his socio-economic ideology. By the same token, the whole world welcomed with great deference the support given by the Catholic Church to the struggle of Polish trade unionists to gain political autonomy and to recast the structures of power in their country.

And so why, when Islam makes its appearance on the political scene, does it provoke such shock, such amazement, and such open disapproval in the world? Religion is present everywhere. Secular France celebrates Catholic feast days as national holidays for its Christian, Jewish, and Muslim citizens. The Queen of England is head of the Anglican Church, to say nothing of the direct influence that the Pope exercises on daily political life in Italy and the more or less occult role of the *Opus Dei* in Spain. Yet one denigrates the title of Commander of the Faithful that the King of Morocco carries. One is surprised that in Tunisia Islam is constitutionally the state religion. One takes as a sign of his backwardness the aim of the Libyan Qadhdhafi to associate the reformulation of power with the reformulation of religion. One cannot understand why revolutionary Algeria is concerned with the problem of reconciling Islam and socialism. One is scandalised by the reference in the international press to Islam that Sadat introduced into the legislation of his country. And one considers, of course, as a manifest regression, even an anachronism, the application in Pakistan, Saudi Arabia, and Mauritania of the ancient penalties of Muslim law.

One can therefore understand the surprise and the condemnation of many whenever the question is broached as to the desired degree of the applicability of Islamic law. Many Muslims are not in favour of summary execution or of stoning. But what annoys them more, whatever the manner by means of which they conceive their adherence to the faith of their ancestors, is the systematic rejection of any place at all for Islam in the life of their countries.

Why does the religion of Muhammad provoke such blind reaction, such a psychological block? People from all walks of life in Muslim countries ask themselves if this might not be the result of the resurgence of a long submerged hatred.

This observation is worth discussing. In Western intellectual circles it is recognized that the culture which from the eighth to the fifteenth centuries gave the history of Islam its splendour also contributed, since it alone was able to accomplish this task, to the progress of humanity. The way in which rich Muslims can effect the renaissance of the Islamic heritage is sometimes viewed with sympathetic interest. The Agha Khan, as Imam of the Ismaili Shi'ites, evokes neither repulsion nor criticism. The same lack of concern is shown about the fact that it is a school of religious thought, however literalist, that governs Saudi Arabia. And if one does not like what is going on in Mauritania, this does not prevent one from treating it with indifference.

Iran, on the other hand, really frightens people. And, in the war between Iran and Iraq, it is about the fate of the latter that everybody worries for more or less acknowledged reasons. News coming from the Gulf emirates is always analysed with care. Egyptian behaviour is scrutinised with apprehension. The question of the future of Tunisia after Bourguiba was a subject of discussion before recent changes. Yet the children of Algerians who have opted for France are refused first-class French citizenship, whereas one scarcely notices that the Portuguese immigrants – Christians, and therefore assimilable – are more numerous than they.

It is an obvious fact that if Islam does not always frighten people everywhere, distrust turns into rejection as soon as economic and strategic interests are threatened by the first wave of dissidence, inasmuch as this religious-based dissidence baffles analysts more accustomed to juggle with the familiar concepts of political science.

The case of the Middle East, in this respect, is striking. Islam is everywhere on the political scene. The Sultanate of Oman is the only place in the world where Kharijitism, the puritanical branch of Islam which represents its first historical schism, is the state religion. Power in Saudi Arabia is exercised under the direction of a council of *ulama*[1] who represent the Wahhabi school. The civil war in Yemen opposed from 1963 to 1967 the conservatives, supported by Saudi Arabia, to the partisans of socialism, maintained in place by Nasser's troops. The republican regime was protected – surely no one can doubt this – by Saudi Arabia. And we have already spoken about an understanding between King Hussein of Jordan and the Muslim Brethren and have mentioned as well the fact that the Syrian leadership belongs to the Alawite sect, a very odd branch of Shi'ism.

What worries the adversaries of Islamist activism therefore is not that power is exercised in the name of religion or in conformity with it, but that these regimes may collapse. All well and good if their fall is the work of a secular movement. One can always define a policy when one deals with politicians, even if they are military men. This happened in Iraq in 1958 after the extermination of the royal family by rebels under the leadership of Colonel Qassim. It happened again after the seizure of power by the military in Turkey. But how can one deal with men galvanised by faith and drunk with triumph? Without a doubt, the supply of petroleum to the West, the fate of Israel, and the balance of spheres of influence between the superpowers cannot be left, from the viewpoint of the West, to the mercy of theologians whose ideas are unfathomable.

These worries, let it be clear, are not the prerogatives of Americans and Europeans alone. The Soviets, too, seem no less worried. The Egyptian journalist Muhammad Hassanain Haykal has evoked in his book *The Sphinx and the Commissar*[2] the difficulties that the Moscow leadership has experienced in understanding the Arabs. It does not take much to imagine the perplexity into which Islamist movements, inspired by frankly antediluvian ideas, have been thrown. They have devoted themselves, of course, to laborious political analyses which take into consideration local circumstances. Their writings, their declarations, and their positions prove that they begin by congratulating themslves on the fact that their movements are for the most part in opposition to American hegemony. Very quickly, they back off. The anti-Americanism of Khomeini's partisans is – and this was proved by the arrest of Tudeh leaders – far from manifesting any pro-Sovietism whatever. Even Mu'ammar Qadhdhafi, the Public Enemy Number One of the United States, has not become the rival of Castro, nor a hero (or a herald) of the Soviet Union. Moreover, the Soviets face difficulties on several fronts. In Afghanistan, the revolt launched against them is directed by Islamist movements and is financed and supported by the Muslim world. In Syria, where the power elite is their declared ally, the leadership is exposed to a murderous activism. Finally, it should not be forgotten that the Soviet Union includes seven Muslim republics. Hélène Carrère d'Encausse, in *L'Empire éclaté*,[3] does not hesitate in writing:

> The reestablishment of the *umma* (nation-community of Islam), where those who are Muslims because they believe stand side by side with those who are Muslims because they belong to the community, must be *henceforth* a reality of the Soviet world.

Henceforth, she says after sixty-five years of a communist regime!

Finally, having made an abstraction of its strategic and economic interests, and of the international dimension of its problems, the Soviet Union cannot help but consider Islamism a potential internal threat, especially if Islamism carries its success to the very doors of the Soviet Union as it has done in Iran, or if it puts into question Soviet hegemony in Afghanistan.

Can one speak, also, of an internal threat in China? Not for the moment, of course, but in the event that Islamism gains new ground in Asia, such a situation could evolve. How can regimes founded on the unity of faith and the fraternity of all Muslims not interest themselves in the fate of their coreligionists in the People's Republic? Not long ago I was accorded an interview with the comrade Minister of Culture of the central government in Beijing, who was also a member of the Executive Bureau of UNESCO. I asked her how many Muslims there were in China. She answered me that there must be about 10 million. I was astonished by a number that represented half of what was published thirty-five years ago. Should not that number, at the very least, have doubled like the rest of the Chinese population since the victory of the revolution? My interlocutor invoked at that moment the lack in her country of confessional statistics. This answer gave little satisfaction since the regions of China where Muslims traditionally live are well known, as they are in the Soviet Union.

Observers of the China scene have offered their impressions in various publications. W. Zafanolli has not hesitated to write in *Le Monde*, apropos of the province of Xinjiang (Sinkiang before the orthographic reform): 'The categorical affirmations of the Chinese cannot mask the truth, to wit, that the control of the authorities over Xinjiang is of the colonial type, the same in nature as the former annexation of Algeria by France.'[4] How many Uigurs and Kazakhs are there in that province which used to be called Chinese Turkestan? About 7 million, claims Zafanolli. But Marie-Ange Donzé and Claude Sauvageot, who visit China for three months each year, have given another figure. They maintain the existence of 5 million Uigurs. But they remind us that there are no less than six different Muslim minorities in China and that they live in the four corners of this vast territory. Beside the Kazakhs, Uzbeks, Tadjiks, and Uigurs of Xinjiang, there are the Mongols, the Huei, who belong to the majority Chinese ethnic group, the Han, and the Muslims of Ningxia, of Beijing and the coastal regions of the south: Canton, Fujian, Hangzhou. 'Officially 13 to 15 million, the Muslims of China might number today 45, even 50 million people'.[5]

One cannot be sure of the figure, but what one can be sure of is that during the Cultural Revolution the 'Gang of Four' made Islam, among other religions, the target and closed the mosques of China. However prudent one may be, can one not see that as a sign for the future?

If Islam has been pushed aside as a religion, culture, and tradition in the many countries with Muslim minorities – immigrants or natives – it is because it represents an extraordinary force of resistance to assimilation. This is the case in China as well as in the Soviet Union. It is assuredly fear of this which permits the easier acceptance of non-Muslim immigrants in Europe and in Canada. In the liberal democracies it is not a question of asking immigrants to renounce their faith (the Jews have indeed preserved theirs), but of accepting complete assimilation into the population of the countries in question.

The fears that Islam evokes, it is true, are not only of this order. In the countries not directly involved, Islamist activism provokes even greater rejection since it appears to attack, patiently and painfully, a system of values already rooted in place. The rights of man, the emancipation of woman, for example, belong to the entire human race. What has shocked international opinion is not so much the number of deaths due to the Iranian revolution but the justice people call Islamic where the accused cannot attend his own trial and where trials proceed without any rules of order; it is the unbelievable list of crimes whose definition is so vague that any act at all can be considered reprehensible.

For example, what is this 'corruption on earth' which figures so prominently in the Quran but whose juridical description needs a clear explanation published well in advance? The rights of children, of the wounded, and of prisoners are considered today as so belonging to humankind that no civilisation can scoff at them without exposing itself to general reprobation. Militant Islamism frightens people because to cut off the hand of a thief is proof of barbarism. And when this is done, as in Mauritania, by licensed surgeons, it is a problem for medical ethics, ethics which are considered the result of the evolution of civilisation. One cannot at the same time denounce doctors who, in totalitarian regimes, associate themselves with the political chicanery of psychiatric internment and yet accept others who have become executioners. And if one can convince oneself that throughout the course of history corporal punishment may have been at times considered the only remedy for infringements of the social order – the *lex talionis* does not exist solely in the Quran; one finds it in the Bible as well – one cannot admit, on the other hand, to any modern man that just when the abolition of the death penalty is being seriously discussed, a penalty already banned in numerous countries, some people approve of corporal punishment and have given a place of honour to practices condemned for centuries.

If for all these reasons Islamism frightens people, foreigners are not alone in dreading its success. In Muslim countries, it must be said, the same fear exists. What is, in fact, the situation in these countries? Let us remember first that many regimes suffer from a dangerous fragility that underdevelopment, with its long train of problems, does not suffice to explain. Geographical location often counts for a great deal. The conflict with Israel, quarrels with neighbours, border squabbles, superpower rivalry; occasions do not lack for concluding precipitous alliances which make agreement difficult on essential issues. Thus one of the frequent accusations made against men in power is that of causing alienation abroad. America has not been the only country alienated. The alliance of Syria or South Yemen with the Soviet Union was welcomed by no one but those two countries. Nasser was in trouble from the moment of his entente with Moscow; Sadat, in breaking relations with the Soviet Union, could not help but please the Americans. A segment of Egyptian public opinion, in particular the Islamists, was delighted. No doubt nonalignment was the way to salvation. Nevertheless, for countries threatened from the outside, help, or at least assistance, could come only from a great or medium-sized power. And so all regimes had to choose whether to align or not. The result was a hardening of police control, even repression. At any rate, wherever one turned, one had to deal with power on the watch if not actually at bay.

What does it matter, as in the story of the chicken and the egg, which comes first? The precariousness of regimes is measured by the degree of their despotism and their alienation. The more time passes, the more the establishment consolidates and its preservation becomes *raison d'état*. Whenever the Islamist menace appears on the horizon this establishment feels itself in danger.

Without a doubt, the established regimes in the Muslim countries are not all reactionary or in the pay of the foreigner. But even if they are other than reactionary – progressive or modernising – they feel a still greater apprehension in the face of an Islamism on the rise: in Senegal, Algeria, Tunisia, Turkey, Syria, they seek to protect already-won social benefits – the emancipation of women, socialism, secularism, tolerance according to the situation – for they have every right to fear a retreat that could provoke a simplistic appeal for a return to original sources. This apprehension is shared by all militants or by those who wish simply to modernise society quickly; and by many women who have acquired the right to education, to work, and to judicial and even political responsibilities.

Because the intentions of its leaders are not always clear, Islamism frightens government officials and simple citizens alike so much the more. When, on 12 January 1974, the rapidly terminated union between Tunisia and Libya was declared, one of the least expected reactions came from certain Tunisian women who asked: 'And what will happen to our personal status?' Since 1957 there has existed in Tunisia a code of personal status forbidding polygamy, requiring divorce in a court of law, and recognising for women rights which tradition formerly denied them. Certainly the union of these two countries did not have a religious character, but calling the new state an Islamic Arab republic justified the fears of the beneficiaries of social progress: which of the two countries' law codes would be applied to the union?

This fear explains why the most extreme forms of Islamism provoke such opposition, even among certain Islamic militants. It would be a mistake to think that Islamism is a homogeneous movement. It has its own factions and the differences among them do not lie only in the choice of means: armed combat or political struggle. Doctrinal differences oppose the partisans of cultural action to those of political action, progressives to traditionalists, modernising reformers to conservatives, universalists to particularists, and, naturally, Islamists in power in Saudi Arabia, Oman and Pakistan to dissidents. There is quite a large gamut of 'parties' that fear the Islamism of total revolution.

It can be said that in practically every Muslim country and within all the minority Muslim communities in America, Europe or Africa, there exists an Islamism that one may call in one place cultural, in another missionary. To teach the Quran to the young, to organise conferences on *fiqh* (law and jurisprudence), to educate prayer leaders (imams in the mosques), and to organise funeral services are the tasks to which associations devote themselves, associations whose importance is in inverse proportion to the activity of the official authorities in these educational and social matters. From this can emerge, as we will see later, the sudden appearance or the consolidation of a veritable clergy – more precisely, of a structure favourable to religion – that plays a considerable role. At the beginning of the century, Abd al-Hamid Ibn Badis created the Association of Ulama in Algeria. Between the two world wars the Tunisian Shaykh Muhammad Salah al-Naifar led the Association of Young Muslims and created the School for Muslim Girls whereas at the end of the 1960s in the same country, another association for the 'preservation of the Quran' was established. In Lebanon, Shi'ite, Sunnite, and Druze associations exist. In Senegal there are the two great brotherhoods of the Tijaniyya and Muridiyya that play the same religious, cultural, social, and economic role. In 1938, in China, the association of the 'Five Ma' was founded. And among all these Islamist movements, at least in Tunisia, Egypt and Iran, progressive factions exist. Their declared goal is not to restore the tradition inherited from the rather sombre past five centuries, but to adapt Islam to the world of tomorrow. The representatives of that view in Tunisia, for example, have chosen for their journal a title which in itself is a program: *15/21* (15 for the Hegirian century that began in 1980 and 21 for the years after 2000!) Some of them, like the Mujahidin of Iran, have declared themselves non-Marxian socialists.

The modernising reformers, who believe they must reconcile a new society with a religious legacy, do not constitute, moreover, movements, properly speaking, and are generally close to political power whenever such power, as in Algeria, Tunisia, Libya, Egypt, Indonesia and Black Africa adopts the objective of peaceful social change. For them, it is a question of giving priority out of respect for religious law, to codes of Western jurisprudence in the corpus of which legal prescriptions that correspond best to modern life are clearly distinguishable.

Finally, the Muslim world counts among its members also, as does Christianity, ecumenists who are careful to stress the universal character of

Islam, to throw up a bridge between its various branches, and to seek encounters with other 'people of the book' and quite simply the entire world. These people are recruited from among the elites. They have formed the associations one finds scattered at the four corners of the earth. The Islamic Conference, which on 19 September 1981 in Paris promulgated a 'Universal Islamic Declaration of the Rights of Man', is a union of associations in the mainstream of global thought and benefits from the aid of several countries such as Pakistan and Saudi Arabia.

These men, these elites, these groups, those with these tendencies regard with jaundiced eye the rising perils represented by obtuse traditionalism, idealised obscurantism, and legitimised violence.

The diversity of those for whom Iranian Islamism is a mortal danger invites us, therefore, to be discerning in our judgments regarding the events that are now shaking a large part of the Muslim world. They must convince the zealots to be more modern, if only to show the zealots why their call does not always produce the mobilisation they expect. Throughout history the majority of Muslims have resisted extremism. They may be stirred up in moments of social chaos, especially when multiple reasons coalesce to push them to revolution, but once the party is over, an accounting is made and moderation carries the field. Why did Ismailism not succeed in rallying the majority of Shi'ites? And why did Shi'ism itself not unite the majority of Muslims? Why did Kharijite fundamentalism or Wahhabi puritanism not succeed in expanding beyond narrowly circumscribed limits? This is a big subject of meditation for those who believe that the hour is come for hundreds of millions of Muslims to take the path of war.

And yet rulers would be wrong to wager on the number of partisans of non-violence, on the fundamental moderation of their subjects, and on the help of either the West or the Soviet Union to influence destiny. The revolution is slowly incubating. It has broken out from time to time, violently and destructively, in certain parts of the world. Fear of revolution serves no purpose. It would be better to succeed in eliminating the causes. To kill or imprison the revolutionaries has never prevented the systems that no longer rely on an authentic popular consensus from bursting into pieces.

Notes

1. *Ulama* is the plural of *alim*, literally 'learned'. Although this word has a general meaning, it is used in the Islamic context especially to designate the doctors of religious law. We will write it without an *s* here because it is already a plural.
2. Muhammad Haykal, *Le Sphinx et le commissaire* (Paris: Editions Jeune Afrique, 1980).
3. Hélène Carrère d'Encausse, *L'Empire éclaté* (Paris: Editions Flammarion 1978).
4. W. Zafanolli, 'Les Musulmans de Chine', *Le Monde*, 20 January 1980.
5. Marie-Ange Donzé and Claude Sauvageot, 'Entre Mao et Mahomet', *Jeune Afrique*, no. 993, 16 January 1980.

4.   The Magic Potion

The French take great delight in a comic strip which celebrates the achievements of the Gauls who resisted the Roman invasion. The central character, an imp of a man and for that reason called Asterix, acquires instantaneously a prodigious power each time he drinks a magic potion prepared by the religious leader of the village, a venerable druid who, of course, jealously guards the recipe for this extraordinary concoction.

Naturally, we are only talking here of a comic strip. Nevertheless, in the adventures of Asterix, we find all the ingredients of a communal struggle: revolt against oppression and the foreigner, defence of traditional ways and customs including dietary habits, solidarity with basic principles – under these circumstances, racial solidarity – and finally recourse to the religious weapon represented by a potent liquor.

Well, this is a bit like what occurs among the militant Islamists. It is not too difficult to grasp that the return to the totality of religion, to which some people cling without seeking to distinguish essences from what is only the silt deposited by centuries of stratified customs, constitutes in certain cases what the psychiatrists call a return to the womb. The militants think that they can recover there the peace that reason no longer brings them since reason has lost all its points of reference, a communal sympathy displaced by unbridled individualism, a spirituality eclipsed by what they define as an omnipresent materialism – in a word, moral comfort here below such as is offered in the hereafter. Moral comfort is not a negligible commodity at a time when people may go easily astray. Men are quite happy to leave the beaten path of proven reason to follow the road of a well-worked-out religion.

The battle cry sounded by the Islamists of the world is 'The Quran is our constitution!' (al-Quranu Dusturuna). This says all, and it says nothing. The statement is clear and unequivocal. The communal lifestyle must be sought in the Quran as well as the organisation of the state (Dustur meaning here constitution), the principles of legislation, the definition of relations between individuals, personal statute, and the ordering of economic life. The work of exegesis, interpretation, judgment, and the elaboration of precise answers to precise questions is left to those who know, the Ahl al-Ilm, or Doctors of Islamic Science. Allahu Akbar! they scream in Iran. To that reaffirmation that God is most great, the old and young, pious men and women, believers and nonbelievers, followers of the political left and right answer with one huge swell of emotion. The journalist Marc Kravetz, who has followed all the stages of the Iranian revolution, tells how he was approached one day in Teheran by a certain Abbas, a man of critical intelligence and of sovereign detachment from what was happening in his country. This man gave the impression of being able to explain everything to the foreign observer. Suddenly the two men crossed the path of a demonstration: *Allahu Akbar*! Swallowed up in the crowd, Marc Kravetz lost his companion. When he found him again Abbas was moved to tears. 'It was incredible,' he said to the French journalist.[1]

Are we witnessing in Islamism the proclamation of a primitive preaching, the inspiration of a faith that moves mountains? At this point, we might take the time to look again at several notions that up to now have been somewhat muddled here and in the Muslim world; that is, the revival of Islam, the awakening of the Muslim world, and political activism with its Muslim referents. In the preceding pages the question of the political character of the movements that manifest themselves in violent action has been treated at length as have the several reasons that seem to justify this move toward religion. But the question remains to be answered what the person seeking shelter finds in the faith and what he makes of it. If we understand by revival of Islam a return to religiosity, then the facts are strikingly obvious and are explained by the reasons that have already been advanced. On the other hand, we would change our tune very quickly if we seek to find in this popular movement an attempt to regenerate the faith, an adaptation of the credo to the world of today, a new union of the destiny of man or a program of social reform.

The expression 'return to the sources' seems to us equivocal in itself. A return, agreed, but to what sources? To the Quran alone? To the Quran and to the *Sunna*: that is, the tradition of the prophet? To these two sources expanded and enlarged by the works of the Shi'ite imams or by the codifications of the imams who founded the four juridical schools of Sunni Islam, or to a Kharijitism withdrawn into itself? Ought we consider too as a return to the sources actions which consist in reestablishing the *status quo ante* as if the European colonisation of the nineteenth and twentieth centuries had accomplished nothing more than to disturb an exemplary stability? As for the 'reawakening', did it not begin culturally in the nineteenth century, and did it not draw from the struggle for national liberation a new vigour?

In truth, to each of these questions not only the Islamist movements but the governments and the elites of Muslim countries bring extremely varied answers that will be broached as this book progresses. Let us state first of all that the movements of religious militants that have the greatest chance for success are those that are scarcely embarrassed by subtleties. The magic potion has so much more of an effect because it is a worldwide phenomenon that makes people feel safe. It is not a dissertation subject or an object of research that the militant seeks when he joins an Islamist movement; it is an organisation that takes charge of him and gives him orders. Interrogated by the court that passed sentence on them, certain members of the organisation that had President

Sadat assassinated confessed having scarcely read at the time a single book recommended by their immediate superior. They had acquired their culture essentially by listening to sermons or by occasionally chatting with those among their comrades who were known for their wisdom, however summary. They had no need for more in order to commit themselves, even unto death, to a revolutionary movement.

Many are the prophets who, throughout history, have sung the glory of the struggles of a man who espouses a cause and pledges his life to defend it. In a religious party, the militant accedes, in addition, to the sacred. This sacralisation of his struggle is all the more marked since in his soul he is acting to rehabilitate the believers by giving them more respect and to exalt religion by imposing its law.

A common example, because it is so frequent, illustrates this transfiguration of the religious militant. In Tunis, a woman working in a company where the majority of the employees were Europeans was caught smoking during Ramadan by the messenger boy. Despite the difference in position which put the messenger boy far below her on the social ladder, he publicly and vehemently chastised her for being both a miscreant and a traitor to the cause of Islam. Not to observe the obligatory fast was already, he said, a violation of the law but to do so in public before foreigners was to exhibit herself to unbelievers in a performance that smacked of irreverence for Islam.

Thus the sacred confers on the humblest of militants a power that transcends social, political, or economic hierarchies. In their simplicity the arguments of the messenger boy illustrate very well the two aspects of the defended cause: the internal cohesion of the Islamic community whose members must obey the law and the image that this community must project on the outside. The sacred character of the cause emphasises the power of the militant, and the grandeur that he acquires makes him spurn the respect of the principle of tolerance or of the rights of the individual. Does not Islam make it obligatory for the believer to command the good and to forbid evil?

And so the militant Islamist draws from the cause he defends this power to judge between good and evil and, having made an abstraction of the difference, defends the right and the obligation to exercise that judgment. He is called to engage in an unfaltering struggle for the triumph of the faith, a daily *jihad*. Many Islamic organisations bear the name *Mujahidin*, or Strugglers for the Faith. And this *jihad* is the sublime act that transfigures man completely. Are not those who died on *jihad*, on the field of honour in the struggle for the divine cause, assured of gaining paradise as martyrs? An Iraqi, commenting on the war between his country and Iran, declared once that it was impossible to fight soldiers convinced of going not to their death, but to Heaven.

The idea of *jihad* has caused much ink to flow and it is taken in the West for a defect of Islam. Translated generally to mean holy war, it invariably refers to that previously evoked image of the man who, sword in hand, crosses the steppes and the mountains on horseback carrying death to those parts of the world where the cause of God is unknown. Holy war evokes a spectrum of attitudes made up of fanaticism, narrow-mindedness, cruelty; in a word, of the inhumanity that underscores the anachronistic character of religious wars.

Consequently, Muslims who have come into contact with the West have always felt embarrassed by the obligation to go on *jihad*, confusing the idea and the image to which it has given birth. Their very elaborate explanations are often contradicted by the facts and the deeds of movements that certainly justify reproach. Still, some clarification is in order.

Whether holy war or daily struggle, *jihad* actually constitutes a duty for the believer. *Jihad* implies a struggle which can take multiple forms. The Arabic language, which is composed of thousands of roots themselves multiplied by fixed derivational models, does not possess this one lone word to designate the clash of men. War corresponds to the word *harb*; the fact of killing one another is rendered by *qital*; struggle by *kifah*; combat by *sira'a*; battle by *ma'araka*, etc. That in so large a spectrum of words Islam chooses *jihad* to denote the action required of the believer merits a less summary definition than what is suggested by the general expression 'holy war'.

Jihad derives from the root *j h d* which signifies physical, moral, or intellectual effort. The English word that most closely approximates *jihad* is 'struggle' and can be interpreted in a number of ways. From the same root we derive another word which we shall encounter further on, that of *ijtihad*, or a display of effort, judgment, discernment, and comprehension. The student who in school shows a continuous effort to learn is recognised by his teacher as having exercised *ijtihad*. Scholars regularly recall the words of the Prophet who declared upon returning from battle: 'We return from the little *jihad* to confront the great *jihad*,' by which he meant the daily struggle to live and survive. The display of effort in conforming to the doctrine of the faith, in living in peace with one's conscience by observing the rules of religious ethics, in preserving the community, and in promoting the cause of God can take various forms. Armed struggle, or if you like 'holy war', represents only one form among others. To follow the Prophet's words to the letter of the law, armed struggle could only be the minor form of *jihad*. Moreover, the Quran is careful whenever there is the possibility of a bloody encounter to use the term *qital* or one of the derivations thereof. No matter what form their militancy assumes Islamic activists lead a true *jihad* for their faith and no one ought to be surprised at the use of the word.

This being said, it is not our intention to involve the reader in the quarrels of exegetes and of linguists. Whether one means here *jihad*, *qital*, or martyr, Islam recognises the idea of war, and its most noble form is the war for the defence of the faith. But as an armed struggle properly speaking, *jihad* is located on the lower end of the scale of combat in which the believer must partake.

Now it is this form of *jihad* that worries the non-Muslim in particular because the days of the wars of religion are considered to be over and, consequently, recourse to these kinds of confrontations is thought to be dangerous and anachronistic.

Let us pause a moment to contemplate a short article published in the newspaper *Le Monde* in June 1982. The text was signed by the Jerusalem correspondent for this Paris daily, and under the explicit title 'Holy War?'

Francis Cornu reported, during the Lebanese crisis, that 'the Grand Rabbinate of Israel [had just] decided to pronounce that Operation Peace for Galilee conformed to Jewish law (*halakha*).' The rabbinate indicated that participation in this operation 'in all its aspects [corresponded] to a duty or commandment (*mitzva*) to make war which was expressed in the Scriptures and the commentaries.' The correspondent of *Le Monde* went on to ask: 'Holy war? It all depends how you look at things. The Israelis have so often denounced in Arab speeches the abuse of the call to *jihad* [holy war, according to Cornu's translation] against the Jewish state that they now distrust these words and their possible sacred character.'

Is holy war outdated and anachronistic? The Scriptures are an inexhaustible source for all those who wish to find a sacred justification for acts that break with the morality of their times. At any rate, for those Islamists who wish to throw themselves into a vengeful struggle, the notion of *jihad*, understood here in the sense of a total war against the enemies of the Muslim community, assumes a character of burning contemporaneity. There more than elsewhere the sacralisation of struggle has great importance for the candidate of the militant cause. To fight in Iran, or on the Iraqi frontier, in Syria, in Mecca, in Afghanistan or in the Philippines is to join in a sacred fight with the help of an omnipresent God. The fighter sees himself as the rival of the first Islamic *mujahidin* who consecrated themselves to the purification of Arabia, carrying the Good News to the edge of the Taurus and the Zagros mountains and to the banks of the Nile.

Fighters dismiss with disdain the objections of those who would wish to demystify this primitive expansionism and to recall the circumstances that constrained the first Muslims from making war and the conditions dictated by the Prophet concerning the manner of conducting it. Among these are the prohibition against killing another Muslim, the reasons that justified geographical expansion, the reluctance of the second Caliph Umar to undertake the conquests called for by those who wanted war and, finally, the weakness of the third Caliph Uthman before the appetites of his close associates and the pressure of the tribes to push out in all directions. This explanation is hardly worth repeating. One must recognise the truth: the abusive call to *jihad* is a simplistic solution to which Islamist organisations often have recourse. Of course, recalling the least debatable data concerning the early times of Islam imparts various nuances to the abstract explanations by means of which the Islamists wish to justify their choice of extreme action. But is not the principal characteristic of a mass movement precisely the simplicity of its ideas, the clarity of its order, and the designation of a single objective? It is evident that Muslims themselves, at least the most activist among them, make more confusing the notion of *jihad*. Nevertheless, for the militant in the arena there is the sought-after sacralisation of struggle because it dignifies his acts. Better to die for the sake of dying according to the Divine Plan, he thinks, or for what one believes to be the Divine Commandment, than to get oneself killed like others, for Marxism, socialism, or democracy of God knows what persuasion! The struggle that draws its meaning from religion is an act of purification, of the individual and of society. When they denounce, moreover, as did the secular movements inspired by contemporary ideologies, the corruption, the extortion, the westernisation, even the treason, the exploitation of the people, the inequities, the nepotism, the squandering of public funds, the arrogance of the ruling classes, the ostentatious materialism, the misery of the proletariat and the peasant as the ways despotism protects the system, how could the Islamists not feel obligated to preach the establishment of a pure and unyielding society where behaviour would be regulated by a rigorous morality and where punishments for infringements of the law would be all the more harsh since the disease to be cut from the social body was so great?

Where can we find this morality, this rigour, this ideal social organisation, this transfiguration of men called daily to become angels, if not in the essentials of a total religion, in the Islam that governs all aspects of the lives of the individual and of society?

The magic potion, then, has many consequences. It not only exalts the feelings of the fighter and increases his power tenfold; it forces him to see the sickness of his society and the cure that must be applied to it.

An argument reappears often in the discourse of Islamists that cannot help but hit the mark among those who have witnessed the weakness and the physical and moral misery of the Muslim peoples. 'We were great when we were faithful to our religion,' they recite everywhere.

Fidelity thus glorified is highly debatable. Each century had its vehement critics of a lapsed faith. But the idea of grandeur corresponds nonetheless to a reality. In the course of centuries Islam has not realised territorial expansion alone. By bringing together into one single community people of diverse origins, Islam brought about a fusion of civilisations that turned out to be fruitful and that leaned for support on the Arabic language. Islamic culture and civilisation had a Golden Age that counts for much in the history of humanity. Whether in belles lettres, linguistics, lexicography, mysticism, philosophy, history, geography, mathematics, astronomy, chemistry, medicine, architecture, art or craftsmanship, Islamic civilisation represents a considerable gain for human culture. The twentieth century, enamoured at the same time with mysticism and science, has discovered once again the great men of Islam. Farid al-Din Attar, Hussayn Mansur al-Hallaj, Mohiy al-din Ibn Arabi, Jamal al-Din al-Rumi, among the mystics: Ibn Sina (Avicenna), Ibn Rushd (Averroes) among the doctors and philosophers; Ibn Hawqal among the geographers; Nasir al-Din Tusi among the astronomers; al-Fazari, the maker of astrolabes; al-Khuwarizmi, who gave his name to the logarithm, to cite only some, all of whose works have reappeared on the shelves of Western libraries. Muhammad Abd al-Salam, physicist and Nobel Laureate of 1979, recalls the classification made by George Sarton in his monumental *Histoire des sciences*. The author, says Abd al-Salam 'divides scientific evolution into epochs of a half-century in duration. Thus the years 450 to 400 BC constitute, according to Sarton, the epoch of Plato. The half-centuries of Aristotle, Euclid, and Archimedes follow. The seventh century AD is placed under the sign of China with Hsang Tsang and I Ching, then from 750 to 1100 it is the uninterrupted succession of the epochs of Jabir, Khuwarizmi, Razi, Mas'udi, Biruni, Umar al-Khayyam, all of them Arabs, Turks, Afghans, Persians – chemists, mathematicians, physicians, geographers, physicists, and astronomers - belonging to the Islamic culture and community. In Sarton's history, it is only after 1100 that the first European names appear, such as Gerard of Cremona and Roger Bacon. For a century and a half once again the honours were shared by such men as Ibn Rushd (Averroes), Nasir al-Din Tusi, and Ibn Nafis, the precursor of Harvey and his theory concerning the circulation of the blood.'[2] For five centuries Islam was at the forefront of progress. That is twice as long as the current period of Western supremacy.

It is necessary to underline here that these are the names of persons who, throughout their lives, eclipsed all their contemporaries and that if one sticks to the date 1350 AD at which Abd al-Salam puts the beginning of the eclipse of Islam in the field of science, one could, from 1100 to this ringing down of the curtain, cite other illustrious representatives of Islamic civilisation who have left an imperishable memento without having had the distinguished privilege of giving their names to their epoch. Most of them, whose fame spread during the Middle Ages, are known under the Europeanised forms of their names. Hence, one can evoke the names of Ibn Tufail (Abu Basir), Ibn Zohr (Avenzoar), Bitrugi (Al Petragius) for the twelfth century; Abu al-Fida (Aboulfeda), Ibn Baytar for the thirteenth century; and bringing the list to a temporary end, Ibn Khaldun for the fourteenth century.

If scientific growth suddenly ceased, artistic activity continued to develop on a local level with the Persian miniatures of Tabrizi and Qasim Ali in the fifteenth century, of Mir Sayyid Ali, Abd al-Samad, and of Wali Moneiminaati in the sixteenth century; with the architecture of Sirian (fifteenth century); and Khayr al-Din (sixteenth century) in Ottoman Turkey. The Masjid-i Shah (The Mosque of the Shah) in Isfahan dates from 1611 and the Taj Mahal in Agra (India) from 1632.

Muslims and Arabs must not forget that apart from the well-known works of these men of world culture there are other illustrious persons who, ignored in the West, have made their mark on the evolution of literature and especially Arab letters, of theology, of exegesis, of thought, and of law. As their fields of study are of greater importance for Islam than for the outside world, Muslims sometimes value them more than they do those who, by their scientific activities, have a universal significance.

Islamic civilisation is not dead. One cannot speak of the Islamic world as one speaks of the pre-Columbian civilisations of the Americas. Its energy was sapped by the dissolution of empires, the Crusades, and the Mongol hordes. Its political strength has been frittered away. The difficulty in communications and the gradual shifting of the trade routes brought about the progressive impoverishment of the Muslim countries. Islamic civilisation fell by stages into a profound sleep. Having fallen back on themselves, entire regions endeavoured to accomplish nothing more than the preservation of the faith, the teaching of the Quran, the rote learning of certain chosen exegetical and juridical works, and, naturally, the maintenance of religious ritual. Soon, to be a scholar became precisely that and nothing more: to be the curator of a museum.

The Muslim has, with respect to the Golden Age of his civilisation, the feelings of an exile. These feelings are supported by a mixture of pride and bitterness. Certainly, the mass of Muslims know neither the names of Biruni or Khuwarizmi, nor the splendours of the Alhambra in Granada, or of the Taj Mahal in Agra. But they know that there were Muslims once before whom nothing stood in the way of when they gave rein to their purebreds, whose supremacy was recognised in everything they did, whose boats and caravans reaching out to the four corners of the globe brought fabulous riches back to Basra, Baghdad, Samarkand and Kairouan. The idea of time is suppressed and the collective memory confuses the period of the great flowering of Islamic civilisation with that of the first century of the faith.

Thus historical truth begins to resemble a story from *The Thousand and One Nights*, a book whose writing – could this be by chance? – began in the thirteenth century and whose final Arabic version probably dates from the middle of the fifteenth century at the moment when the decline begins. The popular image of the greatness of yesterday transformed into myth the Islamic age and into supernatural heroes the people who lived in those times. Thus history became a song of heroic deeds.

Rationalists may take offence at these distortions, but myth has played an essential role in maintaining the links with the past, just as traditionalism today is denounced quite rightly as a brake on progress. The former Tunisian president, the same Habib Bourguiba who did so much for the emancipation of women, liked to recall that in 1930 he led a campaign to defend their wearing of the veil. In the trough of the wave of history, nations cling to whatever preserves their personality and their uniqueness so as not to be absorbed by a system that oppresses them.

The call of Islamists to defend the cause of Islam not only sets spiritual strings vibrating. The candidate for activism also feels imbued with the historical mission to rehabilitate Islam with all its power over men and all the splendour of its civilisation. The militant is convinced that he is taking up again a torch that has been left to sputter but which has never gone out. The conflict does not revolve around this point whenever Islamists oppose rulers. It revolves around the question of which road to follow, around the real objective and the ways to realise it. The requirement to act is shared by all Muslims who consider themselves the inheritors of an indivisible patrimony which they are sworn to protect. The wife of an ambassador from an African country to Paris wept hot tears on 21 August 1969 after a certain Michael Rohan had set fire to the al-Aqsa Mosque in Jerusalem. Her country was located at a great distance from the Middle East, yet the act was felt as an unacceptable humiliation, because like the Dome of the Rock built on the same esplanade in front of it, this mosque is one of the most venerated sanctuaries for Muslims the world over. It was for the same reasons that the winning of the Nobel Prize by the Pakistani Abd al-Salam was hailed as a great event by the Muslim press.

The Muslim world is not alone in these feelings and this behaviour. From the fifteenth century in Italy first, then in France, and finally in all of Europe, what was the Renaissance if not an enterprise to rehabilitate Greek civilisation and the Graeco–Roman legacy? The word itself suggests that the preceding thirteen to twenty centuries represented a dead period. Assuredly the movement had begun with the search in ancient Greece for forgotten aesthetic norms and then for the rediscovery among the philosophers of the reasons for ignorance and obscurantism during the centuries of superstition. But the movement also gave a new impulse to Graeco–Roman mythology, to linguistic studies, and to political ideas. We call all this the humanities. And Europe became the sole legatee of the empires of Alexander and Caesar.

When the Greeks revolted against the domination of the Muslim Ottoman Turks in the middle of the nineteenth century, the sympathy felt throughout Europe was dictated by the conviction that the cradle of civilisation had to be liberated. And when the same Europe undertook to colonise the southern shores of the Mediterranean there was in this enterprise, besides the immediate political, strategic, and economic interest, the publicly expressed desire to reconstitute the Empire of Rome and Byzantium. This feeling was so strong during the colonial period that the endeavours of archaeologists in North Africa, for example, were limited essentially to Roman antiquities since the Islamic period was considered no more than a historical parenthesis.

In our times the sentimentality that Americans exhibit toward the birthplace of their ancestors in Europe or Africa demonstrates that the desire and the will to renew with the past are not unique to Muslims.

After all, the Muslim has more reasons than any other to start a 'renaissance'. The Arabic language and Islamic culture have never been forgotten and buried. One can speak in the strictest sense of a civilisation in suspended animation. The essential thing is that, at its awakening, this civilisation must meet the challenges of the times and that the men who give it form do not find themselves in the situation of the Seven Sleepers of Ephesus who, upon their return to the city, discovered that events had passed them by.

All this mobilises the Islamic militant. We see him devouring any and all publications that glorify Islam, even if they are intellectually simplistic. The schools have for a long time neglected the history of the Muslim world, and especially the history of its ideas, and today's militant does not easily find his way back to the sources. How many times has a lecturer been questioned by North African Sunni Muslims about the nature of Shi'ism – exactly the same questions that have been asked of him by a European audience in Paris, Geneva or Brussels. And this says nothing of the differences between the Shi'ism of Khomeini, that of the Agha Khan, that of the Syrian Hafiz al-Assad, and that of the Druze! They throw themselves into the work of Ibn Taymiyya (thirteenth century) on *fiqh* (law and jurisprudence) without knowing that he reformed the Hanbali schools, because they were ignorant of the nuances among the four Sunni schools of law: the Maliki, Hanafi, Shafa'i, and Hanbali, about which we will speak later. In this way, they find themselves in really laughable situations. A Sunni who rejects the fundamentalist doctrine of the Kharijites might cite in support of a thesis on electoral democracy in Islam the elected kingship of the

Kharijite state in Tiaret in ninth century Algeria. Another Sunni would hardly be embarrassed to invoke the example of the Qarmathian revolts in Lower Mesopotamia and the Gulf in the ninth and tenth centuries to prove the existence of socialism and even of a form of communism in Islam. He forgets, or simply ignores, that these unfortunate Qarmathians were taken for heretics, annihilated by the armies of the orthodox, and continue to this day, in retrospect, to be the object of general vilification.

This confusion explains to a certain degree the dogmatism and the intolerance of certain Islamist movements. Not being prepared to entertain an open debate about ideas, and believing that the regeneration of the entire community constitutes the primary objective, they block all ideological discussion. To them, the heritage must be taken as it is, and as one package, because they believe that the most important thing is to 'reconstitute' the state in order to govern men and manage their affairs according to tradition.

Now what Islam offers as a whole to the militant seeking both peace of mind and the energy necessary for the struggle is, in a word, total control over his life and his acts. It matters little to him that the doctors of the law – those *ulama* – may be the product of a system of education frozen for centuries and dedicated to the preservation of the necessary minimum, to the perpetuation of the faith. These men of traditional knowledge are the frame of reference. They are not ready to reply to the challenges of the times, but they know nevertheless that the mass of men is stupid. And so one arrives at this paradoxical position where the rejection in Islam of an institutionalised clergy accommodates itself to the existence of a religious hierarchy; that is, to a group of men to whom one yields the right to pronounce on religious matters and who recognise among themselves degrees of preeminence.

For the Muslims as well as for the non-Muslim reader these two questions are important and deserve further discussion in order to avoid misunderstanding. The totalism of Islam has for fourteen centuries caused much ink to flow. The fact that this religion claims to extend its control over all aspects of individual and collective life has not always been gladly accepted and has posed numerous problems in all historical periods which many modern people are unaware of.

The question of the secularism of the state, which has no precedent in Islam, will not be settled in a single day. Indeed, it raises not only theological queries but philosophical and juridical ones as well.

By the same token, the existence of a religious hierarchy was not the work of the present era. The clerics have sometimes insisted on the validity of their own judgments and at other times have submitted to secular power. And the opponents – once again, in all epochs – have kept secret their own religious hierarchy. Although this may be a Shi'ite peculiarity, the Iranian mullarchy does not constitute a singular phenomenon. The structure of religious power elsewhere possesses other ranks than that of ayatollah, hojjat al-Islam or mullah.

Finally, the conflicting relations between ruling and religious hierarchies have sparked many debates and have given birth to many solutions as varied as the differences between the Muslim states of the past and the present.

Notes

1. Marc Kravetz, *Irano Nox* (Paris: Editions Bernard Grasset, 1981).
2. Abd al-Salam, 'Pour une renaissance de la science dans le monde islamique', *UNESCO Newsletter*, August-September 1981, p.51.

5.   The Totalism of Islam

The unique role of the Arabs is not sufficient to explain the expansion of the religion of Muhammad in space or in time. Whatever the importance of the part played by the Arabs in the diffusion of the faith and of Islamic culture, one can understand the conversion of the Turks, Mongols, Hindus, Chinese, Malays, Africans and Europeans only by looking at the religion itself in order to underline the import of the message received by all these populations and peoples who themselves were not without culture nor a legacy of civilisation. To be sure, Islam caused the crystallisation of a true Arab nation after a desperate and often antagonistic tribal history. This concentration of energies directed the warrior impulse toward martyrdom and military conquest. But we have already seen that Islam fought several wars and was more than once thrown into disorder. Yet it hung on as a belief system and tenaciously put down roots, even under the Soviet yoke; moreover, it continued in times of peace and of colonial oppression to exercise a strong attraction to many peoples and communities.

The West does not understand the reasons for this seductiveness. The influence that this dual image of the Muslim – that of the swordsman and the fatalist – exercises on the minds of men has not helped to make understanding easy.

Let us attempt, then, to put aside for a moment the undeniable need that men feel from time to time to believe, and let us see what Islam offers. This approach seems more promising than all sociological, materialist, or pseudo-scientific analyses put together. It can help us understand the conversion of the Arabs in Mecca around AD 610 as well as that of the new adherents to the faith in the 1980s.

Islam is a faith, an ethos, a cosmogony, a cult, and a way of life. One may add that in the course of history, by the action of men who adopted it and because of the weight of the nations that joined the community, it became a culture, a civilisation, and a temporal power. All these elements have had their moments of intense brilliance but also their moments of relative weakness. They continue to occupy a place in the consciences of Muslims in various degrees.

Islam as a cult is *one*. All its branches, schools, doctrines, even sects, agree on the essentials. The fast month – Ramadan – is the same for everyone. The pilgrimage to Mecca brings together, on the same day, men and women from the four corners of the earth. And to pray in the mosque, the Muslims never ask if the imam, the prayer leader, is a Sunni, a Shi'ite, or a Kharijite. Muhammad was opposed by no one and his message was accepted by all as Divine Revelation. The text of the Quran is unique and its corpus everywhere contains the same number of chapters – *surat* – established in an immutable order. Translations are allowed today, but the document of reference remains that which was initially recorded in Arabic. Divergences are found on other levels which will be determined later on.

The creed is the same for all and it is simple. Thus simplicity has certainly played a decisive role in the conversion of the first Arabs and in the revelation even today of the universal character of Islam. To be a Muslim one must believe that the universe has a single creator. Chapter 112 of the Quran commands: 'Say: He is God, the One and Only; God, the Eternal, Absolute; He begetteth not, nor is He begotten; and there is none like unto Him.' One must believe that God will demand reckonings from men on the Day of Resurrection and Last Judgment. And that before, to give men their chance of salvation, He has commanded prophets – in Arabic, *nabi*, plural *nabiyin* – or special messengers – *rasul*, plural *rusul* – to spread the Good Word and to guide men along the Straight Path – *al-sirat al-mustaqim* – that leads towards God. These prophets, guides for men whom God had sent to earth, have followed one after the other since Adam with the same message of the unity of the Godhead, of purity, and righteousness. This message has regularly been met with derision, scoffed at by miscreants or even worse, altered by generations of dunces, hypocrites, the arrogant, or of opportunists seeking to put religion at the service of their personal interests. Untiringly, God has again and again given humanity a new chance. Notice here that the message transmitted by Muhammad was the last call addressed to men. He is the last of the prophets in whom the cycle of prophecy is brought to a close.

This is the profession of the Muslim faith, the one which every person converting to Islam must pronounce: *Ashahadu an la Ilaha ila Allah, wa ashahadu anna Muhammadan rasulu Allah*. I bear witness that there is no God but the One God, and Muhammad is His Messenger.

To believe in one God, in the Day of Judgement, in the message of the prophets of which Muhammad's is the last, this is to be a Muslim; that is, to submit to the will of God. In Arabic, this submission is called *Islam*.

Naturally, there flows from this a very rich theological corpus of works concerning the Divine attributes and Creation which there is not space here to explore. But the principles of belief are summed up so well in these doctrines that Muhammad forbade Muslims to continue the struggle against anyone who pronounces the profession of faith, the *shahada*: literally, the testimony.

This creed is amplified by a vision of the universe, a cosmogony that takes up the thread of the universal history taught and developed in the Bible: the creation of Genesis, Paradise, Adam and the fall of man, man's redemption, Satan, good and evil, the successive prophecies from Noah to Jesus, the end of the world, the Last Judgment, the role of the angels, and so on. It is coherent global vision that makes room for all elements in the universe: the heavens, the stars, the sun and the moon, the earth, the natural elements, the plants, the animals, men and their destiny, with a delicate balance between determinism and free will. In this vision, nothing escapes the omniscience and the power of God.

Man endures alone the tests to which he is put. There is no intercession. No one can take upon himself the errors of others. The prophets can ask pardon of God for men, *shafa'a*, but cannot take upon themselves the burden of men's sins. God alone will decide whether to forgive or to punish. Human acts also have a decisive importance. A Muslim ethic exists which in its fundamental aspects does not differ from Christian morality but on which Islam insists – more than the observable behaviour of Muslim organisations or the programs of Islamic movements lead us to believe is indeed being practised. In fact, ethics is of such importance that acts which conform to an ideal of goodness are often associated in the Quran with faith and belief, *iman*, to the point that certain theologians do not hesitate in integrating them into the creed.

The enumeration of these acts is edifying. They constitute the basis for a life that conforms to divine prescriptions. To live one's faith every day is, according to the Quran, to free slaves, not to kill, not to steal, not to commit adultery, not to lie, to show charity towards the captive, the orphan, the poor, and the beggar who must never be humiliated, towards the one who must be helped, to preserve one's relationship with one's parents who must be succoured to the end of their days, to respect the rules of propriety, to show oneself righteous and decent in one's dealings with others, to have a sense of good judgement in the spending of one's income as well as in the expression of one's piety, to have probity in commerce, to respect contracts, to keep one's word, not to accumulate wealth as an end in itself but to use it for charitable purposes and to accomplish the acts cited above, to believe that all Muslims are brothers and are expected to show tolerance, to be indulgent and at the same time avoid infatuation, arrogance, pride, vanity, ostentatious behaviour and haughtiness but also to steer clear of stinginess and pettiness and, in general, to command the good and forbid evil.

The Islamic ideal is not limited to individual moral behaviour. It also encompasses economic activity by the exaltation of effort, of honesty in work, and of bringing to fruition the blessings with which God has endowed the world. 'Do ye not see that God has subjected to your use all things in the heavens and on earth, and has made His bounties flow to you in exceeding measure, both seen and unseen?' (Quran 31:20) It is not to passivity, but to action that man is called: 'Say: Work; (righteousness) and soon God will observe your work, and His Apostle, and the Believers.' (Quran 9:105) It is the Quran that insists on man's responsibility in the growth of his attitudes: 'Verily never will God change the condition of a people until they change it themselves [with their own souls].' (Quran 13:11) These changes can only come about at the price of effort, and the first thing man must accomplish is to increase his knowledge, to observe the physical and animal world, and to give himself up to meditation of it.

Muslim morality does not only fix the norms of conduct that imply, on the behavioural level, the submission to religious precepts and which are manifest in a nomenclature of prescribed and forbidden acts. It demands of those who are capable of exceeding the common norm that they acquire a supplement of virtue. Moreover, the word which in the Roman languages signifies etymologically power is, in Arabic, 'a surplus': *fadhila*. One does not become *fadhil*, virtuous, by conforming strictly to the rule. One must do something more. And in this respect, the Arabic language and the Quran make the distinction between this concept and that of morality, which is expressed by *khuluq*, a word that derives from the verb *khalaqa*, to create. And so these are the innate qualities that must be cultivated by the *adab*, that is, by those who would possess social grace and distinction. The appeal addressed to man to rise above mere contingencies is of such great import that God likens these acquired qualities to divine attributes. Thus, for example, forgiveness is necessary for domestic harmony, social reconciliation, and coexistence of nations. The Quran uses no less than six words to translate the various nuances of forgiveness. In a particularly striking verse, one finds three of them linked to a human attitude of which one, that of *ghufran*, is generally reserved for God because it means absolution: 'But if ye forgive (*afw*), and overlook (*safh*), and cover up [their faults] (*ghufran*), verily, God is oft-forgiving and merciful,' states verse 14 of chapter 64. The appeal is the more striking since, in this chapter, it deals with members of the same family who have prevented their Muslim parent from fulfilling his religious obligations. Family harmony is thus raised in value.

Furthermore, when reviewing the concepts of morality (of which one can present here only a partial list), one is correct to ask oneself about the order of real priorities that Islam establishes between one's life and the hereafter. In the Quran there is such an insistence on what men must do on earth that the hereafter appears as the Last Judgment; in a word, everything happens first in this life and will be judged in the next.

In another verse of chapter 28, it is written: 'But seek, with [the wealth] which God has bestowed on thee, the Home of the Hereafter, nor forget thy portion in this world.' (Quran 28:77)

It is in this context that the problem of freedom is placed, a problem that has divided so many Muslim thinkers. The latitude left to man is so great that one cannot know with precision where it ends. Unfortunately, the fatalistic option has subsequently made of the ethics of action a simple object of intellectual speculation.

Obviously, we are very far from what is actually practised every day in Muslim countries. This ethic, these values were in former times considered to be so intimately connected to Islam that their teaching represented, with the verses relative to the faith and to the cosmogony, the most essential revelation of the Meccan period before Muhammad's flight to Medina. The Arabs, who had converted to Islam in response to Muhammad's preaching, who had endured the worst from the Quraysh and had been forced into exile first in 615 to Abyssinia and then in 622 to Medina, had responded to this universal message. We can understand the effect that this high moral teaching was able to have on men living in a milieu of rape and raiding where only the tribe, riches, and force counted. We can understand even better the atmosphere of brotherhood and solidarity that had marked, after the *hijra*, the community in Medina and that this message must have struck similar nerves in other peoples despite the differences of language and culture. These universal values had a permanent impact.

It was during the Medinan period of the life of the Prophet that what Muslims considered essential would be laid out: ritual and juridical organisation. What one called the basic duties, *qawa'id*, or the Pillars of Islam, *arkan*, were the foundation stones of the cult and the concrete manifestation of the faith. They were ranked according to the ability of each believer to observe them.

First came the *shahada*, the bearing of witness, the sacramental formula by which one professes the faith. No one may be dispensed from this obligation since all can accomplish it, even if one is dumb, in the silence of the heart, or in the raising of the index finger on the right hand to indicate the unity of God.

Second, there is prayer, *salat*, the greeting of God, the physical and moral act of submission. Muhammad used to pray in Mecca twice a day and used to prepare for prayer by ablutions in such a manner as to present himself before God in a state of physical and moral purity. Some time before his flight the number of prayers was fixed at five. But it was at Medina that the ritual was to require for each prayer a certain number of bowings and prostrations. No one may be dispensed from this obligation but, depending on one's abilities, one may pray alone or in a group, in a mosque or elsewhere, seated or lying down if one is sick or weak by imitating the movements of the body.

Third, and occupying a pivotal position between what is indispensable and what can be done without, is the fast to be observed during the month of Ramadan, the ninth month of the lunar year. One must abstain from drinking, eating, and sexual relations from dawn to dusk, until the instant when one can distinguish a white from a black thread in the sunset. But already the accomplishment of this duty allows for some latitude. One must be physically mature, resident in one place, in good health, and in a state of moral and physical purity. And children are not required to fast, nor adults while travelling, nor those who for reasons of health fear the consequences of the fast, nor women during their period, or while they are pregnant or nursing. But the religion attaches such importance to social and moral acts that it necessitates compensatory acts as a matter of ethics. If one does not observe the fast without good reason, one can free a slave or feed sixty beggars for each fast day missed. Once again, for Islam, social behaviour is more important that the act of devotion.

In fourth position comes *zakat*. The word is generally translated as alms. The Arabic language and Islam have yet another word that is usually used for alms: *sadaqa*. The root of the word *zakat* suggests more the ideas of increase and purification, or probity and integrity. So the word means to purify the wealth of this world acquired during the preceding year or belonging to a patrimony by putting aside a portion for the needs of the poor. It is a tax both on income and on goods! To approximate the Islamic sense of the word, orientalists define *zakat* in European languages as legal or sacred alms. This purification is a duty, certainly, but even more one must have at one's disposition goods to be purified. Thus the poor and the underprivileged are exempt. In fact, they are the designated beneficiaries of this duty. Here again community welfare is linked to the act of devotion.

Finally, and in the fifth and last position, comes the pilgrimage to Mecca, an obligation to be accomplished once in a lifetime 'if one has the means'. Exemption is based as much on material resources as it is on physical health or other impediments.

When one thinks of the millions of Muslims who are hardly concerned with the vision of life and of the universe that their religion offers them, who cavalierly ignore Islamic values while at the same time seeking at any price to observe the five pillars of the faith, one is obliged to come to the conclusion that when a religion is reduced to a gesture, it resembles more a soulless skeleton than the faith that can move mountains. As has been mentioned before, Islam has certainly known periods of oppression when retrenchment has enabled it to survive attack. But since men desire to reinvigorate Islam through militant action, why do they strive also to maintain it reduced to its simplest expression?

We come now to the question which has generated the most abundant literature, that of the practical organisation of Islamic life as defined by the *shari'a*, the law.

The root of the word, *sh r 'a*, means to open, to begin to commence, to go forward, to make clear. The *shari'* is the straight path. In Old Arabic it was said that 'the shortest way to water is to go directly to the source,' and this action was called *tashri'*. Also the use of the words *shar'* and *shari'a* to denote the divine law refers back to these notions of the straight line, the open road, the beaten and upright path. The word law and its corresponding translations in European languages refer to ideas of agreed-upon proposals, contracts, pacts; in sum, to what is termed positive law. To suggest the divine origin of a prescription, one must necessarily have recourse to the adjective and so one speaks of divine law. In Arabic, the word *shari'a* already signifies the straight path. This has nothing to do with a contract. One cannot change the direction of the path or change it in any way; one can only conform to it. One strives to understand it and the need to interpret it. And one learns the *fiqh* that signifies knowledge and comprehension of the *shari'a*, not legislation in the European sense. Moreover, the *faqih*, the learned person versed in *fiqh*, is an exegete of the *shari'a*, a legalist in the sense that Littre's Dictionary gives to this word ('someone who knows or who studies the law'), but not someone who has the power of decision. If, for convenience and to follow common usage, the word *shari'a* is translated here by 'the law', it is nevertheless necessary to remind the reader of those characteristics that are particular to Islam.

To conform to the law, however, without violating any of its prescriptions is not so simple. Where is this law found and who defines it? The answer is invariably the Quran. The reality is somewhat more complex. When the *faqih*, the legalist, invokes the *shari'a* to forbid or approve an action, the word does not cover in its spirit only the prescriptions contained in the Quran. It extends over a whole spectrum of references and it is there that one encounters the real problem of Muslim societies. All believers agree that the Quran is a sacred text. On the other hand, they have never agreed on the attitude to adopt with respect to its legal prescriptions and we shall see why. Moreover, the Book of God does not cover in an explicit manner and in detail all situations. Furthermore, a law and juridical code developed from sources other than the Quran.

What then are the other sources of *shari'a* and what value should they be given? In the place of honour stands the Quran. Then comes the tradition, the *Sunna*, of the Prophet composed of his sayings, the *Hadith*, and his acts, the *Sira*. Following, there is the tradition of his companions and immediate successors known for their wisdom and piety. Their acts, their judgments, their writings constitute the original consensus, the *ijma'*. To this consensus another *ijma'* is added, that of the great scholars of juridical science, whether or not they were founders of schools of thought, when there are no divergences among them. Now the divergences begin precisely when appeal is made to two methods: that of analogy, *qiyas*, and that of systematic personal judgment, *ijtihad*.

The Quran for the Muslim is, as we have already said, the Word of God revealed to Muhammad who transmitted it faithfully to men. In this respect, it constitutes a sacred text, inviolable, unalterable, and having a permanent importance. It was not revealed all at once in a fixed order, but in graduated steps (*munajjaman*) over a period of about twenty-two years: thirteen years from 610 to 622 during the life of the Prophet in Mecca, and ten years after his flight to Medina until his death in 632. The stages of revelation varied in intensity and in duration. The verses were written down little by little by scribes, on various materials: skins, stones, shoulder blades of camels, and other materials. But they were all committed to memory, a widespread practice in an environment where illiteracy and the love of beautiful poetry existed side by side. The Prophet indicated to the faithful to which preceding verses everything that had just been revealed was to be appended, but while he lived he never ordered the assembling of the recitation into one volume.

This question was to prompt much discussion after his death. His first successor, the *khalifa* (caliph) Abu Bakr al-Siddiq (632–4), accepted only the collation of the writings that he kept piously at home, without putting them into a single book. This collection, which was passed on at his death to his successor 'Umar Ibn al-Khattab (634–44), was preserved intact and at his death his daughter, Hafsa, a wife of the Prophet, inherited it. Twenty-one years went by after the death of the Prophet before the third caliph, 'Uthman Ibn Affan (644–56), decided in 653 to fix the order of the chapters and thus to make the writings into a book. He ordered copies to be made which he sent to the various provinces of what had become an empire, with the order to destroy all private collections and not to permit copies to be made that did not conform to the model of what was called the *mushaf'Uthmani*, that is the 'Uthman Codex. The first two caliphs had hesitated scrupulously to carry out an act that Muhammad in his lifetime had not ordained. The third had to confront a new situation: the growing number of converts, the dialectical differences among them, and especially the quarrels that broke out among the professional reciters of the Book who, according to tradition, were reported to have incited veritable battles in 653 between Syrian and Iraqi clans, each claiming to recite the authentic Quran. It was therefore necessary to put an end to a debate that risked becoming extremely dangerous for the unity of Islam. Here 'Uthman took up the work where Abu Bakr had left it. A commission of experts was assembled and from its methodical and scrupulous work came the text that we possess today. Given that the word of God is one and indivisible and that the faith is an indissoluable whole, the chapters, *surat*, were arranged according to their length, beginning with the longest, and not according to their order of revelation.

Now, as we have seen, what referred to the organisation of life corresponds in large part to the Medinan period (622–32). It is there that the Muslim community and the city–state first saw the light of day. It is there that the problems of marriage, of inheritance between believers and polytheists, of association, of commerce, of war, of the dividing of booty, of peace, and of internal social stability in the interest of safeguarding the community against all crimes and misdemeanours were posed. Gradually, the questions were referred to Muhammad. He judged them conscientiously according to the principle of equity and general interest and when a problem appeared particularly difficult he waited patiently for divine inspiration. Then one or two verses were revealed to illuminate the path.

When the revelation ceased at the time of the Prophet's death, the Quran already contained a considerable number of legal prescriptions but these did not respond to all the new situations that had gradually sprung up as Muslim society expanded and social relations became more complex.

The first caliphs, sitting in Medina, had the habit in the first place of referring to the judgments and known acts of the Prophet, to the consultation of the wisest and the most pious among the companions, the *sahaba*, and of exercising in the last instance their own faculties of judgment, *ijtihad*, when no clear answer was offered.

But the Empire was yet to experience a greater shock. The caliph 'Uthman was accused by certain notables of favouring the members of his own family. A revolt started in Egypt and then angry men made their way toward Medina, seat of the caliphate. The caliph was besieged in his own house. Refusing to surrender, he was assassinated by the rioters. This occurred in 656. A successor was elected, the fourth caliph, who was none other than 'Ali Ibn Talib, cousin and son-in-law of the Prophet, father of the only descendants of the Prophet by his daughter Fatima, the first child to be converted to Islam in the early days of the revelation and expert without equal in religious affairs. But 'Ali's election was not unanimously accepted. The governor of the Syrian province, Mu'awiya Ibn Abi Sufyan, cousin of the slain caliph, rebelled. He questioned 'Ali's legitimacy declaring that the circumstances under which he had been elected were not clear and advancing as a condition of his allegiance the punishment by 'Ali of 'Uthman's assassins. Now not only had 'Uthman been killed during an uprising in which hundreds of people had taken part, but the rebels were supported by important Arab clans, especially in Medina, and certain of 'Uthman's opponents had cooperated in the election of 'Ali.

Along with this serious dispute, another appeared, first in Medina, then in Lower Mesopotamia where it gathered strength. It was directed by other Medinan notables and inspired by 'Aisha, widow of the Prophet and daughter of the first caliph Abu Bakr.

The struggle to succeed 'Uthman led to a civil war on two fronts. The 'Great Ordeal', as Muslim historians call it, lasted for five years. In 661, 'Ali was assassinated in turn and Mu'awiya was proclaimed caliph. He took up residence in Damascus, where he had served as governor, and Medina lost its rank as the imperial capital. Mu'awiya succeeded in transforming the elective caliphate into a hereditary system which permitted him to become the founder of the Umayyad dynasty, from the name of the branch of the Quraysh tribe to which he and his cousin 'Uthman belonged.

While it raged, the civil war had other effects on Islam, properly speaking. For having accepted the calling together of a commission to arbitrate his dispute with Mu'awiya, 'Ali was abandoned by a faction within the army one year after his victory in Mesopotamia over 'Aisha's partisans. They were called the *khawarij* or Kharijites, that is, 'those who leave the ranks'. They gave themselves the name *muwahhidun* or unitarians because they believed that by accepting arbitration, 'Ali had accepted, *ipso facto*, that the legitimacy of his election could be challenged, that he had violated the law, and that he no longer deserved to be obeyed. And so 'Ali had to do battle with them also. And if he carried the field against them in 656 at Nahrawan in Persia, he paid for his victory in 661 when a Kharijite slew him in vengeance for his brothers.

Thus, the first schism in Islam was based on an interpretation of the law and of the Quran. The Kharijites, always a minority in the Muslim world, were to prove troublesome to the Empire. In fact, they have survived up to the present day. They are found in Oman, in southern Algeria (the Mzab), and on the Tunisian island of Djerba. It goes without saying that they have developed in the past fourteen centuries their own understanding of the law (*fiqh*) and their own concept of the communal life, and the preference for an elective system of choosing their leaders.

Secondly, after the triumph of Mu'awiya the partisans of 'Ali (in Arabic, the *shi'a* or Shi'ites) did not consider themselves beaten. Certainly military power was on Mu'awiya's side but not, they said, legitimacy. And yet Shi'ism in the doctrinal form we recognise today, was not born immediately. It had a long gestation of more than a century and a half. The concept of who constituted the partisans of 'Ali was initially very large. It extended in the beginning to all those who believed the legitimate power had to be held by the family of the Prophet (*Ahl al-Bayt*). Similarly, those who in 750 created the Abbasid dynasty with Baghdad as its capital were obliged first to combat the Umayyads as Shi'ites, although they did not descend from 'Ali but from 'Abbas, the uncle of the Prophet. The seventh Abbasid caliph, al-Ma'mun (830–3) attempted to make the Alawite Shi'ite Imam Rida his successor. The latter, more attached to his duty as religious guide, refused. Be that as it may, at the death of 'Ali in 661, the 'kick-off', if we can use the word, had already been given to Shi'ite history, a history marked by tragedies: the shift of population from southern Iraq to the Iranian Khurasan in 670; the Alawite revolt in Iran from 683 to 688 which was put down savagely; a new Alawite revolt suppressed in Khurasan in 747; two other bloodbaths in Medina in 762 and 786; and so on.

Little by little, the Shi'ite doctrine of the legitimacy of power, of the pre-eminence of the imams – the descendants of 'Ali – who were supposed to have been initiated from father to son in the esoteric knowledge of religion and law, developed. The movement, by virtue of ferocious repressions, went underground. From time to time it surfaced to create kingdoms, such as that of the Fatimids, first in Tunisia then in Egypt, from 909 to 1172. Meanwhile the Shi'ite tree had, from the tenth century, already multiplied to branches which more and more diverged doctrinally one from the other.

In fact, the Shi'ites had not limited themselves solely to the defence of the exclusive right of 'Ali and Fatima to the caliphate. Some proclaimed that the Quran was composed of two levels of meaning: one visible or exoteric and the other hidden or esoteric. The esoteric meaning masked by the words of the verse itself could be discerned only by the initiated, the first among whom, in the eyes of those who accepted this doctrine, was obviously 'Ali. His successive heirs were reported to have received through a sort of initiatory testament the key to this hermetic knowledge. The majoritarian branch of Shi'ism, that of the Imamites, would never allow themselves to go to extremes but rather contented themselves with defending the high degree of wisdom possessed by their imams. Only the Nusayris, or Syrian Alawites, slipped into sectarianism. On the other hand, the Ismaili branch of Shi'ism made esotericism its basic doctrine and over the centuries put outshoots in all directions, all more and more independent of each other.

The majority of Muslims refused to be dragged into this doctrinal dispute and remained faithful to the tradition, the *sunna*, and so adopted the custom of calling themselves Sunni.

As a third consequence of the transfer of the capital from Medina to Damascus, all political influence was withdrawn from the city of the Prophet. Medina compensated for the loss of prestige by devoting itself to the preservation of the Tradition. The learned doctors of Medina, heirs to a wisdom transmitted from generation to generation, became the legatees of the Prophet's companions, the champions of traditionism[1] and of traditionialism. At the same time, in southern Iraq, which was the theatre of so many military and ideological clashes, a spirit of controversy arose that put down deep cultural roots in the Sunnite environment.

Through these multiple events, one could already perceive the new directions that theology would take. The rigorism of the Kharijites and the legitimism of the Shi'ites were to be opposed by the traditionalism of Medina and the free speculation of the Iraqis while the centre of power in Damascus, and afterwards in Baghdad, reserved for itself the role of arbiter and did not hesitate to resolve conflict by force of arms.

All in all, despite the tragedies and the blood, it was, as far as its ideas were concerned, a lively world. Nothing in that world was yet atrophied. Muslims today cannot conceive that during at least a century and a half, if not two centuries, that is, ultimately for the full length of the great phase of Islamic expansion, their ancestors had only the Quran as an uncontested reference! The first schools or doctrines of Sunnism date from the eighth century. Abu Hanifa (699–767) and Malik Ibn Anas (715–95) developed their teachings more than 100 years after the death of the Prophet. Ibn Hanbal (died 855) and Shafa'i (767–820) were men of the ninth century, like Bukhari (810–70) and Muslim (817–65), the two great codifiers of the Prophetic tradition, along with their contemporaries Tirmidhi (824–93) and the great exegete, Abu Ja'afar Tabari (839–923).

Among the Shi'ites, the teaching of the great masters also appeared late. Musa al-Kazim (745–99) was a man of the eighth century. The founder of the Fatimid dynasty, Obaidallah, was of the tenth century – he reigned from 909 to 934 – as was the codifier of the sermons of 'Ali (*Nahj al-Balagha*), Muhammad Ibn al-Hussain, born in 969, and the Qadi Nu'man, who died in 974.

Recalling these dates may seem tiresome in the context of remarks on the law. But it is indispensable to state what happened from 656 to the end of the tenth century in order to clarify the definitions of the sources of jurisprudence and the use which has been made of them, since it was during these 350 years that the definitions were formed.

Certainly, Muslims admit that after the Quran the *sunna* represents the second material source of the *shari'a*. Recalling history as we have just done brings to light, nevertheless, several facts which are at the origin of the controversies. The codification of the *hadiths*, the utterances of the Prophet, came late. It appeared at a moment when political and doctrinal dissension had already seriously divided Muslims.

From that time forward, each branch of Islam was going to recognise only its own thinkers. And even if there existed a common corpus of *hadiths* that everybody accepted, the additions and forgeries were nonetheless numerous and provoked interminable quarrels among scholars.

Primitive consensus did not remain the object of unanimity for long. Certain Shi'ite factions challenged the first three caliphs, usurpers in the eyes of 'Ali's legitimate power, while the Sunnites accepted this tradition as the extension of a prophetic act, conveyed by wise and pious companions who knew the life and the thought of God's messenger perfectly. For others, the agreement of the wisest scholars, even of the entire Muslim community, sufficed.

There was even a kind of controversy over the use of *qiyas*, the analogic method. Was it an issue of whether to reason, as the Iraqis proclaimed, on the basis of principles established by the Quran or, as the Medinans decreed, on the basis of cases decided by the Prophet, his immediate successors, and the tradition of the city?

Until present times, the notion of tradition differs from Sunnism to Shi'ism and to Kharijitism. For the Sunnites, who constitute the majority of Muslims who did not follow either Kharijite rigorism or Shi'ite legitimism, the tradition is that of the Prophet, his successors and the great teachers. For the Kharijites, it is that of the Prophet and of the austere and intransigent community of early Islamic times. For the Shi'ites, the tradition does not stop at a given date, but includes the teaching dispensed by all the succesive imams who have assumed the management of the community.

Thus we come to the notion of *ijtihad*. As mentioned above, this word derives from the same root *jhd*, which gave us the word *jihad*, struggle. *Ijtihad* signifies therefore the expending of intellectual effort, either to learn as a student learns in the classroom, or to seek solutions to a problem. We prefer to translate *ijtihad* as 'an effort of judgment', but personal, to be sure.

For a century and a half at least, from the death of the Prophet in 632 to the codification of the rules of the first schools of Islamic jurisprudence, between 750 and 795, all Muslim chiefs – military, administrative, judicial, academic – made *ijtihad*. This means that they made an 'effort of personal judgment' by referring themselves to the Quran that they knew by heart, to the tradition of Muhammad or to what they understood of it individually, as well as to their own tribal or ethnic traditions. They obeyed, too, the instructions received from the centre of power. Finally, they would have recourse to the consultation of the honest men of their entourage. In a word, they would legislate without claiming to make dogma of their decisions.

Then came the era of codification, that is, of the *madhhab*, or the proceedings of the founders of juridical schools. Attachment to one or another school rendered each more partisan. Today, for example, the Sunnites accept four schools (Malekite, Hanafite, Hanbalite, and Shafi'ite). But it was not always that way. Truly bloody riots over the generations opposed the adherents of the various schools. It was necessary for the Seljuk Turks to seize power in Baghdad under the authority of the Abbasid caliphs, so that the palace major-domos, who were military officers more concerned with civil peace than juridical controversy, could decide, from the tenth century on, to impose coexistence on the four Sunnite schools. In North Africa there is a popular saying that 'God acquiesces before the four schools.' All at once the Kharijites were commonly qualified as partisans of the 'fifth column' and for that reason often are considered heretics whereas they had nothing whatsoever to do with the Sunnite schools. The ruling establishment wanted to reestablish public order, certainly, but they were not aware of the disastrous blow they had given to intellectual effort. Inasmuch as the four 'schools' had such difficulty in accepting one another, the coexistence imposed on them all ended in the blockage of creative juridical effort. This was called the 'closing of the doors of *ijtihad*', literally the doors of independent judgment. The question has not ceased, in ten centuries, to feed the debates of reformers. Disastrous, no doubt, for majoritarian Sunnism, this halt however did not trouble the Kharijites, whose dogma was already fixed, nor the Shi'ites, whose imams had followed without interruption their *ijtihad* to the extent that a *hujjat al-islam* ('proof of the religion', i.e., a lesser Shi'ite cleric) could easily, and can even today, acquire the title of *mujtahid*, that is, a master of *ijtihad*!

Even in Sunnism, there were some exceptions. Ibn Taymiyya (1263–1328) reworked the Hanbalite doctrine. But he was so ferociously fought by the *ulama* of Cairo that he died in prison. His ideas were taken up by his disciple Ibn Qayim al-Jawziyya (1292–1350), then later by Muhammad Ibn Abd al-Wahhab (1703–87) who founded the Wahhabite school which today prevails in Saudi Arabia.

With these rare exceptions, the effort of independent judgment was blocked, and the beginning for the Islamic world of a period of backwardness from the twelfth century on helped to bar the door to any further progress. In fact, the path to learning was so obstructed that it was not until the coming in the nineteenth century of the *Nahda*, which is most often translated 'renaissance', that the obstacles could be removed.

This question is of such great importance to the majority of Muslims that it would be worthwhile to pause here for a moment. There has never been an explicit or authorised decision to close the famous 'doors of *ijtihad*'. Moreover, neither councils nor papacy exist in Islam to take such a decision. Until now, *ijtihad* continues under certain forms. When a *mufti*, a jurisconsultant, gives a *fatwa*, that is, a juridical consultation, what does he do? He consults the Quran, the exegetical literature, the traditions, makes necessary connections, proceeds by deduction or by induction, and renders his judgment. He 'tells the law' and thus makes *ijtihad*, since his consultation, in the eyes of Muslims, cannot help but enrich jurisprudence. Furthermore, the advice offered by *muftis* differs from one country to another. Hence, it was not long ago in the Iran of the nineteenth century that tobacco was forbidden and in Tunisia that in 1930 Muslims could become naturalised French. The *muftis* who rendered these judgments had used *ijtihad* and were not corroborated by other *ulama*.

What, then, was stifled? In the first place, new juridical schools that produced coherent doctrine were not institutionalised. The fear of innovation was such that the creative effort was condemned to be incorporated into an existing school or to be rejected. Ibn Taymiyya in the thirteenth century and Abd al-Wahhab in the eighteenth century had to make use of the name of the Hanbalite school. They had really perfected new doctrines, but reference was indispensable and despite this connection they were criticised and resisted. Today's *mufti* sees himself constrained by the need to refer necessarily to a single school.

In the second place, the obstacle appeared on the level of method. There was no way that the traditionalist *ulama* would accept the putting into practice of new juridical procedures nor even that accepted techniques be used to change former decisions. Thus Iqbal, the Muslim Indian philosopher, proposed giving to the decision of Muslim parliaments the character of an *ijma* that is, making recognised consensus the basis for legislation. He was not supported in this. Such a thing had never before existed, the *ulama* replied; it would be an innovation, hence a sin! Similarly, the *muftis*' advice can be original only on the express condition that the case under consideration be previously not known. If a precedent exists, it must be obligatorily conformed to, according to the school to which one belongs.

The differences among the four juridical schools of Sunni Islam are, in the eyes of the profane, only subtleties. In reality they are important by virtue of the role each school gives to personal judgment. According to Abu Hanifa, the jurist must remain exacting in the case of the authentification of a prophetic tradition. And if he has doubts, he must turn either to analogy or, as a last resort, to *istihsan*, that is, to the concept he has of the Good.

As a child of Medina, Malik made much of the Tradition and the customs of the Prophet's city. He was demanding only in the case of a tradition transmitted by others than the Medinans. When in doubt he used analogy and, as a last resort, *istislah*, that is, whatever seemed to be in the interest of the community.

Younger than the first two, and considered the true founder of *fiqh*, the understanding of the law, Shafa'i made his goal the fixing of juridical rules. He classed the texts of the Tradition by degree of authenticity and defined a method to arrive at this, based on the quality of the transmitters. He accepted a Tradition transmitted by numerous transmitters and, as opposed to Malik, he did not require that they be Medinans. He denied the usefulness of analogy whenever he found an utterance of the Prophet, even if it were reported by a single *'alim*, and so had recourse to it only in the case of absolute necessity. He rejected *istihsan* because he considered it an opinion having no legal foundation.

Finally, Ibn Hanbal, who was above all a traditionalist, believed that the existence of a text took precedence over all other methods, whether this text was an utterance of the Prophet or simply a consultation rendered by one of his companions. There must be, he said, an absolute necessity reinforced by the complete absence of precedent to justify the recourse to analogic method.

The divergences among the juridical schools of Sunni Islam were therefore born from the attitude of each of the founders toward the *hadith* and the Tradition. These were fundamental because they consequently determined the place reserved for the opinion – *ra'y* – of the scholar. The more the scholar was reluctant to accept a saying attributed to the Prophet, the more he gave free expression to his creativity as a jurist, and vice versa. Thus Abu Hanifa had the reputation for being the champion of *ra'y* and yet on the other hand Ibn Hanbal reduced this procedure to almost nothing. Hence the violent conflicts among their followers, the latter accusing the former of turning up their noses at the acts of the Prophet, the former retorting that tradition might be apocryphal or at best doubtful.

Peace was established in the future only when all Sunnites accepted the entire corpus of these four scholars' work and that of their disciples. Henceforth, references to each school were no longer to be a matter of dispute: scholars would content themselves by making commentaries on the judgments of each school with the result that today the mass of Muslims, being ignorant of the process of verification, accept in its entirety the doctrines of the four schools.

It goes without saying that under these conditions a judgment upon which all the schools agree is considered by all the *ulama* as an *ijma'* – an inviolate consensus.

Thus the law – the *shari'a* – draws its inspiration from many sources of unequal importance: the Quran, *hadith*, tradition, *qiyas*, consensus, the perfected teaching of the great scholars of the past, and the books of commentary and exegesis. The number of references is colossal and knowledge of them demands study that could last a lifetime. Consequently, this knowledge is within the reach of an elite alone, a small number of specialists ready to devote their time to learning, often by heart, a whole library. The hierarchy among them was easily established according to the knowledge of each. Those who occupied top rung on the ladder deserve an unhesitating admiration for the work accomplished during their lifetimes. This did not prevent, however, the entire system from weighing heavily on Muslim society.

In effect, and thanks to these developments, the *shari'a* has its word to say in the multiple area of man's life: the institutional, penal, civil, commercial, fiscal, personal, successorial, the rights of man and the rights of the collectivity, the manner of rendering justice, the relationship between power and the mass of believers, and so on. What did not exist in the Quran was added by reference to other sources in terms of doctrines and schools. Throughout fourteen centuries of active or static life, Muslim societies have adapted or coloured the code to conform with their customs, whether they be Arabs, Persians, Turks, Africans or Asians; feudal, tribal or democratic; nomadic, urban, agrarian or maritime. So that when we declare that the *shari'a* touches on all aspects of life, we are speaking the truth, but we must take care all the same not to forget the weight of the centuries and the interpretations of men, even if they are specialists.

Why should the Muslims of the twentieth century and of the future not have the right to return to the Islam of the first century of the *hijra* since Arabs, Persians, Berbers and blacks converted at the very first exposure to the call of the Quran? We shall see in one of the following chapters that this idea is not new, nor is the idea either to modernise the law, to legislate with respect to the traditional, or to borrow from other legal systems whatever does not violate a Quranic principle.

What remains to be answered is where to stop in this return to the sources. We can wager that the present debate that has indirectly contributed to the rise of Islamist movements will end up by bringing forward a definitive answer, more in harmony with the requirements of the century.

The question is all the more serious because Muslims have, as we have already mentioned, adopted the habit of reducing religion to a cult, still worse, to a meaningless gesture. Now, to live one's faith is to reconcile an ultimate vision of life with a renewed vision of the world that surrounds us in which, as producers or consumers, we participate; it is to reconcile one's ethos with a changing society; it is to keep or safeguard the permanent values that rest on a solid foundation amid perpetual evolution. An example that illustrates this debate is the manner of rendering justice. The *lex talionis* exists in Islam. But each time the Quran mentions it, it does so by recalling that it was prescribed to the Children of Israel in the Bible but followed immediately by an exhortation for clemency. In the second *sura* of the Quran, called 'The Heifer', verse 178, we read: 'O ye who believe! The law of equality is prescribed to you in case of murder: The free for the free, the slave for the slave, the woman for the woman.' But the verse does not stop there, it continues:

> But if any remission is made by the brother of the slain, then grant any reasonable demand, and compensate him with handsome gratitude. This is a concession and a Mercy from your Lord. After this whoever exceeds the limits shall be in grave penalty.

In the chapter called 'The Table Spread', the Quran recalls once again, in verse 48, the *lex talionis* such as it was prescribed in the Torah and mentioned above. But after having enumerated the intentions of the rule, 'Life for life, eye for eye,' etc., the verse ends this way: 'But if anyone remits the retaliation by charity, it is an act of atonement for himself.' And in conclusion: '. . . if any fail to judge by [the light of] what God hath revealed, they are [no better than] wrongdoers.'

An uncontested *hadith* of the Prophet reported by Bukhari established that no one ought to render a legal opinion between two persons under the influence of anger. Serenity was thus established as the *sine qua non* condition for sitting in judgment. Another *hadith* stipulates that testimony must be presented before a judge at the moment of the examination of a complaint. And 'Ali, the fourth caliph and supreme reference for the Iranian Shi'ites, refused to render a verdict without having first assembled a tribunal. One day, the tradition tells us, 'Ali was stopped by a man who demanded justice against an enemy. 'Ali forbade him to speak, asked him to follow in his footsteps, stopped in turn a companion of the Prophet who was passing by and requested him to serve on a court which gathered in the caliph's house before hearing the case of the plaintiff.

These are the principles that we find at the heart of all respectable justice: a real tribunal that hears testimony; serene judges; and intelligible law; mitigating circumstances; and above all, charity. Today, what does respect of these seventh-century principles mean in practice? Does this respect conform to what is called Islamic justice which denies all legal procedure and excludes lawyers from the courtroom?

In another vein, certain rigorists reject even the idea of evolution whenever it is a question of interpreting the Quran. For them the Word of God was not a gradual revelation transmitted by Muhammad to men taking into consideration their intelligence but rather a global text to be understood such as it is without any questioning. Yet the exegetes recognised that there exist in the Quran verses that contradict or cancel the intentions of other verses. These are called the *rasikh* and the *mansukh*, and the exegetes have gone so far as to develop a whole new branch of Quranic science for the study of these discrepancies. The reasoning of the rigorists often took the following form: from the time of Muhammad, God in his wisdom wished to facilitate the conversion of miscreants. But the message had come to an end and the prophetic mission was accomplished. What was received ought to be taken as it was and applied to the letter of the law without discussion.

This reasoning, however respectable in its form, did not cover all the possible contradictions. Take for example the question of the Islamic attitude toward slavery. There is no doubt that the faith opposed it, founded as it is on the equality of all men before God. The faith made the manumission of the slave an act which gained absolution for him who accomplished it and required that the compensation for certain violations of the rules be precisely the act of freeing a slave. The second caliph, 'Umar, said: 'How is it that you are allowed to enslave a man whose mother brought him into the world a free being?' And yet, the Quran, despite the many exhortations that it contains concerning the freeing of slaves, has never forbidden slavery in an explicit way. For generations Muslim societies had concluded from this, and wrongly, that the maintenance of this system was authorised for certain of them, at least, until the twentieth century. Now the argument of the theologians in this case consists of saying that the Quran avoided running foul of societies in which slavery played a great economic role. The Quran, they say, has sufficiently insisted on the importance of manumission so as to indicate the direction of religious preferences. Why, in this case, would it not be possible to adapt this reading of the Quran to the present time any less than it would be, by following the partisans of rigorism, to allow slavery to perpetuate itself?

As we can see, the questions that refer to the totalism of Islam are not simple. All life's acts being envisaged in one text or another, the candidate for Islamist activism knows that it is lawful to find in his religion an answer for anything – even if this allows him to come up with simplistic solutions. But what kind of an answer? One conforming to the letter of the law or to its spirit; to the universal and enduring message or to the encyclopaedias of commentary; to the frozen tradition or to that of *ijtihad* renewed?

Notes

1. *Traditionism* is the discipline that relates to the authentication of the prophetic tradition, the *Sunna*. It is not to be confused with *traditionalism*, which is an approach that preaches respect for the traditions and the imitation of the first Muslims.

6.   The *Ulama* of Power and the Power of the *Ulama*

There are neither priests nor ecclesiastical orders in Islam. This affirmation to which all Muslims agree flows from the creed that makes every human being responsible for his acts and is based on a saying of the Prophet.

The question is really posed in practical rather than dogmatic terms. The dogma is unequivocally clear. No one can atone for another, nor baptise him, nor absolve him, nor give him extreme unction, nor confess him, nor represent God, nor replace Muhammad or set himself up as a repository of God's power. The office of Apostle or Vicar of Christ, for example, has no correspondent in Islam. Those who had the privilege of accompanying the Prophet during a part of his life, or of receiving directly from him religious instruction, are only the companions (*sahib*, plural *sahaba*). Those who after him directed the community are only the successors (*khalifa*, plural *khulafa*). Without a doubt, those among them who were also companions benefited from a special authority, but whenever that authority exceeds the stage of respect, it smacks of veneration. From the dogmatic point of view, there are no saints, no beatification, no canonisation. But human society is such that its functioning always produces hierarchies.

There are no monks – *rahib* in Islam. So be it! Nevertheless, Islam has known the pious personage, *nasik*; the ascetic, *zahid*; the warrior–cenobite devoted to the defence of the community, *murabit*,* (plural, *murabitun*); the convent–fortress of the *murabitun*; the *ribat*, the brotherhoods which we call *turuq* (plural of *tariqa*, path or method), such as the Qadiriya, the Shadhiliya, the dervishes,the Aissawiya, the Baktashis, the Naqshabandiya, the Hurufis, and so on.

Certain practices and certain rules observed by these men are comparable no doubt to those of the Christian hermits or of the Catholic monastic orders. Still, we are speaking here only of the varied forms of mysticism that majoritarian Islam began to combat before absorbing and normalising them. Whatever the relationships of understanding or of confrontation that these orders had with power, the occasions when they played the role of clergy or religious judge are rare.

---

* The French word *marabout* has been generalised into English.

It was quite otherwise for those whom we can place under the rubric of men of religion, *rijal al-din*. Certain ones acceded to the rank of doctor of the law, *'alim* (plural, *ulama*). Others were charged more modestly with the regular observation of the ritual; still others watched over the proper application of the law. They all had social functions linked to religion.

The *muaddib*, the teacher, generally on his own initiative, took care of the *kuttab*, that is, a Quranic 'nursery' school where he taught young children the Quran. On higher levels existed the *mudarris*, or professor. In early Islamic times and in certain cases up to the present day, they were men of knowledge who voluntarily gave lessons in the mosques after prayers. Circles of listeners would form around them and the success of each depended on his talent and what he knew. Little by little this free instruction yielded place in the large cities to an organisation of education which itself gave birth to the celebrated Islamic universities such as the al-Azhar of Cairo.

The *imam*, literally the one who shows the direction to follow, was originally the prayer leader. He was not a priest belonging to an order. He could be anyone at all. It was enough that the faithful designated him as such or agreed to line up behind him for collective prayer. Still the custom very quickly came to mean the imams of large mosques – and in our day every permanent place of prayer has its imam – were appointed by the official authorities or by the leaders of the Muslim community in the case of minorities living in non-Muslim countries.

The *mufti* is a jurisconsultant. He renders judicial opinion by means of which he interprets the law. Without this being systematic, it often happens that this dignitary plays the role of an appeals judge. But a *mudarris* of reknown may be consulted as well and 'read the law'. Still, as in the first case, he is always a high functionary.

One of the first religious positions to have been instituted in Islam was that of *qadi*. The *qadi* was at all times named by the highest authorities of the Muslim community after having been chosen from among men reputed for their understanding of the subtleties of the law and, most of all, for their integrity. It often happened in history that great scholars were designated to exercise this responsibility and many declined. They were generally forced to accept and certain were even imprisoned for disobedience.

But with the evolution of the Muslim empire we began to see appearing the titles *qadi al-qudat*, judge of judges, and *bash mufti* or chief jurisconsultant, or as the Americans say, chief justice. Today we use more modest titles such as mufti of the country, this last word being translated more precisely as 'kingdom', 'republic' or 'territory': *mufti al-mamlaka*, *mufti al-jumhuriyya*, or *mufti al-diyar*. More simply, we might say grand mufti.

On the same level we find also the position of *shaykh al-Islam*, that is, the position of patriarch. However, this title has been used only in the context of the Ottoman Empire, either in Istanbul or in the outlying provinces, to designate the highest dignitary in the hierarchy of Hanafite scholars.

Finally, there existed at certain times in Islamic imperial history the equally official position of *muhtasib*, or moral censor. His disappearance was due to the evolution of the prerogatives associated with the ministries of the interior and of the police.

In Iran, the *mullah* holds sway today. The word derives from the Arabic *mawla*, lord or master, a title given in reality to anyone exercising a religious function, whereas Africa remained the domain of the *marabout*, of whom we have already spoken, with the difference that in North Africa this word meant a holy man dead and buried long ago, while in sub-Saharan Africa he was a living *mullah*. Moreover, this conforms closely to history since the *marabout* whose name was preceded by the title of respect, *sidi*, was he who dedicated his life to the service of society.

But while anyone at all – since there are no priests in Islam – can be *muaddib*, *imam* for prayer, or may carry out any other socio-religious function such as funeral rites, a level of education was needed in order to accede to the other ranks.

With the rank of *qadi* we begin to speak of the *ulama*. To read the law, to judge an appeal, to render juridical verdicts and to guarantee the community that it was not about to stray from the straight path, a degree of knowledge was required.

The *ulama* of Sunni Islam are therefore generally *qadis*, *muftis*, *shaykhs al-Islam*, teachers in a religious university such as al-Azhar in Cairo, al-Zituna in Tunis, al-Qarawiyyin in Fez, or rectors of one of these schools.

The *ulama* of Shi'ite Islam are the *hujjat al-Islam* (Proof of Islam), the *mujtahids* (jurisconsultants who render systematic personal judgment), and the *ayatollahs* (Sign of God). These three degrees are strictly regulated. They require proof of a research effort showing the extent of the candidate's knowledge. One does not apply for the positions. They are conferred by the community of scholars and, as for ayatollahs, their members are very limited, not exceeding five living title holders.

Beyond these degrees there exists the sublime one of imam. The word, of course, was applied to the prayer guide and so it could mean just 'guide'. In Sunni Islam, the supreme dignity of this title was accorded to the great scholars, founders of schools of jurisprudence, compilers of the Prophetic traditions, and propagators of the faith. Malik, Abu Hanifa, Shafa'i Ibn Hanbal, Awza'i, Sahnun, Bukhari, Muslim, Tirmidhi, Shatibi, Ibn Araba, Juwaini, among others, had the right to this title. In the twentieth century few persons have acquired this privilege, except when they were the object of great veneration by their disciples, as was the case of the Imam Hassan al-Banna, founder of the Muslim Brothers. Sometimes, through abuse of the language, the first imam of the great mosque of the capital of each country has this title attached permanently to his name because of social considerations.

In Shi'ite Islam, the title has an even more limited meaning. It designates the supreme leaders of the community, descendants of the Prophet through his daughter Fatima, designated to succeed their father after his death, the first in chronological order being, of course, the Imam 'Ali, son-in-law of the Prophet. In the Imamite branch, sometimes called the Twelvers, the title disappeared with the twelfth imam, Muhammad al-Mahdi al-Mukhtafi, who disappeared in

878. For the Ismaili branch, sometimes called the Seveners, the imamate ended with the death of the seventh Imam Ismail, who died before his father Ja'afar al-Sadiq (699–765). But the title reappeared with the Fatimids who were descendants of that branch and whose fourteen imams reigned over a part of the Muslim world, first from Tunisia and then from Egypt, from 909 to 1171.

The definition of the Shi'ite imamate is found again in all the boughs of this branch. Thus the chiefs of the Zaydis of Yemen carried this title until the disappearance of their monarchy in 1963. Similarly, the Aga Khan, chief of the Nizari Ismailis and of the Khojas of India, has an equal right to the title of imam.

Finally, as did Sunnism, Twelver Iranian Shi'ism happened to give this title to eminent scholars whenever they had to take charge of the destiny of the community. This is the reason why the Ayatollah Khomeini became, in turn, imam.

The Shi'i imamate made no distinction between imam and the other title carried by leaders of the Islamic community since the death of the Prophet, that of Amir al-Mu'minin, Commander of the Faithful. Although at this level one errs more on the side of secular affairs, the title indicates clearly that it is in the hands of its holder that the direction of the community must be sought inasmuch as the community constitutes an assembly of believers.

These social functions were deemed necessary from the beginning at the moment when, during the lifetime of the Prophet, it was important to send missionaries to preach the new faith outside Medina. They became even more necessary as the territory of Islam grew. One had to learn the Quran, educate the converts, assure the saying of prayers in all corners of the empire, have justice rendered, and counsel governors who could be valiant conquerors and excellent administrators without, however, having a deep understanding of the law.

Hence, the problem of the relationship of this hierarchy with power was quickly posed. Only twenty-four years after the death of the Prophet the civil war opposing 'Ali to Mu'awiya and to the Kharijites broke out. The young community of believers, the mass of whom were not ready to take sides in the conflict, faced at that time a grave problem of conscience. The Muslim state extended already in 656 from Tripolitania to Baluchistan and from the Caucasus to the Upper Nile. The results of conflict, as we have already mentioned, had practical consequences. The Sunnites, the Shi'ites, and the Kharijites were each their own judges, jurisconsultants, and scholars. The Shi'ites, now in deep hiding, were also their own *da'is*: propagandists who would later represent the Hidden Imam.

In the first instance (Sunni), the community evolved a religious structure that accommodated itself to power. In the other instances (Shi'ites and Kharijites), it was organised outside and against all central authority.

All the regimes that established themselves in the Islamic world on a religious basis counted on their *ulama*. Their goals were first to gather together partisans, then to give themselves legitimacy, and finally to expand, or quite simply to safeguard a threatened authority. The Fatimids had their *da'is*, their propagandists who spread throughout the Muslim world in order to preach allegiance to the Hidden Imam. It was the success of one of these preachers in the Berber country of the Kabylia that permitted them to seize power in North Africa before conquering, *manu militari*, Egypt. From Cairo they attempted to rally to their cause the Qarmathians, sectarians who were rebelling against the Abbasids of Baghdad from their well-established stronghold in the Gulf. They engaged them in long theological discussions in which the *ulama*, as much as the Fatimid imams, played an essential role. The day their undertaking failed they anathematised the Qarmathians. Since then, every time a bough broke off the Fatimid Ismaili branch, the *ulama* were required to justify these divergences with the dynasty in Cairo. And so it was for the Druze, Nizari, and Taybi, as well as many other branches which majoritarian Islam subsumed sometimes under the generic rubric, *ghulat al-sh'ia*, Shi'ite extremists.

Finally, wherever Islam found itself in the minority and isolated, whether in Europe, China, or today in America, the believers formed a bloc around 'those who know', their *ulama*, the only reference possible to guarantee the correct observance of the faith and the cult.

The very same present-day Islamist movements are headed by leaders embellished by the titles of imam, such as the founder of the Muslim Brothers, or of *murshid al-'am* (general guide) or *amir* (commander), the last title being found everywhere, from Tunisia to Syria, via Egypt.

It is worthwhile to point out that throughout history this hierarchy sometimes experienced changes in the order of precedence. Thus an author of the fifteenth century, the Andalusian Ibn al-Azraq, ranked the *ulama* according to a protocol which might astonish us today.[1] He cites in descending order: first the imam who leads prayer because he replaced the Prophet himself in a duty which he yielded only at the time of his final sickness to his companion Abu Bakr; then the *mufti*, interpreter of the law; the teacher because he makes religion known; the *qadi* who judges litigation; the notary because he is expected to conform to legal prescriptions in the official acts that he draws up; the *muhtasib* because he is charged with the overseeing of morals and the punishment of infractions; and, finally, the master of the mint.

We know that this latter function disappeared with the appearance of paper money, as well as that of the *muhtasib*, but we do not understand very well how the role of an imam of a mosque can be more important than that of a *mufti*, unless the imam officiates in a large mosque in the capital city of the country and theoretically offers the prayer in the name of his prince.

The formation of cadres, the organisation of society, influence over men's minds, reference for knowledge, social linkages, whatever the functions we attribute to them (and all of these correspond to historical realities), there has always existed in Islam men who have devoted themselves to the understanding of religion and have played a role in society at the same time.

Whether these men were (or are) *fuqaha* (plural of *faqih*, legalist), *ulama*, scholars in all religious disciplines, or simple imams of local mosques, they are all found within the same hierarchy, that of specialists in religious affairs.

One had reason to hope, in the light of what happened at the beginning of the Islamic era, that no crisis would emerge. The caliph was commander of the faithful and the judges, like the governors, were only his representatives: he alone in fact occupied the top position in the religious hierarchy.

But not all the successive leaders of the state possessed sufficient authority in matters of *shari'a* to impose themselves without opposition. Certain ones, like 'Umar Ibn Abd al-Aziz, the eighth Umayyad caliph, left an indelible imprint despite a short reign (717–20). To a governor who wrote him to complain of the conversion to Islam (!) of certain of his people who sought by this means to avoid the head-tax (*jiziya*) to which non-Muslims were subjected, he responded in a laconic and peremptory way: God sent Muhammad to be a guide, and not a tax collector. The seventh Abbasid caliph, al-Ma'mun, who reigned from 813 to 833, interfered in 827 in the doctrinal quarrel between the orthodox *ulama* and the Mu'tazilites over the Quran and took the side of the latter. The founders of the North African Almoravid (*al-Murabitun*) Empire, from 1055 onward, and the Almohad (*al-Muwahhidun*), a century later, had their say concerning religious matters. The examples of temporal leaders whose religious authority was recognised remained, despite everything, very few.

The caliphs, too, from the Umayyads to the Ottomans (from 661 to 1924), and the sovereigns of the great kingdoms from Córdoba to Delhi, sought to ensure permanently the support of the men of religion. European colonisation, for its part, practised an identical policy. In Africa, in the north and to south of the Sahara, it depended on the brotherhoods. In India, Great Britain courted the great scholars and did not hesitate to knight some of them. The states born from the independence of colonial territories generally had a bone to pick with the religious hierarchy but all, at one moment or another, wanted to have 'their' own *ulama*, religious scholars who would play in the game of secular power.

We have already mentioned the court paid by President Sadat to the religious authorities of the al-Azhar University and the conflicts he had with them. As for the Tunisian President Bourguiba, he simply suppressed the religious hierarchy but maintained the post of Mufti of the Republic and gave it to a man picked by the government. Without going to extremes, all Muslim states proceed in the same way in nominating high religious dignitaries. The King of Morocco regularly consults the *ulama* of Fez University. A council of doctors of the law exercises the right to oversee the Saudi state. The Khomeinist revolution did not have to have occurred for religion to interfere with the conduct of public affairs in Iran. The Constitution of 1906 had already made the *ulama* censors of the government and it was for having ignored this fact that the last shah found the men of religion raised in revolt against his government.

There has always been a relationship of force between the power of government and the power of religion, between men charged to look after the safety of the state, even when they themselves came from *ulama* families, and those whose mission was to watch over men's consciences. On several occasions, violent quarrels have opposed *'alim* against *'alim* and have provoked the intervention of power on one side or the other.

In the seventh century the debate over determinism and free will took on such proportions that the partisans of opposing viewpoints ended up by forming 'parties'. The Jabriyya, who took their name from *jabr*, compulsion, professed that man was not free, that his fate was determined in advance and that he had only to submit to his destiny by imploring God's mercy in the hereafter. A sub-group of this philosophy called the Jahmiyya, from the name of its founder, pushed this reasoning to extremes when they proclaimed that man was 'constrained' to act as he did, hence the impossibility of being responsible for his actions. The Jahmiyya were condemned by the central power before being annihilated in a battle in northeast Iran where they had taken refuge.

Opposed to them was a philosophy which appeared under the name of Qadariyya. Although the word *qadar* means destiny, the partisans of this movement believed that man was free to act as he chose. They accepted as given that everyday actions could be either good or bad and that to claim that man is not free was to intimate that God is not just. How, they asked, could the Creator demand a reckoning from man if man was not responsible for himself? In fact, central power never decided in a clear manner between the Jabriyya and the Qadariyya. To believe in the responsibility of man was to confer in that way even more coherence on the actions of the state which was thus able to legitimise its justice, its repression, and in general its role as controller of the lives of its subjects. On the other hand, to be forced into believing in determinism was to admit that power had eluded the descendants of 'Ali: 'God wished it so,' they could say.

One single concern in the ninth century illustrates best the relationship between public power and the *ulama*, and that is what, in Muslim history, was called 'the trial of the creation of the Quran'. Responsible for this affair were the thinkers known as the Mu'tazilites who developed the ideas of the Qadariyya with respect to the responsibility of man and those of the Jahmiyya on the negation of the attributes of God.

The Mu'tazilites, who were rationalists rather than traditionalists, believed that God should not be defined by human attributes. The Quran could not be the 'word' of God. Sense perception, they said, was inspired by the Creator, but the word was human. The logical conclusion was that the Quran was 'created', and that it was not the manifestation of an eternal celestial archetype.

To this affirmation, which contradicted the convictions of a good number of believers, the traditionalists replied with arguments declaring that they had always held as an inviolate dogma the eternality of the Quran, that it was literally the 'word' of God, that through it God had 'spoken' to Moses, that the verses had been revealed to Muhammad by the angel Gabriel, and that to deny this fundamental fact was to fall into heresy.

Now it happened that from 813 to 833 the reigning prince was the Abbasid caliph al-Ma'mun who got mixed up in the quarrels of the scholars. Moreover, in 827, he himself accepted the thesis of the Mu'tazilites who, having obtained official sanction, did not hesitate to persecute the traditionalists whom they in turn accused of anthropomorphism. 'The trial of the creation of the Quran' was thus to develop over many years and many scholars were to suffer its consequences. It was at this time that the Imam Ibn Hanbal was thrown into prison for championing the literalists, thereby condemning all discussion on expressions such as 'the Hand of God,' or 'the Word of God', or 'God the all-Knowing, the Omniscient', which figured in the Quran.

But the second successor of al-Ma'mun, the caliph al-Mutawakkal, condemned the Mu'tazilite thesis and rehabilitated traditionalism. Then it was the turn of the classical *ulama* to launch a campaign of purification against the Mu'tazilites, whose school of thought eventually disappeared.

The Fatimid leaders were Shi'ite imams. In Tunisia, they had come into collision with the Sunnite clerics of Qayrawan whose permanent resistance succeeded in detaching the country from the Fatimid Empire in the eleventh century in order to bring it back into the bosom of the *sunna*.

In reality each time a secular power proved capable of obtaining the support of a religious hierarchy, one divine or another sought to raise the population to revolt. If ever the opposition developed by virtue of a schism, a doctrine, or a political choice, it invariably gave birth to its own hierarchy.

Movements of national liberation have had their own religious leaders or, at least, their jurisconsultants. In the Sudan, opposition to the British occupation was sparked by the Mahdist movement. In Somalia there were the activities of Muhammad Abdallah, whom the English called 'the Mad Mullah'. In Algeria there was the resistance of the Amir Abd al-Qadir, both a religious and revolutionary warrior. In Libya, it was the Sanussis, members of the brotherhood founded by the Algerian Muhammad al-Sanussi and closely related to the Wahhabite doctrine, that led the opposition and endeavoured to put religious reform into operation. In Guinea, anti-colonial action was led by al-Hajj 'Umar Tall. As we see, what is happening today in Afghanistan cannot help but recall the past.

To a certain extent, the logic of Islamist movements is similar everywhere. They attempt, through a concept of faith and law, to kick an established power out of the country but – as compared to the past – with a significant difference: the dissidents in most cases are dealing nowadays with a national power.

Ulama in power, *ulama* in opposition; in either case they rarely enjoy a good reputation. 'Old turbans' and 'ragheads' are the kindest adjectives attributed to them. The most current words used to insult them are obscurantists, reactionaries, backward fanatics, fools, and so on.

It must be said that for centuries the *ulama* have been especially marked by their intellectual prudence and their practical intransigence. The concurrence of these two attitudes engendered a religious intolerance from which neither branch of Islam was totally exempt. Certainly, we must be fair to the majority of *ulama*. Their conservatism was not simply negative. At the darkest moments of Islamic history, they were the guardians of the faith, the promoters of a continuing rather than limited literacy, the archivists of a knowledge whose disappearance would have relegated Muslim culture to the rank of an object of archaeological study. Without these conservatives – and the word must be taken in the broadest meaning of the term – without this discredited body of men, the small flame that remained lit in the midst of shadows would have been extinguished. We must officially recognise them for their work.

But the tragedy of the Muslim world is that this religious hierarchy prefers the flickering light of the candle to the blazing flame of the spirit. The great Malik was, in the eighth century, condemned to be whipped, as we will discuss more fully later. The unfortunate Hussain al-Hallaj (858–922), celebrated today as a great mystic who did honour to the spirit of Islam, was martyred and crucified. The Imam Ibn Taymiyya (1263–1328), who was the progenitor of the Wahhabism that flourishes today, died in prison. And we ought also to include that matchless thinker Abu Hamid al-Ghazali (1059–1111), a man whose works form part of the scholastic program of Islamic philosophy and who was rewarded with an *auto da fé* of his works in Córdoba. The *ulama* have judged the teachings of their masters as heretical, sectarian or even dangerous.

Closer in time to us, the reformers and champions of Pan-Islamism, Jamal al-Din al-Afghani (1838–98) and his disciple, the Egyptian Muhammad Abduh (1849–1905), encountered their worst difficulties with the *ulama* who reproached them for being innovators because they preached the return to the sources of early Islam, that of the *salaf* (the predecessors), and for drawing from this a teaching in harmony with the modern world.

At a still more recent time, the Algerian thinker, Malek Bennabi (1905–73), author of eighteen works in French and in Arabic treating Islam from the political and philosophical point of view, was systematically ostracised. In 1980, a leader of the Muslim Brothers recounted to us with bitterness how twenty years before the Brothers passed the word around that the reading of Bennabi's books should be banned. And he added with regret: 'Yet it is by means of the renewal of Islamic thought that we should begin our action.' This was said to us in Amman, in Jordan, at the moment when the news of the Aleppo massacres was arriving on the hour from neighbouring Syria.

Condemned, Bennabi was thus guilty like his predecessors, the Egyptian Qasim Amin and the Tunisian Tahar Haddad, of having dared to demand the emancipation of women! Their works were blacklisted in the interwar period. A professor at the Zaytuna University in Tunis flattered himself for having written a book that refuted the theses of Haddad without having read as much as a single line of this 'impious' book.

Good or bad, possessors of encyclopaedic or superficial knowledge, the men of religion represent a force that must be reckoned with. Even if they do not constitute a body having permanent ties among its members except when they create a party as in Iran, they belong nevertheless to a particular hierarchy with its own set of rules.

But why this power, we may ask, since in Islam there is neither priest nor a well-defined clergy? Who may say one day that a certain individual shall have the right of excommunication which permits him to cast anathema in a world where only dogma establishes the direct relations between man and God? The simplest answer might consist in saying that it is history which confers on these men a considerable power. The examples cited and the controversies recalled above show well that from the end of the second century of the Muslim era onwards religious scholars exercised a strong influence on society.

But one must go beyond historical fact and state that certain social functions have to be performed and that these are tied to a solid understanding of religion. Now we cannot forget that the sum of references has multiplied, that the number of books of exegesis, of commentaries, of law, and of jurisprudence has become quite considerable so that the ignorance in which the mass of Muslims live confers an uncontestable authority on those who know these works. In this way, knowledge becomes power.

The less we reflect on the fundamentals of faith, the more different doctrines, as well as their commentaries and their avatars, acquire importance. In the beginning a tree grows straight. Then the branches, the boughs, and the twigs proliferate. The vigorous foliage ends up by hiding the sky. Knowledge that is thought necessary surpasses in scope what a single human life can possibly apprehend. The importance of men is measured in library shelves swallowed whole. Society abdicates and, to ensure the functions which it cannot do without, yields to those of its sons who propose to take it by the hand until that moment when it revolts, cuts back, prunes, or chops down entirely the lush foliage.

Moreover, this is what certain Islamic movements claim to do which deny to the *ulama* all rights to oversee religion. It is what certain reformers, thinkers, and secular leaders tried to do. On the other side of the coin, it is against precisely this that the established hierarchies rise in indignation whenever they have the possibility of mobilising troops to put a stop to reform.

Notes

1.   Cf. Ibn al-Azraq, *Bada'i al-sulk li taba'i al-mulk* (Some Characteristics of Power), critical edition by Muhammad Ibn Abd al-Karim, vol. 1 (Libya–Tunisia: Maison arabe du livre, 1977), pp. 240–65.

7. The Shipwrecked Mullarchy

Towards the end of the twentieth century things are beginning to stir. Political tensions are stretching the fragile fabric of young states. Economic difficulties are bringing promising plans to a halt. Social cohesion is bursting asunder and is being replaced by multiple forms of human relationships. Present-day technology is providing new weapons for violence. The dissemination of information is drawing all peoples on the planet into the vortex of ideas, discoveries and conflicts. Governmental authority is contracting and hardening. Discontent feeds the grumblers and the conspirators. What will Muslims choose? Disaster or salvation?

The conditions for revolutions have been or are in the process of being created in numerous countries. The desired change is political, as the insistence of the dissenters on the reasons for, and objectives of, their movements clearly indicates. The choice of means for the aspiring activist is not innocent. Availability stimulates the recourse to violence, on which the Islamic countries have no monopoly, and a particular concept of authenticity encourages the preaching and the practice of a return to the sources of the faith. A welcoming structure is always available to receive those who have made their choice.

The Islamists are elucidating the notion of the *umma*. The *umma* does not represent the nation in the European sense. The word derives from the root *amm* which is also related to *imam*, or guide. The *umma* is the totality of persons who take the same direction, the path of righteousness and salvation, the community of believers. The bond which ties together these men and women is that of faith; of adherence to a morality and of submission to a law. There is nothing territorial about this at all. The American Black Muslims make this rupture clear by choosing, as a name for themselves, the expression, the 'Nation of Islam'. They have broken with the notion of allegiance to a state limited in space by its frontiers, in time by a history common to its inhabitants, and socially by its own organic laws. Citizenship, according to them, is a juridical statute, an administrative situation which permits the accomplishment of certain acts such as that of travel. It does not imply any obligations toward a society to which one is not convinced that one belongs. Elijah Muhammad, the founder of the Black Muslims, refused to serve under the American flag and was condemned to prison, as was the boxing champion Muhammad 'Ali, the former Cassius Clay. Yet, for a Muslim to associate him/herself with the

Egyptians, Iranians or with the Indonesians even when born a Tunisian, a Senegalese or an American does not pose any problems.

One of the great rectors of al-Azhar in Cairo thirty years ago was Shaykh Muhammad al-Khidr Hussain, originally from Tunisia. The Egyptian *ulama* are today Saudis. Certain North African Arabs finished their lives at the beginning of this century as dignitaries of the Ottoman Empire in Istanbul.

Consequently, and without going as far as physically changing one's residence, one can commune with one's brothers in Islam in the Philippines and fight against one's own government should that government be guilty of helping the authorities in Manila crush the Muslims of that country. It follows that the notion of 'fatherland' becomes ambiguous. One loves one's place of birth, the environment of one's childhood, and the social milieu that issues from it without the patriotism of territory justifying, as was the case in Europe, 'national' wars.

On this foundation, which has never disappeared from the Muslim psyche, have been deposited the unstable sediments of ideas that have flooded the world for four centuries. In former times, Christian Europe recognised these transnational sentiments which propelled the Crusades on the road to Jerusalem or pushed the bishops of Germany to evangelise the Hungarians and the Poles. Once again, these sentiments appeared in the nineteenth century as the Marxist appeal for the unity of all proletarians. But the nationalism of territory had by that time already replaced in the West that of religious or ideological faith. A similar evolution has also manifested itself in Third World countries, among which are ranked all the Islamic nations. The appeal for the resurrection of the *umma* of Islam has also been perceived as subversive, not only by the governments in place but also by all those for whom the struggle to end colonialism has had a patriotic and national meaning.

The war between Iran and Iraq, launched at the end of 1980, illustrates tragically the opposition between two nationalisms. The two governments had committed a gross error from the beginning, the Iraqis in believing that the Arabs of Iranian Khuzistan (called Arabistan by the Iraqis) would react like Arabs, the Iranians in counting on the reaction of the Iraqis of the south as Shi'ites. But the Iraqis showed themselves to be Iraqis and the Iranians Iranians notwithstanding culture on one hand, religious obedience on the other.

In this case it was nationalism of the modern kind that proved decisive. It was citizenship that gained the upper hand over the two communal ideologies: Arabism and Islamism. Nonetheless, it happened that fidelity to ethnic origins showed itself stronger than citizenship, especially when it was a question of conflicts breaking out between ethnic groups living in the same country.

The two examples of Pakistan and Iraq prove this point. Pakistan is a country founded on Islamic principles after the partition of India in 1947. Pakistan was composed of two large provinces, western and eastern. The eastern province, populated by Bengalis, had the advantage of racial homogeneity. Moreover, as a simple province, it was separated from western Pakistan by a good thousand kilometres. Without a doubt, Dacca, the capital of eastern Pakistan, was considered the second capital of the state. In reality, everything was decided in the West, in Karachi or in Rawalpindi and in Islamabad. Because of this fact the ethnic factor, reinforced by provincial frustrations and the desire for secession, revealed itself to be more powerful than Islamism which had nevertheless caused the separation from India. From this Bangladesh was born in 1971 as the state of the Bengalis.

In Iraq it was the Arabs who found themselves quarrelling with the Kurds who refused to join a state where their ethnic nationalism would not be permitted to flourish. And yet, since the other Iraqis were in part Shi'ite or Sunnite, the Kurds, who are all Sunnite, might have been able to find either in Islamism in general or in Sunnism in particular sufficient reasons to justify their belonging to a single and unique *umma*. Ethnicity and culture outweighed the *umma*. Finally, in the Sahara, it was the desire for independence and political calculation which turned out to be more powerful than the lip service given to Arab unity. This is to say that one must be careful not to exaggerate the power of the appeal for the unity of the Islamic *umma*.

Furthermore, each time an Islamic movement has attempted to encroach upon state frontiers, it has come up against new nations determined to defend themselves. Intervention from the outside is considered an interference in the internal affairs of an independent country. The activists inside are liable to be condemned for passing information to foreign powers. In 1958, the Muslim Brothers of Syria, not wishing to fall like their Egyptian rivals under the yoke of Nasser, who had just had himself recognised the supreme authority over the destiny of the two countries brought together in the United Arab Republic, allowed their leaders to emigrate to Jordan where they formed an important core of the association. Thus they could not help but increase the distrust of the Cairo and Damascus regimes with respect to the Jordanian monarchy. More recently, the Syrian regime openly accused King Hussein of Jordan of encouraging this religious movement in its war against the government of President Hafiz al-Assad. As for the countries of the Gulf, all those, whether Shi'ite or not, who suspect that a collusion exists here with the Iranian mullarchy are immediately branded traitors.

That is not the only question to which militant Islamism brings no acceptable answer. In seeking to lay siege to the state with an uncompromising Islam all activist movements, despite their great divergences, promote an extremely dangerous confusion in the mind. Instead of bringing about a real Islamic renaissance, they drag their countries through a dialectic of violence towards what might best be called regressive tendencies.

Among the peoples of the world old demons lay dormant. They have many names: fanaticism, intolerance, xenophobia, machismo, racism, and so on. These diseases have no specific Islamic content. They are even contrary to pure Islam. But wherever they appear they are fed by ignorance, obscurantism and the will to take power. They are still more dangerous when we seek to justify them by religion, for if we can demonstrate the aberration of Nazism or of Fascism by relying on 'scientific', historical, or rational arguments, how can we convince a religious activist who answers, 'Such is my faith'?

It is tragic to see how certain Islamist movements put into motion social mechanisms, sometimes without reflecting on the consequences, which result in the liberation of forces for evil that all the efforts of civilisation have sought consistently to suppress, if not to eliminate, from the body of human society. The absence of reflection on what Islam ought to be today is at the origin of this regression.

The expansion of knowledge, of which we have already spoken, has had two serious consequences: the impossibility for people in general of laying claim to a profound knowledge of Islam which has become the monopoly of a minority of clerics; and the ignorance, even by a part of the religious hierarchy, of fundamental religious texts. Faced with the impossibility of digesting all the encyclopaedic works of the exegetes, of the jurisconsultants, and of the thinkers, one falls back on the abridgements, on the sometimes inadequate commentaries or, still worse, on popular pamphlets when it would be so much simpler to reread the Quran in order to try to understand it with the mind of a man of the twentieth century. For more than five centuries, primary instruction in the religious universities of Fez (Morocco), Zaytuna (Tunisia), al-Azhar (Egypt), Qum (Iran), and in many other cities was dispensed by means of *mukhtasarat* (abridgements). One reads the *mukhtasar* of Shaykh Khalil rather than the work from which he popularises the law, the *mu'atta* of the Imam Malik. For the Hanafites, it is the *mukhtasar* of Tahawi; for the Shafa'ites that of Mazani, and for the Hanbalites, that of al-Kharqi. These are the preferred works of the masters and the disciples and yet these works are still studied in editions which bear the commentaries of jurists of many centuries past so that the personal point of view of the last author, being added to that of the editor of the abridgement and to that of the thinker whose views one is supposed to have popularised, becomes an integral part of the law. Only the privileged few with access to higher levels of knowledge delve into the reading of the original sources which themselves, as we have already mentioned above, are really works of more recent vintage.

We have reached the point where it takes singular courage for a member of the community of *ulama* to write today a new exegesis of the Quran. There are still others who, like the Tunisian Shaykh Tahar Bin Ashur, having joined the twentieth century, have nonetheless taken care to imitate the older exegetes so as not to transgress against the tradition and to incur the condemnation of their peers. This was also the case of the exegesis taught by the Egyptian reformer Shaykh Muhammad Abduh, which was written down and propagated by his disciple, Shaykh Rashid Rida, who turned it gradually into a form of conservatism.

One must add to this legacy the laziness of the reader and the confusion that reigns in the mind between the notion of what is modern and what is contemporary. Why bother to take the time to read primary source documents when one has at one's disposal a recent book that claims to be a commentary on them? And yet, what treasures of tolerance, of humanity, of openness of spirit, of simplicity and of good sense one discovers in reading the first works relating to the life of the Prophet.

Once upon a time, reports the traditionist Bukhari (810–70), a man came before the Prophet in the middle of Ramadan and declared to him in the mosque and in the presence of the congregants: 'I am not observing the fast.' The Prophet asked him if he were sick. The man was content to repeat his first declaration. Muhammad ordered him, as a punishment for his laxity, to free a slave. 'I cannot,' the man replied. 'Feed sixty of the poor, then.' The tiresome fellow replied again that he could not. The Prophet turned away from him and began to talk of other things. Another man came who offered Muhammad a basket filled with dates. The Prophet then asked where was he who had first sought his counsel. When the man arose, Muhammad presented him with the dates: 'Offer this as alms,' he said. The man picked up the basket, took several steps, then asked: 'May I offer these dates to my family?' The Prophet, realising how needy the man was, allowed him to do so. Taking several more steps, he asked a last question: 'May I eat some?' And the Prophet responded, 'Eat.' What jurisconsultant today would give these answers?

The same traditionist Bukhari reported that the Prophet, when he made his ablutions during Ramadan, cleansed his mouth by gargling. The listener asked Bukhari, 'Did he clean his teeth with *siwak* [a supple wood, used especially for oral hygiene]?' 'Yes,' replied Bukhari. Now, today, most Muslims think that brushing the teeth with toothpaste during Ramadan is to break the fast. Moreover, in sub-Saharan Africa, certain pious people do not even swallow their saliva but prefer to spit it out.

We should underline here that these are only some examples relating to the observance of the cult whose rules are clearly spelled out. The examples of tolerance and of open-mindedness are much more numerous in the realm of social relations, of the conduct of public affairs, and even of morals.

Now it is at the beginning of the fifteenth century of Islam that Muslims have been bidden to adhere to the political vision of the Pakistani Abu Ala Mawdudi, in some places to put into practice the doctrine of the Egyptian Sayyid Qutb, in other places to give way before the mullahs of Iran. Their concepts of the seizure of state power by religion have seduced many militants in various Islamic countries. Men deserving of respect and sometimes of admiration give life or have already given life to these three inclinations. Mawdudi has known prison, was condemned to death in 1953, and was saved only by an international campaign of amnesty; Khomeini lived sixteen years in exile; and Qutb was hanged on Nasser's orders. No one can reproach them for the lack of a professed doctrine or for a hesitation to sacrifice themselves in its defence. The knowledge of these three persons was immense. When he brought out in 1923 the French translation of his work, *Towards Understanding Islam*, written in Urdu in 1932, Mawdudi was underlining that his goal was to make the 'real Islam' known to those 'who did not have access to the basic sources of Islam in Arabic'. Qutb had written, among other works, a seminal book entitled, *In the Shadow of the Quran*. The culture that formed Khomeini had already permitted him, before becoming the master of Iran, to accede to the highest rank of the hierarchy, that of ayatollah.

What is in question here is therefore not the knowledge of these men but a concept that is personal to them regarding the relationship between the state and Islam and the role of Islam in society. That their disciples present their works as a contribution to an interpretation of Islam no one will deny. When they say that such and such is Islam and that everything different from it is heresy, they fall into a sectarianism so much the more dangerous since from time to time it has led to bloodshed.

Abu Ala Mawdudi, born in 1903 in the south of India, led, until his death in 1979, an unrelenting struggle for the Islamicisation of the government of men. To this end he wrote more than eighty works and monographs and edited a number of newspapers in Urdu, a language mostly spoken by the Muslims of the Indian subcontinent. The partition of 1947 ought to have brought him great satisfaction since Pakistan, which he made his country, was formed according to a religious formula. He believed nonetheless that Islam was not being properly applied there and the struggle that he led so vigorously aimed at 'recasting the state along Islamic lines'. Today, it is to his ideas that many Islamist movements refer – in Tunisia for example, but also in Egypt and in many Asian countries. An Islamic foundation in London, an association of Islamic students in France, an international Islamic federation of student organisations in Kuwait, a union of Egyptian students, participate, exclusively or partially, in the distribution of the works of Mawdudi. Better yet, a well-polished propaganda technique gives this distribution system an exponential scope. For example, a pamphlet entitled, *The Islamic Point of View*, has been printed in Arabic by an Egyptian committee. It concludes with this appeal from the editors: 'Brothers and Sisters . . . when you finish reading this brochure, lend it to others so that its benefits can be passed on. God will repay you.' Tunisian readers did better. They took this same text and brought it out in Tunis. The book cover bore the name of the printer and stated that the work had been produced in 7,000 copies. Such faith deserves admiration.

Yet the theory – and it is finally nothing more than a theory – is debatable. Mawdudi rejects with reason any cult of personality that would place those who govern above the simple citizen. All more or less divinely appointed despots are condemned, from the pharaohs to Mussolini, including Stalin and the American economic magnates. That said, he considers that the Islamic credo 'withdraws all power of command and legislation from men, either as individuals or collectivities'. The fact of believing in the One God must entail the refusal to submit to all other authority. God has made known His law to men. It defines the framework in which liberty can be exercised. 'Life,' he says,

> may be compared to a winding mountain path between dizzying heights and bottomless chasms. Would we say of someone that he impedes the progress of the climbers if he were to build railings so as to prevent them from falling into the abyss?

These railings 'constitute what we call in Islam the limits imposed by God (*hudud Allah*). They are the ramparts of liberty.' Furthermore:

> The Muslim state can be founded only on the law, which remains valid

under all circumstances, and governments deserve allegiance only insofar as they put into practice what God has prescribed. It is from this fact alone that they draw their legitimacy.

How is Islamic government constituted? Mawdudi stresses that 'the state can be directed only by those who believe in this fundamental law.' He reminds us that Islam uses only the word *khilafah* (the responsibility of the *khalifa*, in other words, the successor, substitute or deputy), and not that of *hakimiyya* (sovereign power), 'because sovereignty is an attribute that belongs only to God.' The government of men cannot be administered except 'under limits designed by the sovereign'. Thus government is theocratic. And it is up to Mawdudi to make clear what he means by 'democratic theocracy'. Western democracy is an aberration because it gives to representatives, elected thanks to disreputable methods and advertising lies, the right to loosen and to bind, whereas there are rules that arise from God alone that no one has the right to change. Theocracy is founded on the rigorous respect for these rules within the framework of which the will of the members of the community of believers can be exercised.

The establishment of this democracy is furthermore subject to other conditions: the *amir* (leader) can be chosen only after applying the verse of the Quran which proclaims that 'the most honoured among you is the most pious.' He cannot present himself as a candidate without nullifying his election. He is not given precedence over others because all believers are the repository of the law by virtue of the application of the Prophet's word: 'You are all shepherds and are responsible for your flocks.' Moreover, the law makes it obligatory for him to consult others. Although early Islam, Mawdudi points out, was not subject to formal constraints, this consultation can be organised within the framework of a consultative council. But this assembly cannot be composed of parties or factions. This is forbidden since the believer is called upon to give his advice in good conscience and with his heart.

One must admit that these ideas have had a certain impact on a part of Muslim public opinion. The relatively short text where these ideas are developed issued from a conference held in Lahore in 1939. Since that time the text has been translated from Urdu into the many languages of India and into English. The Arabic translation that we possess dates from 1946. And it is impossible to make the exact count of its editions – there have been several hundred thousand copies. In fact, the simplicity of the style, the clarity of the ideas, and the decisiveness of the statements have made these little pamphlets a remarkably effective instrument of propaganda.

The problem that these ideas raise has two aspects: the first is theological and the second practical. If Muslims knew – let us say most Muslims so as not to demand the impossible – their religion as well as Mawdudi, the formula proposed could serve as a basis for a constitutional Socratic method. After all, states ascribe to themselves a fundamental law. Why should not that of the Muslim community be the *shari'a*? But Mawdudi, like other *ulama* before him, juggles the Quranic verses and gives a very personal interpretation of them.

Thus, to establish that government (*hukm*) can only be of divine origin, he cites the verses where the words *hukm* (judgment, authority, verdict) and *amr* (order, command) do not relate to what is commonly called government today.

The key sentence, 'The Command is for none but God: He hath commanded that ye worship none but Him: that is the right religion,' is drawn from the fortieth verse of the chapter of Joseph in which the Quran reports Joseph's quarrels with Pharaoh. The complete quotations read:

> If not Him, ye worship nothing but names which ye have named – ye and your fathers – for which God hath sent down no authority. The Command is for none but God: He hath commanded that ye worship none but Him: that is the right religion, but most men understand not . . .

Whether one gives the meaning of power, authority, judgment, or even sovereignty to the Arabic word *hukm*, it is clear in the context of the verse that polytheism is being condemned and not the conduct of public affairs that we call government. The power to govern the universe is recognised by all monotheists – and not only Muslims – as being the exclusive attribute of God.

The other key sentence used by Mawdudi is the one in which the word *amr* (order, command, affair) appears as 'what affair is this of ours? Say Thou: Indeed this affair is wholly God's.' Now, once again, this sentence drawn from the one hundred and forty-fourth verse of the chapter of Imran refers back rather to the notions of destiny, fate and finality. The verse reports, in point of fact, the debates which the issue of the Battle of Uhud stirred up among the Muslims: the warriors, believing in certain victory, had disobeyed the Prophet and abandoned their posts to seize without delay their share of the booty. Because the withdrawal from the field was taken advantage of by the enemy and because the victory soon turned into defeat, certain believers had begun to doubt God's favour:

> If we had anything to do with this affair, we should not have been in the slaughter here; 'Say. Even if you had remained in your homes, those for whom death was decreed would certainly have gone forth to the place of their death.'

Furthermore, if there had been a precise form of government in early Islam, that of the Quran and the practices of Muhammad, those who would have been the best acquainted with it must surely have been the companions of the Prophet. No risk of disputes, then, after his death as far as choices to make were concerned. The first caliphs would not have been opposed by the Shi'ites later on. And the majority of Muslims would not have accepted the change from the elective procedure adopted in 632 to the hereditary system established by the Umayyads after 661.

There was, of course, opposition at that time, but it was the opposition of the Kharijites whom the Sunnites, like Mawdudi, specifically rejected. Not only do the Sunnites condemn the Kharijite opposition as it appears in history but, even more so today, they refer to none of the theories to which this opposition has given birth. The oldest authors to whom the Sunnites refer the reader were men of the end of the second century of the Hijra (first quarter of the ninth century AD) exactly as if, for 180 years, Muslims had lived in perfect harmony without any problem of power being posed, or as if these Muslims did not know the verses that Mawdudi cites.

Apart from this appeal to the Quranic text, Mawdudi postulates that the law is a fixed code of which, he repeats indefatigably, men can change nothing. But because he is too well informed about theological history to expunge entirely the work of subsequent codification realised by men and not formalised by the Quran, he does not fail to insist in certain books on the importance of the work accomplished by the men of the Tradition. 'It is thanks to them', he recalls in *Towards Understanding Islam*,[1] 'that Muslims everywhere in the world can follow the *shari'a* easily, whereas their knowledge of religious subjects would never have permitted them to interpret correctly by themselves the Quran and the *hadith*.' And so the card was played and the Tradition alone became sacred.

This is the most serious aspect of the problem which Muslim societies have to confront. By proclaiming that only the *shari'a* can govern the community and by admitting that the work of the traditionalists, the jurists, and the founders of the schools of law is indispensable to its 'correct' understanding, one logically reaches the conclusion that the only government possible ought to be that of the *ulama*. 'Democratic theocracy' is rendered structurally by mullarchy.

The system of the diffusion of knowledge described in the preceding chapter shows clearly that for fourteen centuries we have passed from the Quran as sole reference, to the collections of the Traditions, then to exegesis and the commentaries, then to the glosses on the commentaries before arriving at the summaries and finally at the pamphlets.

The accumulation of such works discourages the best intentions. It implies in practice a delegation of power to a minority among whom real scholars can be counted on the fingers of one hand. This elite possesses an absolute authority since this system requires us to yield to them in order to obtain 'correct' interpretations of the texts.

Such is the tragedy of Iran and of Islam because of Iran. Everything is called Islamic, from the most rational decisions to the acts of pure barbarism. Should one take it into one's head to cite a Quranic verse which manifestly condemns such actions, the adversary would find himself in opposition to the classical dictum of the Muslim world that states: You are not prepared to interpret the Quran correctly. You must belong first to the body of the *ulama*.

Sayyid Qutb, the leader in hiding of the Egyptian Muslim Brothers, did not put forward his ideas with the same effectiveness as Mawdudi. Whereas the latter was a master of the art of advertising, the former was more erudite and wordy. And his work was not reducible to pamphlets for large-scale distribution. But he was more categorical and, dare we say, more candid. From his point of view, he wanted to form an elite who knew Islam thoroughly and was ready to fight for its success with a view to founding an authentically Islamic state. His school of thought is often called 'the educative school' for this reason, and, in contradistinction to his master al-Banna, is defined by its propensity for mass action.

Hassan al-Banna, the founder of the Muslim Brothers, when he spoke of the ties that bound his followers, used to evoke 'a reformist movement (*salafiyya*), a Sunnite belief, a mystical truth (*sufiyya*), a political organisation, an athletic club, a cultural and scientific association, an economic society and a social doctrine.' Hence, the accent placed by the organisation built under his leadership on those activities aimed at the widest possible public. With his companion, Sayyid Qutb, he employed the techniques of an activist minority.

Let us examine for a moment the ideas of Rashid al-Ghannushi, leader of the Tunisian Movement of Islamic Tendency (MIT), who, before finding himself sentenced to ten years in prison in 1981, compared in this manner the work of the two men in a Kuwaiti newspaper:

> Has what we call mass action in the Islamic struggle (the al-Banna school) failed to the extent that today we are no longer required to follow it, but to replace it with what we may call the hard-core school (that of Sayyid Qutb) which professes a selective, elitist action that turns away from the masses? . . . The actions of al-Banna had taken for a target large segments of the population and attracted more particularly the classes at the bottom of the social ladder, those of the disadvantaged such as the students . . . al-Banna's movement had concerned itself to a large degree with the struggle against colonialism and the national cause much more than with the establishment of an Islamic state. So we may say that the movement led by al-Banna was primarily a movement of national liberation.

After having underlined that the Muslim Brothers of that time were preoccupied more with questions of morals than with social problems, Ghannushi added:

> Al-Banna's movement had committed a terrible political error – which was continued elsewhere – by proposing the Islamic movement as the guardian of the whole society and not as a political and intellectual partner that drew its legitimacy from the force of its arguments and from the adherence of the masses to its programs. The Islamic movement remained reluctant to put itself on the same level as other partners in political action whether they be communists, socialists or democrats.

And Ghannushi concluded his judgment on the Egyptian Muslim Brothers in these terms: 'After the death of al-Banna the movement changed. It neglected the national dimension. It despised the masses and it turned towards selective and elitist methods or what we might call [the creation] of a hard core.' In other words, towards the path envisaged by Sayyid Qutb.

This judgment, that of someone who has studied the question, reveals the political option of the Tunisian Movement, which considers itself a mass action movement, and explains at the same time why the toughest Islamist factions, notably in Egypt and in Syria, follow Sayyid Qutb rightly or wrongly. It is a question here of an elitist tactic inspired by the loss of hope in the rising of the masses and in the conviction that it is necessary to create the future leaders of the Islamic state. For if the analyses and the styles differ from one country to another, the objective remains the same: the seizure of state power.

The works of Khomeini are little known among those who do not read Persian. On the other hand, his actions, especially since 1979, have been followed with interest by many observers. One does no injustice to the Imam Khomeini in stating that the Shah helped him a great deal. When, after 1976, the Shah blocked all possibility of legal opposition in the context of established institutions, without realising it, he channelled the opposition movement towards the mosques. In this way, he provided troops for the best organised and the richest religious hierarchy in the Muslim world whose members received funds from their parishioners and disciples. The mullahs, who were educators on all levels as well as preachers and instigators of social action, became the brains behind a populace in a state of latent rebellion. Suddenly, the old man exiled to Najaf in Iraq since 1963 turned out to be a dangerous fellow indeed.

The Ayatollah Ruhollah Khomeini, who had not ceased to oppose the Shah for more than twenty years, continued from his place of exile to maintain direct and indirect relations by letter with his followers who used to visit him frequently in Iraq. It was not until 1978 that his activities were judged threatening enough to justify an agreement between Baghdad and Teheran which ended in a new exile, in France this time. The accords concluded in Algiers in 1975 between the Shah and the Iraqi Saddam Hussein with respect to frontiers alone made this possible (by stopping the aid furnished to the anti-Iraqi Kurds, the Shah had thus obtained an important concession on the frontiers). In fact, the Shah believed, at the beginning of the seventies,that the problems caused by Khomeini's propaganda were of little importance. But as of 1976, these problems grew to unusual proportions. Why? The only answer that corresponded to Iranian realities was that from that moment on the mosques had become the principal focal point of opposition and that the influence exercised by Khomeini had transformed itself into a political fact with which one had to deal. This situation could have paved the way for the leadership of progressive religious chiefs like the Ayatollah Taleghani, who had spent nearly thirty years of his life in prison (at different times). But the mass of mullahs preferred the more classical, the more traditional of the *ulama*: Khomeini.

The head of the Mujahidin-i Khalq (the People's Strugglers), Masa'ud Raja'i, tells how in February 1979, after the return of Khomeini to Iran, Khomeini's son Ahmad paid him a visit to propose two conditions laid down by his father for the recognition of the Mujahidin: admit the absolute leadership of the imam and share in the struggle against all enemies whom Khomeini might designate. Recognition seemed entirely likely. The first condition in particular had been regularly advanced by Khomeini as a rallying point for all the representatives of Iranian political currents who visited him or who contacted him indirectly during the period when he was a refugee in Neauphle-le-Château in France.

The objective – that is, the control of the state – could only be attained if a certain number of conditions were met: the absolute leadership exercised by an imam who professed a traditional doctrine, the adherence of the majority of mullahs, and the mobilisation of the armed forces which would be eventually called in to intervene.

What happened is history. In August 1979 a 'council of experts' was elected to write a new constitution. Clause 111 established the *wilayat al-faqih* (the authority of the religious legalist to govern) under terms of which the imam held absolute power, including authority over the elected president of the republic. Moreover, Khomeini forbade certain candidates from running for election and ended up in June cashiering President Bani Sadr.

Although Iran possessed one of the best armies in Asia, the regime established after the fall of the Shah was also endowed with two parallel armed forces: the first, a regular force, consisted of the revolutionary guards, and the second, camouflaged and called the Hizbullahi (the party of God) was represented by the militia of the IRP (Islamic Republican Party).

Still more serious and illustrative of the process of regression described above was the manner by which 'Islamicisation' was carried out. The arbitrary arrests, the kangaroo courts, the denial of the right to counsel, the summary executions, the abrogation of codified laws, the latitude left to the judge to interpret judicial principles, the repression of minorities, the elimination of officials who did not accept the authority of the IRP, the subjugation of women, the repeated closing of schools of higher learning, the dissolution of revolutionary organisations, the creation of SAVAM to replace SAVAK, the Shah's feared secret police – all this was decided in the name of an Islamic law which the majority of Muslims throughout the world no longer recognise.

Hence the following paradox: 'the Iranian Islamic revolution' does not constitute a threat to other Islamic countries to the same degree that it represents a serious obstacle for the success of Islamist movements, the distressing spectacle that the revolution offers not being one which by nature would lead the crowds elsewhere to join parties that might involve their countries in the same predicament. Nevertheless, not only is the Iranian revolution the sole Islamic revolution to have succeeded in the seizing of power, but it contains all the ingredients that are found in the doctrines professed by Islamic activists, and although it projects an indefensible image, one cannot help but consider it a model of what could come about in an Islamic country shaken by revolution.

We have said that Khomeini was categorically opposed to the use of violence in the struggle against the Shah. Masa'ud Raja'i, leader of the Mujahidin and adversary of the imam, recalls this fact in order to illustrate the role played by his own troops, who took up arms to hasten the fall of the regime. We have also said the spiritual leader had taken some time during the summer of 1981 before admitting the validity of the impeachment of the president of the republic. If this is true, then what we see here is an added proof of the contention put forward by some to demonstrate that the process unleashed by radical

Islamism has quite rapidly escaped all reasonable control. It is not so much the man as the system that he put into effect which is in question here. It is useful to recall, following this line of thought, that at the end of the fourteenth century Tamerlane pillaged the countries from north of the Caucasus to India in the name of 'orthodox' Islam. Wherever he went skulls were heaped into pyramids. In Damascus the historian and great religious scholar Ibn Khaldun interceded in favour of its citizens. As a consequence, he succeeded for a short time in being welcomed to the court of the bloody conqueror. The purest of intentions can have disastrous results. By the same token, it was aforementioned how the peace sealed between Baghdad and the various Sunnite schools in the tenth century brought to an end all intellectual effort. In the former case the will to restructure the world led to carnage, while in the latter it institutionalised mediocrity. Alas! History teaches us that we can, and with the best intentions, bring about two misfortunes at the same time.

The error of the Iranian political forces that had consented to join the Khomeinist ranks and to accept his conditions (absolute obedience) originated in the contempt that had been cultivated in the Muslim world towards men of traditional religion. By labelling as 'old turbans' the fanatics, the obscurantists, and those who were hopelessly behind the time, and mocking the influence they could have ('Never will our educated people accept their reactionary absolutism!'), we forget that when new men come to power, they use the instruments of the preceding regime, even if they take care to change the name. For example we have seen how the secret police were no longer called SAVAK but SAVAM. We forget too that what permits the 'Islamic' resistance to last longer than other forms of political protest is precisely its remarkably efficient ways of creating cadres: a network of localities (the mosques), hierarchised personnel (the mullahs), a doctrine of reference (the *shari'a*), a devotion to the cause (the faith), and the incommensurate hope of erecting the Heavenly City on earth. Finally, we forget the mediocracy, the end product of all processes that tend to put the individual into a mold where thought and freedom of action are denied to him. Why should the Soviet *apparatchik* be more ferocious and more stubborn than his Iranian *maktabi* counterpart since both renounce all personal attributes in favour of a superior ideology and content themselves to remain under the order of a charismatic leader? Iran has consistently underlined this fact by distinguishing the *maktabi* from the specialist to whom alone the right to think is given. To believe that simply because the society in question is Muslim things would happen differently is a delusion.

It is vain to hope for new creative departures when one advances historically only to take a step backwards in the belief that everything has already been decided and accomplished ten centuries ago and that it is sufficient to adopt the old model and to form contemporary society to it as if society were a mould. Neither by their education nor by the nature of the power they exercise over the mind are the mullahs prepared to set free the creative genius of society. Mawdudi declared that in the context of the law the liberty of the Muslim is achieved. He eliminated totally from his thought the obvious fact that the most brilliant centuries of Islamic civilisation have been those from the eighth to the twelfth when the society of Islam was open to outside influences. He forgot to say exactly why the Muslim empire entered into a period of decline the moment when thought in all its forms became frozen, when mimetism, that *taqlid* to which the Muslim is once again urged, replaced *ijtihad*, that effort which is no longer encouraged.

Stronger than the best intentions, the process that leads to the placing of the destiny of a society in the hands of an organisation, even if it is directed by the most pious and most learned men, results in the swallowing up of civilisation. Once that organisation is put in the service of a total doctrine, the system that has 'an answer for everything' quickly becomes totalitarian.

Many observers, intrigued by the events in Iran, have begun to study Muslim law with passion. They have been profoundly disappointed; they have understood what has been happening even less. Their task might truly have been easier if they had broached the problem from the standpoint of the way power was seized and exercised. Khomeinism is to the *shari'a* what Stalinism is to Marxism. And the fatherland of triumphant Islamism is today what the 'fatherland of socialism' was for the communists of the thirties: a country in the grip of the worst internal and external difficulties that tenaciously supports a machine whose wheels pulverise everything in its path. After the elimination of declared enemies, the proper functioning of the machine requires the purging of those who have not understood that the system admits only the total submission of the individual conscience. Ghotbezadeh, the former spokesman of Khomeini in France, was shot in August 1982. Bani Sadr and Raja'i live in exile. They have not ceased to reflect, as Trotsky did before them, on the mechanisms that allow the transformation of a just revolution into a monster that devours men.

Note

1. Abu Ala al-Mawdudi, *Towards Understanding Islam*, from the French translation published under the sponsorship of the Islamic Foundation, United Kingdom, 1973, p. 135. The volume which I have consulted, printed in Tunis, bears the double date 1397 Hijra 1977 and mentions, along with the foundation in the United Kingdom, the Association of Islamic Students in France, without making precise the role of this organisation in the publication of the work.

8.   The Impossible Secularism

The Republic must be nationalist, unitary, and secular, proclaimed Mustafa Kemal, the father of the new Turkey, on 3 March 1924. At his instigation, a constitution was promulgated on the following 20 April. It brought to a close the long struggle of the Turkish nationalists against the Allies and their hostage, the Ottoman Sultan Muhammad VI Wahid al-Din, then against his successor, the Caliph Abd al-Majid.

We must remember that the Ottoman Empire had sided with Germany during the First World War and that it had lost all of its European and Arab territories as a result. The territory that Turkey occupies today would have all but been dismembered and divided up amongst Greeks, English, and French had it not been for the nationalist uprising provoked by the military action organised by Mustafa Kemal and his comrades-in-arms.[1]

On 1 November 1922, Mustafa Kemal had already had the abolition of the sultanate proclaimed by the Grand National Assembly sitting in Ankara. Until that time, that institution had played the role of estates-general assembled to express the popular will before a power which, in Istanbul, found itself under the direct control of the Allies and agreed without protest to its manoeuvres with a view to safeguarding what appeared to it essential: the throne.

'There is only one way of getting out of the trouble we find ourselves in,' declared the leader of the 'rebels' in Ankara, 'and that is for parliament to make a law separating the sultanate and the caliphate and expelling Muhammad VI from the country.' This was accomplished in early November 1922. Seventeen days later the Sultan left Istanbul under British protection and took up his exile in San Remo, in Italy.

The sultanate disappeared in a storm of troubles but the caliphate survived, with the office falling to the Crown Prince, Abd al-Majid. Many Muslims, in fact, confused the two titles and could not easily find a secure footing among the vicissitudes of Islamic history.

It was in Baghdad in the tenth century at the moment when the Abbasid caliphs decided to entrust the defence of the regime to the armed forces that the title of sultan made its appearance. Literally, the word signifies in Arabic authority, power. Henceforth, moral and religious authority was vested in the caliph as successor of the Prophet and the authority to govern remained with the sultan. In principle, the latter was only the secular arm of the caliph.

But little by little, he represented real power so much so that the title began to exercise a kind of fascination on the masters of the various countries who seized it. Nevertheless, the figure of the caliph held great prestige in the eyes of the people. When the Mongols took Baghdad in 1258, a survivor of the Abbasid dynasty was received in Egypt by the local sultan Baybars who conferred upon him the title of caliph, heir to the Prophet.

Thereafter, the title passed to the line of the Abbasids in Egypt and until the sixteenth century was purely a religious dignity. In 1517 the Ottoman Sultan Salim, representing the greatest Muslim power in the Middle East, put an end to the reign of the Mamluks in Egypt and arranged for the last of the Abbasid religious leaders to transfer the caliphal title to him. From that day, the heads of the Ottoman Empire carried the two titles of sultan and caliph.

For most Muslims, and especially the Sunnites, this meant that from the death of the Prophet to the twentieth century, the community – the *umma* – had never ceased to have a commander of the faithful, a supreme spiritual chief. But the separation of sultanate and caliphate had already existed. At least on the formal level the sultan was invested with power by the caliph. Thus consecrated, he was guaranteed a legitimacy that arms alone did not suffice to confer on him. In Baghdad, the sultans certainly named the caliphs and did not hesitate to dethrone some and execute others. The need, however, to obtain the approval of the holder of religious authority was such that its function was maintained to the end. Thus when the Arabo–Islamic Empire collapsed, the governors of Egypt arranged to have among themselves and as their puppet a legitimate successor of the Commanders of the Faithful. This explains the insistence of the Ottomans, at the height of their temporal power, on obtaining this religious title carried by a poor heir who lived in Egypt on an allowance often stingily meted out.

Was Mustafa Kemal sincere in only suppressing the sultanate in 1922? Does it really matter? The sequence of events clearly demonstrates the difficulty in reconciling the two offices. The republic was proclaimed a year later on 29 October 1923, but the organisation, or more exactly the creation *ex nihilo* of a truly Turkish state on the European model came up against so many stumbling blocks that the opponents regrouped themselves very soon around religious leaders who had claims on the caliphate. The man who lived in Istanbul had not a single soldier at his disposal and was involved in no affairs of state, but he showed himself more powerful than the powerful conqueror of Anatolia. Ataturk's struggle to build a modern Turkey was transformed into an open war against Islam, and in the first instance against its supreme representative: the caliph.

This disestablishment of the caliphate in 1924 was to traumatise Muslims well beyond the frontiers of Turkey. It remained the centre of a debate until the Second World War. We have already mentioned that the Muslim Brothers in Egypt made one of their objectives the reestablishment of the caliphate and it would not be unusual to see in the various Islamic congresses organised here and there some attempts to resolve by consensus the problem posed by the absence of a central authority.

'The republic will be . . . secular,' said Mustafa Kemal. So be it! But was it? No, if we understand by that that the state does not concern itself with religion. The 'secularisation' of Mustafa Kemal's Turkey quickly resembled a repression of Islam. The Sufic brotherhoods and their convents were closed, the number of mosques was limited, a new lifestyle was imposed, all those who openly practised religion were persecuted, and an impressive number of them were hanged. The homogenisation of the new country, moreover, impelled republican power towards a proclivity for the systematic persecution of religious and ethnic minorities. Kurds, Armenians, and Greek Orthodox were put to the sword or deported en masse. Our intention here is not to denigrate Ataturk. His resistance to all the encroachments of the imperialists and his will to bring Turkey out of the Middle Ages were admirable. The facts are evident, however, which attest to the ferocity of the repression – a ferocity equal to that which the defenders of absolute Islamicisation are today the proof. The West admires Ataturk and condemns Khomeini. From the standpoint of respect for the rights of man, for freedom of conscience, for the right of peoples to self-determination, both men are equally culpable.

Today the Turkish republic remains formally secular. In truth, it resembles more Poland or Italy than France. The religious 'party' is strong there. Secularism can be achieved, can triumph only when it becomes part of the individual psyche. It assumes that man/woman sees him/herself as citizen of a nation-state and not as a member of a transnational community. It means that they place religion on the level of a personal and direct relationship with God without interference in the life of society. It implies that belief is an act of faith and religion is a moral code of conduct, not a system of social, economic, and political organisation. It suggests ultimately peaceful coexistence within the context of citizenship with those who do not have religion or profess another faith.

Nothing of this exists in a clear manner in the psychology of the Muslim, for whom Islam is not only a belief but also an identity and a system. Also, to remove religion from the control of the state is tantamount in the end to delivering men up as a flock to a religious hierarchy that will always finish up by returning to take them in hand, with all the risks that this entails.

In 1969, I went on an official trip to Bulgaria to attend a congress of the Agrarian Party. One day, having expressed the desire to meet some Muslims, I was permitted, once the first shock of surprise had passed, to satisfy my curiosity. I knew very well that some *apparatchiks* would be introduced to me, but I wanted to know what Muslim communists had to say. A meeting with two deputies, a woman and a man, was accordingly organised. I expected them to recite a speech that I would be called upon to interpret as I wished. Very quickly, it was the woman who monopolised the conversation. She asked me all sorts of questions about circumcision, marriage, names given to children, the fast of Ramadan, prayer, in a word about all the cultural and social aspects of Islam in Tunisia. To each question my answers always provoked enthusiastic reactions if not a genuine response from the heart such as, 'That's the way it's done among us,' even when a slight difference was underlined. The interview lasted longer than expected. The joy that could be read on the faces of my interlocutors was not faked. When we said our goodbyes, they told me how happy they were 'to have met a brother and to have found out that we practise the same religion'. I had never hidden my socialist and humanist convictions and had said nothing that might make me pass for a 'fundamentalist' or a devoted believer. Representatives of this isolated minority simply wanted me to verify that they were still Muslims. They had used me as a reference. For them, I was first and foremost a brother.

A friend who had gone to Albania faced an attitude diametrically opposed to what I had discovered in Bulgaria. He made the same request that I did. They answered that no one believed anymore but that he could speak to whomever he wanted. During one of his trips in the countryside, he observed that the mosques were either closed or turned into ordinary quarters. He asked questions of numerous people. They snubbed him. One man went so far as to mimic the gestures of Muslim prayer and, contorted with laughter, punctuated his story with these comments: 'This is how my father used to do things.'

On the other hand, another friend, a victim according to him of a misadventure in Yugoslavia, gives a different image of Albania. After a series of misunderstandings, he found himself incarcerated in a prison camp in the south of the country near the Albanian frontier. Now the majority of the detainees there were Albanians who, seeking to flee their country, had illegally entered Yugoslavia. Learning that my friend was Tunisian, and so a speaker of Arabic, they brought him a Quran and requested that he read it aloud, observing that he could perform this task without hesitation. They made him their imam and required him to lead them in prayer. He had never had that job in his life and he had to rely on childhood memories so as not to make mistakes in the gestures. He was barely able to pull it off but the prisoners were happy. From that day onwards until his release two months later, he lived in that sinister camp, pampered and venerated like a pope. According to his flock, the Muslim religion has always been secretly practised in Albania.

It is difficult to know which of the two stories best reflects the Albanian reality. The second, it is true, goes back almost twenty years while the first dates from 1979. But in any case, we have here the proof that when people affirm their attachment to a persecuted faith they are ready to accept any guide at all provided that he can establish a bond between them and the sacred text. From that moment onwards his decisions are accepted as indisputable judgments, hence the danger of a systematic secularisation decided by government and not assumed by ordinary citizens.

Between 1922 and 1924 Ataturk came to understand that he could not build a state without reference to religion if he permitted spiritual guides and traditional leaders to exercise a considerable parallel power over the minds of people. Not only did such leaders turn out to be the declared opponents of his policies but they succeeded in dividing the ranks of his followers. Several of his closest companions stood themselves at the head of the plotters.

Ataturk reacted violently and came down hard on those who schemed against him. His forceful action made him the absolute master of Turkey, but fifty years later, it cannot be said that his policy of secularisation has succeeded. Already in 1945 parliamentary competition had pushed the Democratic Party to align itself with the Islamists in order to gain the upper hand with Ataturk's Republican People's Party which he had led until his death in 1938. At a stroke, this alignment was obliged in its turn to soften it position so as not to lose its majority status. Under the secular regime, Islam was not forgotten by the state which in reality had brought it under its control. During the lifetime of Ataturk, the government had already named men of religion to occupy cultural functions. It was the government which provided for their education. In 1947 the government authorised the setting up of private religious schools and two years later permitted the inclusion of religious programs in official primary schools. With Adnan Menderes, leader of the Democratic Party, the government went even further in the fifties. Religious instruction became an integral part of secondary education.

After a military interlude, the new Justice Party revealed itself after 1961 to be even more Islamist. And when its leader, Sulayman Demirel, became head of state, religion made its official debut in the university. Finally, after 1973, a real Islamist party, the National Salvation Party, appeared on the scene and played a determining role in the political equation.[2]

A curious situation, that of this officially secular state, where the law prohibits all reference to religion but where all parties, in different degrees, flatter the religion of the masses in order to assure themselves of a certain political weight. It is a fact that not only has secularism not eliminated religion from public life but it has provoked the ghost appearance of a religious hierarchy which, although nonofficial, is nonetheless visible. Besides, secret societies and even sects have come into being. This underground Islam was so strong that the 'secular' leaders could not ignore it for a long time. They judged it more prudent to soften their positions inasmuch as the risk of fanaticism was not the privilege of the religious movements. The clandestine organisations of the extreme left have nothing to envy the Islamists for by way of violent action. As in other Muslim countries, the successive Turkish governments thought it useful and efficient to avert the Marxist threat with generosity towards the Islamist movement. Without wishing to judge Turkish domestic politics, which are exceedingly complex, let us simply note that the practice of traditional Islam is today in that secular state more flourishing than ever.

For large segments of the population, the Westernisation pushed forward at great pace under the banner of Kemalism was resented as an alienation, a violent uprooting for which Turkish nationalism compensated only in part. More often wrongly than rightly, the word alienation returns to the lips of those who criticise the forced march towards 'modernism', as much in Turkey as elsewhere.

In a society cut off from its roots, the individual has the impression of undergoing a disagreeable mutation. The chrysalis dies before becoming a butterfly. On close examination, what one denounces with the word alienation in Muslim countries is equally condemned in the West: the dislocation of social structures, coercive industrialisation, the proletarianisation of the peasant masses, the greed for wealth, the consumer society, the culture of gadgets, the overthrow of morality, the disappearance of traditions, or quite simply the difficulty of living. Certainly, and even more so for Muslim societies, these diseases seem to be imported from the West. Let the West denounce them and seek a remedy; it is the West's affair. These diseases prove at least that the model is far from being perfect. But from there to the experiencing of a violent desire to resurrect a tradition unwillingly abandoned is only a step which the traditionalists happily help the people to take.

The problems of the secular state are of two kinds: on one hand, the state must invent a model of rapid and balanced development and, on the other hand, it must assure its citizens that their personality will evolve without causing them to break with their roots. In other words, the state must find the ideal equation integrating the economic, the social, and the spiritual.

The Turkish experiment proves that the spiritual cannot be eliminated in favour of the political and the national. The Iranian example confirms – although the Shah's regime never declared itself secular – that the spiritual and the social can never be neglected in favour of the economic.

However different, the Soviet example illustrates to perfection the impossible secularism of Islamic countries. Hélène Carrère d'Encausse, in *L'Empire éclaté* already cited, analyses the difficulties that the Soviet authorities encountered with their Muslim republics. 'The USSR', she recounts:

> has more than 200 mosques today whereas it had 45,000 in 1917. For 50 million Muslims, this is laughable. But these figures do not take into account the unofficial places of worship served by unofficial clergy who, everywhere in Central Asia and in the Caucasus, are quite numerous.[3]

As opposed to the Kemalists, the Soviets, while organising an anti-religious propaganda, did not seek a clash with the religious hierarchy. Rather they tried to coopt them by reorganising them. 'Four spiritual centres', Hélène Carrère d'Encausse states:

> dominate the whole (*muftiats*): that of Ufa, whose authority extends over the Sunnite Muslims of European Russia and Siberia, that of Tashkent, to which the Sunnites of Central Asia and Kazakhstan are accountable, that of Buynaksk in the Caucasus for the Sunnites of the northern Caucasus and of Daghestan, and finally that of Baku, which exercises its influence over a mixed Shi'ite and Sunnite population.[4]

The mufti of Tashkent is the most important: he directs the only two Muslim universities of the USSR, the Madarasah Mir Arab of Bukhara and the Baraq Khan of Tashkent, 'where the notables of Islam are educated'.[5] The mufti in question had the Quran printed on the party's presses. He publishes a magazine, *Muslims of the Soviet East*, in Uzbek, Arabic, French, English, and, of course, Russian! And finally he is the spokesman for Soviet Muslims outside the country.

Such is the official organisation of Islam which allows the Soviet Union to affirm before the world that it does not persecute religion and respects freedom of conscience. The reality is quite another thing and the evolution of the situation turns to the advantage of Islam rather than to that of communist ideology despite the untiring activity of the committees charged with the propagation of atheism, the systematisation of control of the individual from birth by social organisations, the mobilisation of sociologists, psychologists, and hard-core militant communists, and the increase in impediments to the practice of religion.

Relying on official Soviet documentation Hélène Carrère d'Encausse analyses in detail the reaction of Muslims to this policy of systematic de-Islamicisation, a reaction which operates on two levels: that of the preservation of tradition and that of the adaptation of the faith to the particular traditions of the Soviet Union.

The signs of traditionalism are numerous. We may state the following facts: endogamy among Muslims; recourse to the mullah for the consecration of marriage despite the obligation to follow a civil procedure; the persistence of the dowry; the circumcision of male children; the choice of given names; the indisputable power, however occult, that forebears exercise; the burial of the dead in Muslim cemeteries; the respect of national and tribal *adat* (customs); and finally membership in religious brotherhoods such as the Naqshabandiyya and the Qadiriyya, although in many Muslim countries, especially Arab, the brotherhoods have completely disappeared. Apart from the brotherhoods, this corresponds exactly to what my Bulgarian interlocutors had told me about their country.

The effort of religion to adapt is still more remarkable. In order to get around the obstacles that aim at the discouragement of religious practices, religious authorities have authorised the Muslim to make only one or two prayers a day instead of five and at home if the mosque is far away. These authorities allow the Ramadan fast to be dispensed with but the *iftar*, the breaking of the fast, must occur obligatorily in the family at the prescribed hour and bring together those who fast and those who do not. All the Muslim holidays are celebrated, and their social aspect is emphasised. The impossible pilgrimage to Mecca is replaced by a visit to the holy places of Turkestan. *Jihad* is exalted but in the form of devotion to work, to brotherhood, and to solidarity with co-religionists. Finally, from communism itself, elements corresponding to the social ideology of Islam have been extracted so that, adds Hélène Carrère d'Encausse, even communism becomes a 'by-product of Islam'. The religious authorities have also encouraged the faithful to be ambitious and to occupy the most important posts in the party hierarchy!

The Indonesian example is entirely different but no less instructive. Since independence, after the Second World War, the Nationalist Party of Ahmad Sukarno demonstrated its preference for secularism. The Indonesian political climate did not resemble that of the former Ottoman Empire of 1918. There had been no defeat. There had been no religious authority allied with a foreign invader. The problems were not posed in terms of sharp, internal conflicts despite the immensity of the territory and its ethnic diversity. Of course, the adherence of ninety percent of the population to Islam could have led so much more easily to an attempt by religion to control the state since Islamist groups, dynamic and sometimes powerful, had been active from the beginning of the century in Sumatra and especially in Java. Yet it was – as in Tunisia and in Algeria – the weight of modern nationalism which was preponderant. Sukarno proclaimed the *Panjasila*, or the 'five principles': belief in one God, democracy, social justice, nationalism, and internationalism. These humanist principles, which make one think of 'the Supreme Being and Architect of the universe' of the French Revolution, were sufficiently vague to rally all tendencies.

Thus it is on these five elements that Indonesian secularism was founded and reaffirmed in the Constitution of 1959, but not without difficulty since at that time it was ratified by only 265 votes against, to 201 for, the Islamicisation of the state. Yet already, as we can demonstrate, this secularism professed by the leaders has scarcely any resemblance to official Soviet atheism nor to the rejection of religion by Turkish Kemalism. Under the circumstances, the question revolved around a syncretism that pursued at the same time the satisfaction of religious feeling and an opening to all the contemporary modernist tendencies up to and including communist ideology. Moreover, Sukarno put forward the Masakom, which was simultaneously a doctrine and a front that united men and nationalist, Islamist, and communist ideas.

Nevertheless this flexible approach did not prevent Islamism from experiencing a continued growth and from exercising an open collaboration in the face of the declared hostility of the government.

First of all, this secularisation had as a consequence the development of religious activities and Quranic instruction in the private sphere despite the existence of a minister of religious affairs. And the maintaining of a hierarchy parallel to that of the state did not cease to pose problems, for contrary to the modern Christian clergy, this religious body, as in French revolutionary times, did not shun public affairs.

There was already in Indonesia a religious association founded in 1912 – the Muhammadiyyah – that had proliferated in Java and Sumatra, had created organisations for young people and women, and had given life to missionary activities: *Mubaligh*. But, with respect to what most concerns us here, it would be instructive to follow the history of another Islamist organisation, that of the *ulama*.

In the beginning, Nahdhatul-Ulama,[6] literally the awakening of the Ulama, better known under the abbreviation NU, appeared as an association in 1926 in reaction against the reformist modernism of the Muhammadiyyah with its power centre in Java. It was therefore at the start a rather conservative movement. The NU, however, placed itself at first between the Muhammadiyyah and the nationalist movement. When the former, issuing from the Sarekat Islam (Islamic Association) which was founded in 1911, parted ways with the communists, who created the PKI in 1920, its former purely nationalist orientation was set, and it gave birth in 1927 to the PNI, which became Sukarno's party. The more the PNI emphasised its nationalism, the more the

NU became a party that welcomed those who wished to give priority to the Islamic character of the movement.

In 1952, the NU became a political party. As such, it participated in the 1955 elections and entered the Sukarno government. For all intents and purposes, as the members of the Muhammadiyyah never ceased to reproach it, it has always been in power. Yet it was its leaders who, in 1967, collaborated with the army in the final fall of Sukarno who, considered by his adversaries as a prisoner of the communists, in fact had been rejected by the rank and file of the army.

When Western and Islamic interests appeared to coincide, the army seized power in 1965 without eliminating Sukarno at first and not without having taken the NU as an ally in the fierce repression of the communists in 1965 and 1966.

As it did elsewhere in the Muslim world, the pendulum swung between the extreme left and the extreme right, in other words, between the radical transformation of society and preservation of an inherited identity. The repression of the communists counterbalanced what in 1958 had accompanied the crushing of the Dar-ul-Islam movement in Java and the Masjumi in Sumatra.

Is the Indonesian state secular? On paper, yes, as it is constitutionally in Turkey. But secularism – which competes to a certain degree with Islamism as a social and political force – appears above all as a simple tool allowing governments to turn against their allies if need be.

The Soviet experience, like that of Turkey and Indonesia, illuminates the problem that governments of Muslim countries face. What to do about the *shari'a*? What to do about the religious leaders? What to do about education? What to do about *asala*, that is, the roots that nourish identity? And what to do at the same time about development? To extol secularism is indeed absurd because Islam is a way of life. If one proposes a different, non-Islamic world view, Muslims will fall back on archaic positions; if one favours, on the other hand, an evolution of the Islamic world view, the approach ceases to be secular. In both cases, nothing comes of the effort.

We can understand better now why a man such as Bourguiba refused to be compared to Ataturk. Being careful not to plunge directly into secularism, he had written into Article 1 of the Tunisian constitution that Islam is the religion of the state. He appropriated it to himself in order better to combat it, regularly taking care to research traditional references to justify his most conspicuous decisions. This has not prevented the birth on Tunisian soil of an Islamism dedicated to battle. The socio-political analyses of the first chapters of this book have presented an explanation of this phenomenon. We will now complete that explanation by treating the difficulties of reformism in the twentieth century.

Notes

1. See for this period Benoist-Méchin, *Mustapha Kemal* (Paris: Albin Michel, 1954), chapters 86–9.
2. See Louis Bazin, *Pouvoirs*, no. 12, first quarter, 1980, Paris, 135–9.
3. Hélène Carrère d'Encausse, *op. cit.*, p. 234.
4. *Ibid.*, pp. 235–6.
5. *Ibid.*, p. 236
6. The Muslims of Asia attach the article *ul* (or *al*) to the first word of an expression formed of two Arab nouns. Thus, for example, instead of writing according to Arabic grammatical rules *Zia al-Haq*, they prefer the form *Ziaul Haq*. The reader who does not know Arabic is led into error. He believes that the name, or its first part, is Ziaul when it is Zia. In the case of the Indonesian organisation, one ought to write *Nahdhatu al-Ulama*, or better *Nahdhatu-l-Ulama*, but not *Nahdhatul-Ulama*.

9. The Many Paths of Reformism

What more extraordinary destiny than that of the enigmatic Jamal al-Din al-Afghani, who in sixty years of life made the Shah of Iran, the Khedive of Egypt, and the sultan in Istanbul tremble; worried the British so that they expelled him from wherever he embarrassed them; bested the Frenchman Renan who painted an exalted picture of him; and won admirers even in America! If his name remains so intimately linked to the birth of Islamic reformism, how is it that a century has already passed since he launched his movement without the fundamental objectives he pursued having been attained?

In the Arab world, we believe that everything began in the nineteenth century with the *Nahda* movement, which is generally translated by the word 'renaissance', but really means 'the awakening' or, better, 'the rising of the sleeper'. In truth the Nahda was specifically Arab and had to do more with the rediscovery of literature and the splendour of a lost civilisation than with the Islamic religion. Furthermore, the promoters of the movement were often Christian Arabs.

On the other hand, the *Islah* movement, translated generally as 'reformism', was Islamic and developed as much in the Arab countries as it did in India, Russia, and Black Africa. It is a religious movement and the word reformism is really insufficient to describe it. That European word suggests an action which is not revolutionary, whereas the word *Islah*, used in this context by all parties whatever their native language, signifies repair, the return to working order of what is defective, the purification of what is corrupt, and so leaves the field open as to choice of methods. It is against the background of these distinctions that the words for 'reformism' and 'reformist' are used here, to conform to the usage established by the European orientalists. One should not be surprised in this context to see certain forms of *Islah* defined as revolutionary in this book whenever, for example, the undertaking of a 'reformist' takes on such magnitude that only this term suffices to characterise it.

Towards the middle of the eighteenth century, two men born in the same year of 1703 woke the Muslim world from its lethargy as much by their ideas as by their actions: Muhammad Ibn Abd al-Wahhab in the Arab Middle East and Shaykh Waliullah in India.

Abd al-Wahhab denounced the *taqlid* – the imitation of the elders – rose up against the *ulama* who kept Muslims in a state of apathy by their obscurantism, rejected the teaching of all the schools, preached the return to the Quran and to the Prophetic tradition, called for *ijtihad*, and led a vigorous campaign against the religious brotherhoods and their meeting places, the *zawiyas*, that is to say, the mausoleums of the saints. He reminded everybody that in Islam people, however pious, were not to be canonised and caused their burial places to be demolished wherever he went in Arabia, Iraq or Syria.

Shaykh Waliullah also denounced the backward traditionalism of the *ulama*, condemned *taqlid* and preached *ijtihad*, the need for which was always felt. He demanded far-reaching social reform, denounced the feudalism established over the centuries in India, declared that the only economic value worthy of respect was work, underlined that the wealth of nations can only come about through the labour of all people, fought against monopolies, required that the working hours of wage earners be fixed, and believed that society had the duty to satisfy the essential needs of all its members. What we are talking about here is revolution. Moreover, to crown his struggle against immobilism of the *ulama*, he translated – what heresy! – the Quran into Persian so as to make it comprehensible to those who spoke this widespread language in India but knew no Arabic.[1]

These two men have exercised a profound influence on numerous leaders of reformist movements and it is sometimes difficult, if one does not engage in detailed analysis, to know who is Wahhabist or who is Waliist among their successors. Often the necessary documents are not available to establish with certainty the spiritual lines of descent. Let us limit ourselves then to the naming of these men and to the evocation of their deeds.

Ahmad Tijan (1737–1815), the founder of the *tariqah tijaniyyah*, previously discussed, merits special mention. An Algerian who emigrated to Morocco, influenced it seems by the ideas of Abd al-Wahhab, he thought the time had come for the purification of Islam. He had as a disciple a man about whom much would be said: al-Hadj Umar, who, in West Africa, established the Tijaniyah on the banks of the Senegal.

Ahmad Ibn Idriss, who died in 1837, is little known outside the Muslim world. Yet his work was furthered through the actions of his disciples. A Moroccan and emigrant to Mecca, well versed in the theories of Abd al-Wahhab yet following his own path, he had as successors the Shaykh al-Mirghani, who founded the Khatimiyyah order in the Sudan, and Muhammad al-Sanussi, who launched the movement which bears his name in Libya.

'Uthman Dan Fodio (1754–1817), who was also influenced by Wahhabist puritanism, launched a veritable war against the 'miscreants' in central and western Africa, the Chad and Mali of the present day.

Two other names deserve mention. The first is Shihab al-Din Marjani, a Tartar from Lazan in Russia. His movement, the Usul-i Jadid, that is, the Principles of Renewal, created in 1855, also preached the reinstitution of *ijtihad* and encouraged the learning of European languages and familiarisation with modern science and technology. He gained a large audience from the Volga to Turkestan.

The second is Ismail Bey Gasprinski, also a Tartar but from the Crimea. He sought to renew Islamic culture by creating a network of schools and joined his work to that of Marjani whose follower he was at the end of the nineteenth century.

Finally, one must invoke the great figure of the Indian Ahmad Khan, incontestably in direct line of descent from Shaykh Waliullah, although he was never considered an official legatee of the master. Whereas the successors of Waliullah allowed themselves to be absorbed by the prevailing conservatism, Ahmad Khan wished to go further on the road to reform. He required a true adaptation of religious thought to his times. Despairing to see the *ulama* act, he founded a school that preached, in the style of Rousseau, the return to nature. Its name twisted by mispronunciation, his movement was called Nitcherya. He was squarely in the Western camp and was knighted by Queen Victoria. A contemporary of al-Afghani, he nevertheless quarrelled with him violently.

The nineteenth century, thus, had already experienced the tremor of an Islamic awakening when al-Afghani arrived on the scene. It could be said, without risk of contradiction, that no part of the Arab world lacked in response to the appeal of renewal. Often purely religious, sometimes social, the idea of renewal incited Muslims always to go beyond the stage of unacceptable underdevelopment. Contrary to the prevailing idea of the time, it was not the shock of colonisation that provoked, at the end of the nineteenth century, the rise of Islam.

It is true that in Algeria from 1835 to 1847 the Amir Abd al-Qadir drew the force necessary to launch his nationalist and Islamist movement from his resistance to French armed might. But it was also at midcentury that the Bey of Tunis, Ahmad I, thrust his country without preparation into the process of modernisation which ended in financial bankruptcy. At the same time, the cultural initiatives of the minister Khayr al-Din Pasha (1810–90) and the dynamic scholar, Shaykh Mahmud Qabadu, began to develop.

It was also during this period that the Egyptian dynasty founded by Muhammad Ali in 1805 attempted to give a new vigour to the Cairene state by competing for power with the Ottomans in Syria (1831–39) and in Arabia (1825–49). Moreover, it was at this time that Wahhabism, about which we have already spoken, began to triumph in Arabia, sometimes thanks to the activity of the Saudis in the northeast, sometimes by the sword of the Banu Rashid of the Shammar confederation in the centre. Finally, it was the epoch when, further east, the Babi movement appeared, followed by its successor the Baha'i, first in Iran, and then throughout the Middle East.

This was the age of the Arab renaissance and numerous are the names of those who symbolised Muslim intellectual activities. The Lebanese Ahmad Faris Shidyaq, the Tunisian Mahmud Qabadu, already mentioned above, and the Egyptian Sami al-Barudi in literature; the Persians Ali Tabataba'i in Quranic exegesis, and Hussain Kashfi in philosophy were well known before the great colonial shock of the 1880s which saw the British establish their authority from India to the Nile, via Aden, and the French impose their protectorate on Tunisia.

But it remained for Jamal al-Din al-Afghani to launch the first vigorous movement that was simultaneously pan-Islamist in ideology, anti-imperialist in politics, internationalist in its methods of action and reformist in its religious doctrine.

His birth in 1837 or 1838 is shrouded in mystery as befits legendary personalities. Was he Afghan or Persian? All that he was willing to admit was that he had seen the light of day on Afghan soil, that he had been educated in India, and that he had a liking for Iran by virtue of what he called 'its proximity and its bonds'. But he put these three countries on the same plane as the Hijaz, 'the land of revelation'; Yemen, 'the land of the kings of antiquity'; the Najd, the Arabian plateau; Iraq of the 'Caliphs Harun al-Rashid and Ma'mun'; Sham, the Arab name for Greater Syria; and the Andalusia of the Alhambra with 'its fate'. He was essentially a member of the Muslim *umma* and recognised no frontiers. If he had been alive today, he would have been, without a doubt, the Che Guevara of Islam.

At twenty he was adviser to the court at Kabul. Twenty years later he took the side of the legitimate heir to the throne against the British candidate. When he lost the battle he went to India, from which he was expelled by the British but to which he returned several months later only to be expelled once again to Istanbul in 1870. His reputation as a fighter and a scholar preceded him there. The sultan named him to the council for higher education. By his audacious ideas he provoked the wrath of the Shaykh al-Islam who succeeded in having him exiled to Egypt. There he quickly became the lion of intellectual and nationalist circles, was surrounded by a court of admirers, and collected a group of earnest followers in the first rank of which stood Shaykh Muhammad Abduh. But, in 1879, he was censured by the *ulama* of al-Azhar, who were outraged by his reformist activities; by the royal court irritated by his liberalism; and by the British, who were preparing to lay hands on the country. He was expelled to Hyderabad in India. But soon the British transferred him to Calcutta and put him under house arrest before sending him off once again to Europe. He had in fact succeeded in founding, in India, a secret society, Al-Urwa al-Wuthqa (The Firmest Bond).

En route he wrote to his disciple Muhammad Abduh, himself exiled from Egypt in 1881 and resident now in Beirut, and asked him to come to Paris. It was there the two friends published a journal in 1884, *al Urwa al-Wuthqa*, which, despite an ephemeral existence (eighteen issues in eight months between March and October), had an impact whose effects are still being felt today. But the enemies of al-Afghani and Abduh were not disarmed. The journal was prohibited in the Middle East and the two revolutionaries had to close shop.

Abduh returned to Egypt, but al-Afghani remained in Europe. In 1886 he responded to an invitation from Nasir al-Din, the Shah of Iran, who wanted to install him in his country. Very quickly he understood that the political climate was not favourable to him. He departed for Russia, where it seems he was better received in intellectual circles. The Shah, who could not do without him, asked him back to Iran in 1889 after a reconciliation in Munich. But his second period of residence was of short duration. With an escort of 500 cavalrymen he was quickly taken to Iraq, from where, after he succeeded in raising a revolt against Nasir al-Din Shah, he embarked in 1892 for London. From there he sent letters to his friends which were veritable firebrands. As he had many followers throughout the Middle East, his activity worried people in many circles. Abd al-Hamid, the Ottoman Sultan, did everything to persuade him to return to Istanbul. He ended up by yielding, only to discover that a golden cage had been prepared for him: a house, a stipend and . . . a restriction on his movements. He died five years later on 9 March 1897. Rumour had it that he had been poisoned. At any rate, he was buried by order of the Sultan in the small hours and his tomb would have to wait long years before an American admirer rediscovered it and made it recognisable.

If the open struggle led by al-Afghani against oriental despots who were suspected, moreover, of being in league with the British can be appreciated correctly only in the specific context of the history of Afghanistan, Iran, Egypt and the Ottoman Empire, his Islamist activities cannot be broached without taking into account his particular relationship with Shaykh Muhammad Abduh. It would not be an exaggeration to say that it was in the Egyptian environment, between 1870 and 1879, that al-Afghani refined his views on religion. Up to that time he had been a revolutionary, a warrior, a fighter against imperialism. Now there he was, after his expulsion from Egypt in 1879, writing an epistle, *Reply to the Atheists*, and engaging in polemics in India.

On the other hand, Shaykh Muhammad Abduh, born in 1849 into a family of the Egyptian Delta, came very early under the influence of one of his granduncles who was smitten by mysticism. Thanks to the encouragement of this old Sufi, he once again took up his studies, left for Cairo, took courses with the great masters of al-Azhar, and there obtained his doctorate of religious sciences (*alimiyya*), but not without difficulty because meanwhile he had become suspect in the eyes of his teachers by virtue of his visits to al-Afghani in the 1870s.

The alliance between the two men was founded on a complementarity that proved fruitful. Al-Afghani had followed an eclectic course of study in the old style; he had taken courses successively in India and in Afghanistan from the masters of Arab letters, theology, jurisprudence, mathematics, medicine, and even surgery. He had a prodigious appetite for reading and was aware of everything published in Europe that was translated into the languages he knew. Abduh, for his part, had received a regular diploma from a classical university. He had the right to count himself among the *ulama* and the *ulama* could not deny him this, nor question the education which they themselves had given him. Moreover, he ended his life as Grand Mufti of Egypt, that is, at the top of the religious hierarchy. The latter brought to this association the security of his education: the former a political dimension and an extraordinary knowledge of the Middle Eastern and Western worlds. Their journal, published in Paris, was the expression of this alliance: al-Afghani was its director and Abduh its editor in chief. The articles were not signed. They explained, as the editors outlined, the point of view of a group of well-intentioned men who were fighting for the triumph of Muslims everywhere. And the name of the journal was significant:

al-Urwa al Wuthqa (The Firmest Bond), which evoked the Quran as the surest means to assure the salvation of those who believed in it.

What were their objectives? One of the disciples of Shaykh Abduh, Mustafa Abd al-Razzaq, summed them up in three points:

1. To liberate the mind from the burden of imitation (*taqlid*) so that reason would not be enslaved by temporal or religious leaders.
2. To consider religion the friend of science and not its enemy, each having its own role to play.
3. To understand religion as did the forefathers (*salaf*), those who lived before differences in doctrine appeared, and to refer always to the original sources of Islam. For this reason, the movement was later called Salafiyyah.

To these objectives, to which all Islamic modernists subscribe today, may be added certain immediate political goals: the struggle against imperialism, the fight for the unity of the Muslim world, the denunciation of fratricidal wars, and so on.

Taqlid – blind adherence to tradition – was attacked by the al-Afghani-Abduh team from all angles.[2] 'Men have appeared among Muslims,' they wrote in their journal, 'in religious dress. They have introduced innovations into the religion and have mingled with its principles elements that do not belong there.' Later, this affirmation became more categorical:

Religion is a divine creation. Those who teach and preach it are men. Minds receive it through the bearers of glad tidings and solemn warnings. It constitutes a gain for those whom God has not accorded the privilege of revelation and is transmitted to them by direct communication, study, instruction, and apprenticeship.

In other words, we must not confuse the word of God with the message of those who lay claim to its communication.

The appeal to be open to the world is repeated, sometimes in the form of an exhortation, sometimes as the denunciation of a situation in which one observes 'heads lowered towards the earth or raised toward the sky so that the gaze is fixed neither ahead nor behind, nor to the right nor to the left.'

But they did not denounce only the *taqlid* of the traditionalists. The mimicry of those who aped the West without discernment was also condemned. Fifty years before Mao Zedong, al-Afghani and Abduh saw them as 'the avant-garde of an army of triumphant invaders'.

For the two revolutionaries a correct understanding of the religion based on the study of the Quran would not allow for any contradiction with science. One did not have to deny one's roots to be modern. 'Religion,' they wrote, 'is the best teacher and guide, leading men to learn science and to enlarge the field of their knowledge.'

Without a doubt, the activity of the two men was limited despite their efforts. They sowed their seeds and had disciples and well-wishers such as the Lebanese

Muhammad Rashid Rida and the Tunisian Muhammad Nakhli. But the opposition was too strong and they had only what one calls in literature an indifferent success.

Their appeal for unity came too late, at a time when Muslim countries had already been divided for centuries. Moreover, at the moment when the European colonisers were parcelling out the remains of the Ottoman Empire among themselves, Western diplomacy could only encourage particularism. And rulers, of course, played this game with the foreigners who portrayed themselves as guarantors of their local power.

As for the reform of Islamic practices, it was against the citadel of the *ulama* that such reforms had to strike. To claim to sweep away in a stroke centuries of traditionalism was to threaten well-established positions and upset habits of thought too firmly rooted in the mind for a handful of writings suddenly to overturn. Moreover, even today, certain activist Islamist movements categorically refuse to take other than the Quran as a basis for study. Al-Afghani and Abduh demanded for their part a return to the sacred book and to 'the trustworthy portion of the Prophetic tradition'. They wanted the behaviour of the first four caliphs to be taken as a model. For centuries the body of *ulama* had been professing that the understanding of the Quran and of the Tradition was impossible if one did not refer to the earlier commentaries. One of the pupils of Shaykh Abduh related that the propaganda campaign mounted against the reformer by his *ulama* colleagues was so intense that students inside al-Azhar avoided approaching the circle where he gave his lessons.

A movement of elitists, the reformism of al-Afghani and of Abduh can be defined as an ideology without a party to put that ideology into practice. Given the dynamism of the two men, we can imagine what might have been the result of their activities a century earlier or a century later. In taking up the staff of pilgrims and in preaching from one town to another, they might have excited crowds hundreds of years before, as the Fatimid propagandists had done during the Middle Ages or the theologian Abd al-Wahhab did in the eighteenth century. Today, they would have profited from the mass media. But at the end of the nineteenth century, local governments were already sufficiently aware of subversive movements and could nip them in the bud. We saw how this worked in Iran, for example, when the Shah, by means of severe repression, brought Babism to heel in six years (1850).

No longer having at their disposal a large margin for manoeuvre and not yet profiting from the instruments of modern communication, the two reformers had to content themselves with conferences given to intellectual circles in the capital cities where the powers in place agreed, for a time, to bear with them. They were lucid and they wrote in their journal that the effects of the many accretions that had perverted Islam 'could not be expunged from the mind of the public by virtue of literacy, so that the proper study of religion was limited to narrow circles and a small proportion of the population.'

We can comprehend why so many regretted that they had not thought of extending their analysis further and of proposing for the future a more thoroughgoing reform. The conditions of the age condemned their enterprise to defeat. There is no doubt that they were both disappointed at the end of their lives. They had sown the seeds and had cared for their garden by appealing to intelligence and the religious ethos for which they had great esteem. Perhaps out of timidity they did not knead these things into a dough by means of which their disciples might have provided the daily bread for their co-religionists. Moreover, and without denigrating their work, it should be stated that they were interested for the most part only in the Mashriq. The 'useful' Muslim world was limited in their view to the area between Egypt and India, Turkey and Aden. The Maghreb was scarcely mentioned. No trace, in their journal, of the Tunisia occupied in 1881, the same year as Egypt. After his Parisian period, Abduh tried to right the balance. He went to Tunis twice, in 1884 and in 1903, and to Algeria as well. But it was too late to help the country, too early to shake the apathy of the *ulama*. Similarly, Black Africa was outside their purview. They did not know of the movement of Osman Dan Fodio that had sprung up at midcentury in Nigeria, made no mention in their journal of the fall of Bamako in 1884, the year their journal was published in Paris, nor of the defeat of Samori. Not a word either of Bamba, who created the Muridiyya order dedicated to work and production. In the end they finished by disagreeing on a fundamental problem. Al-Afghani sanctioned the immediate reform of state structures whereas Abduh, insisting on the primacy of the educational effort for Muslims, preferred to put off the revolution for two or three generations.

Certainly they had some excuses, to say the least. But taken together, the facts establish the limits of a program that attempted to be both radical and universal. Who knows if the torch would not have been better taken up elsewhere than in the region of their activities? After all, the ideas of the Fatimids, born in North Africa in the tenth century, survive today only in India and certain regions of Iran.

And so much remained to be done. With the death of al-Afghani in 1897 and of Abduh in 1905, it fell to others to take up their burden. There were many who tried and many were the reactions according to the plan chosen to fight that battle. Shakib Arslan (1869–1946) became the idol of the Muslim world by choosing to defend pan-Islamism and to recall the grandeur of a forgotten civilisation. Muhammad Rashid Rida, a student of Shaykh Abduh, adopted the policy of careful reformism and furthered the religious work of his master. But it was Ali Abd al-Razzaq who, in 1925, provoked a real public protest when he published a book entitled *Islam and the Principles of Power*, in which he refuted the thesis that the caliphate issued from the religious and not the temporal order. Although he himself was a graduate of al-Azhar and occupied the post of *qadi* (religious judge), he was taken to task by the Shaykh of al-Azhar and by the Grand Mufti of Egypt; even by a Syrian scholar who, still alive today, published a new refutation – in 1973!

Because it was limited to the statement of principles, the Salafist doctrine of al-Afghani and Abduh became a kind of formal catchall in which one could put whatever one pleased. Thus, for example, the Tunisian followers were divided into conservative and evolutionary Salafists; the former, Muhammad Najjar, the latter under Salim Bouhajib. The founder of the Muslim Brethren, the Imam Hassan al-Banna said – as we have already mentioned – that his association followed the Salafist line by means of its appeal to original sources and its pan-Islamism. Yet, it is doubtful that this movement really corresponded to what al-Afghani had in mind; he, as a Freemason, saw no contradiction between the objectives of universal brotherhood and those of the Islam he professed.

We have noted also that Mawdudi himself preached the return to the original sources, but it was for a return to the rule of the *ulama* that al-Afghani and Abduh agitated so that the Salafist movement, as a return to the practices of the forebears, became synonymous in the mind of the public with the archaic.

Al-Afghani and Abduh, Rashid Rida, and before them Khayr al-Din and Qabadu, were ideologists without a following. On the other hand, the Algerian Abd al-Hamid Ibn Badis (1889–1940) understood from the beginning that a work of reform has no chance to succeed if it is not passed on by a network of devoted followers.

Born into a family from Constantine, descendant of Sanhadja princes who ruled eastern North Africa under the Fatimids (tenth and eleventh centuries) and counting among his relatives collaborators with the French colonial administration, he was touched in Tunisia by the reformist spirit. In fact, after having learned the Quran by heart in Constantine at the age of thirteen and having delved into the secrets of the Arabic language and the principles of the *shari'a*, he was sent at nineteen by his well-to-do family to study at the Zaytuna University–Mosque in Tunis, where he spent four years (1908–12). It was there that he attended classes led by the few disciples of al-Afghani and Abduh in the first rank of which was the remarkable professor Muhammad Nakhli. Realising the dimensions of the problem of reform, Ibn Badis resolved to go to the Mashriq, first to accomplish the sacred pilgrimage and then to meet the reformists. When he returned to Algeria, he devoted himself to teaching.

The spectacle that Algerian society offered him at the time was not brilliant. Against the background of economic depression and scarcities, the colonised person was caught between the encouragement to give up his roots and one of the most backward forms of traditionalism. Abd al-Hamid Ibn Badis, imbued with Salafist reformism, believed that one could only resist the former by eliminating the latter. From 1925 on, he published his first journal, *Al-Muntaqid* (The Critic), whose title itself represented already a reply to the rule of the traditionalists: '*Itaqid wa la tantaqid*' (Believe and do not criticise). Then he created another that had a longer life: the *Shibad*, a most positive project if one may say so, since the word meant at once a shining star and the flame that spreads its light afar! Careful to guarantee the survival of the journal, he founded also in 1925 an 'Algerian Islamic press'. Then in 1931, he organised his sympathisers into an 'Association of Ulama'. Here we can plainly see the influence of Shaykh Abduh: to preach reformism through the mouths of doctors of the law whose solid education was not to be questioned. But Ibn Badis, who was both a politician and a scholar, did not lose sight of the necessity for action. Also, when the association published a journal *Al-Basa'ir*

(Clear Views) in 1936, he decided to keep his own journal in circulation in order to safeguard his personal freedom. With companions as devoted as himself, such as Shaykh Tayeb al-Oqbi and the writer Tawfiq al-Madani, he also founded educational associations. These various organs allowed Algeria to be covered with a network of modern Quranic schools that contributed considerably to the preservation of Arab culture in the country. The work of the group had, moreover, the effect of creating – since Ibn Badis's association played primarily a political role – other organisations that, by concentrating on the same political goals, put up competition for his.

The movement took up themes dear to al-Afghani and Abduh by adapting them to the Algerian and Maghrebian context and by enriching them with theological and exegetical developments.[3]

In opposition to *taqlid* – servile imitation – Ibn Badis developed an idea rich in perspectives by distinguishing what one calls 'adopted Islam' from 'hereditary or natural Islam'. He declared that 'hereditary Islam allowed weak nations that adhered to it – like the Arabs – to safeguard their personality, their language, and to a large degree a morality that distinguished them from others.' He added quickly: 'But this hereditary Islam cannot aid these nations to develop because they experience a renaissance only when minds awaken and eyes open. Now, hereditary Islam is based on immobilism and imitation. It has neither mind nor a point of view.' As for

> the Islam adopted by the individual, it is the Islam of those who understand its principles, grasp its splendours through faith, its morals, its ethics, its values, its rituals and deepen – as much as possible – their knowledge of Quranic literature and the sayings of the Prophet. Such men base all this on thought and deep examination, separating what Islam reveals through its beauty and proofs of its validity from what is an accretion by reason of its ugliness and decrepitude. These men live their faith, their thought, and their actions.

In 1931, Ibn Badis published an article on the relationships of Muslims to science, the title of which was 'How far must we go in accepting what exists if that leads us to abandon natural science?' Later he addressed this theme to Algerian intellectuals educated in French universities: 'You must help your people,' he told them:

> by what you have learned . . . and this is not contrary to the acquiring of science from any nation, in any language, to the adopting of what is good in other societies and to the extending of a hand to all those who wish to cooperate with us for happiness, peace, and the common good.

Ibn Badis did not retreat either from a problem that still divides Islamists: that of women. He believed that education was indispensable for women, but he also made it clear that they must aim at the consolidation of the Algerian personality, and to accomplish this the education given to young girls must be both Arab and Islamic.

He defended Mustafa Kemal Ataturk and vigorously attacked the *ulama* who condemned the leaders of modern Turkey. In his eyes, the suppression of the caliphate was only 'the abrogation by the Turks of a regime that was theirs, and the elimination of an imaginary symbol that had seduced Muslims without bringing them any benefits.' He held the religious establishment responsible for the reaction of Ataturk. 'It is the Caliph, the Shaykh al-Islam, and his group of *ulama*, as well as the leaders of the brotherhoods who were guilty.' After having recalled how the sultan had made himself the accomplice of the Allies by proclaiming a *jihad* against his own subjects, he noted that the Shaykh al-Islam and the *ulama* had themselves written up the *fatwa* declaring licit the murder of Mustafa Kemal which was dropped by Greek airplanes on Anatolian villages.

As for the suppression of the *shari'a* by Ataturk, it was justified by the gap between a frozen jurisprudence and the state of Turkish evolution. Ibn Badis was categorical:

> We would like you to note that these fossilised *ulama* were able to understand only what they had the habit of understanding since their youth and, within the context of their doctrine and their limited intelligence, cannot be made to accept more than that.

Coming from the president of an association of *ulama*, such an affirmation could not help but make the argument for all the liberals in the Muslim world.

Ibn Badis did not stop there. Al-Afghani and Abduh called for the unity of all Muslim countries. The Egyptian Muslim Brethren demanded the reestablishment of the caliphate. But neither explained what was to be done with the 'nations' that had existed separately for centuries. For Algerian reformism the question was clear:

> There are those who love only their little parcel of native territory. They are egoists. . . . There are those who recognise only a larger homeland and use whatever means they deem appropriate to enlarge its boundaries . . . They are a calamity . . . Then there are those who recognise only a supranational fatherland obliging them to deny the patriotism of nations, to reject their beliefs, and to consider them divisive factors. These people act against nature . . . And finally, there are those who recognise these three categories of 'fatherland' and give each its proper place. They are those who believe that man finds his happiness and his complete human identity in his native place, his nation-state and his supranational fatherland.

The views professed here are far from the narrowly held notions of interventionary radicalism or even archaic reformism. Ibn Badis, who responded to all the imperatives of the social context in which he lived, was exploring every aspect of modern life.

But what Shaykh Ibn Badis, his followers and his successors at the head of the Association of Ulama – such as the Shaykhs Tebessi and Ibrahimi – did for

Algeria, they could not accomplish on the level of the Muslim world. With the intelligent establishment of a hierarchy among these 'fatherlands', the concern for impact that had taken the form of cultural clubs and schools and, especially, the will to thrust reformist action into the political mainstream and to reconcile it with general industrial, economic, scientific, and technical tendencies, the Algerian reformers had deliberately chosen territorialism rather than universal messianism, a dangerous choice for the survival of the movement. They succeeded – and this must be vouchsafed – to safeguard, for the most part, the Arabo–Muslim personality of Algeria. They educated generations of Muslim scholars open to the contemporary world and free from all fanaticism. They made a precious contribution to reformist thinking. However, by assigning their work squarely to the socio-political context, they secured a place for their movement in the political arena. Therefore it was logical for certain of their positions to be criticised by the political parties and for the movement, which was to gather Algerians together in a true war of liberation, to reduce to almost nothing the followers of all other movements, theirs included, all the while assuming responsibility for the definition of the constituent elements of the national personality among which Arabo–Muslim precepts occupied an essential place.

It would be unfair not to cite also, in this context, the work of the great Moroccan nationalist Allal al-Fassi. His political career has caused the present generation to forget his Islamist activism. But his thought derived directly from Salafist inspiration. He was a reformist – in the sense of the word as it is used in Islamic countries today – and the title of his magnum opus, *al-Naqd al-Dhati* (Self-Criticism), is significant. Like Abduh and Ibn Badis, Allal al-Fassi was educated an *'alim* at the Qarawiyyin Mosque–University in Fez. His work was, in the 1930s, both anti-colonialist and Islamist. But the changeable nature of the struggle led him to give priority to political endeavours. The Istiqlal party that he founded directed the struggle for national liberation, certainly, but always maintained contact with the reformist forces in religious matters. This aspect became more obvious when, after the independence of Morocco in 1956, the left wing of the Istiqlal formed the National Union of Popular Forces, and afterwards the Socialist Union of Popular Forces.

It was just that Islamist reformism in the twentieth century was no longer the monopoly of specialists in religion. In defending *asala* – authenticity – the liberation movements also considered themselves engaged in this vital question. When designing the architecture of newly liberated states, governments established after independence could not afford to neglect the Islamic dimension of their society. Compelled by the logic of power, neither could they take a back seat in this matter to a religious hierarchy that had at times allied itself to the colonising power and often had chosen to remain apart from the struggle. That would have been a withdrawal on the part of soldiers motivated by the fierce will to 'remake' their country.

The challenge that the political leaders of underdeveloped Muslim countries had to, and still must, face is to build a governmental structure able to support economic and cultural growth and social equilibrium all the while safeguarding domestic tranquillity and neutralising external threats. No matter how bloody or costly, once independence is gained territory is sacred. Furthermore, whatever the specific weight given to transterritorial ideas – pan-Arab, pan-African, or pan-Islamic – it is first and foremost within the limits of a defined territory that governmental action must be exercised. On this level, it is no longer a question of intellectual, theological or ideological speculation. The man in charge, legitimately or not, of the state apparatus must make the decisions. And in all Muslim countries the central questions asked of governments can be formulated in these words: What place will be reserved for religious law?

Other essential questions are likewise unavoidable. What idea of education is to be adopted? What will be the personal status of women? Ought religious practices to be encouraged or should their backward aspects be fought? Should places of worship be regulated or left to private initiative? In countries where the religious dimension is also part of the collective conscience, these questions are essential. We have stated that if an atheistic government (this is the least that can be said) like that of the Soviet Union is forced to deal with such questions, how much more difficult must it be for the Muslim leaders of Islamic countries.

The real problem, however, is the *shari'a*. Should we legislate, codify, or maintain the traditional status quo? Three different options might permit us to classify Muslim states today.

The status quo would make the Islamists happy. The state may be reduced to administering the country or to legislating, for example, a code of the road. But penal, civil inheritance, personal, fiscal, and even public law derives from the traditional *shari'a*. Let us say right off that few Muslim countries have arrived at such a point. By deciding to return to that state of affairs, the Iranian mullarchy has taken a giant step back into the Middle Ages that all the reformers had decried for more than a century. Today most Muslim countries possess precise codes promulgated by the authority that represents the sovereignty of the territorial state. Generally, in commercial, proprietary, fiscal, and public matters, countries have at their disposal relatively recent codes. But one must not delude oneself like the French orientalist who contradicted me one day by declaring peremptorily that it was immaterial to talk of the Muslim law because it was nowhere applied! Saudi Arabia always, Mauritania, and Pakistan recently apply the traditional penal code and, in the domain of personal statute, only Tunisia and Turkey have promulgated modern ones.

Nevertheless, let us say for purposes of simplicity that the question may be posed in the following terms: legislate or codify. Those who oppose codification – that is, the action of making precise in articulated laws the rights and duties of every citizen – are less and less heard insofar as it is incumbent upon them to write and publish their views in articles on *fiqh* elaborated in the context of the *shari'a*. Even certain hard-core Islamists leave the application of the law to the mercy of the judge's knowledge as we have seen happen in Iran. On the other hand, legislation – the invention of laws inspired uniquely by temporal considerations – has been categorically rejected by both activist

Islamists and passive traditionalists. It is against that standard that the degree of reformism in tenth-century states measured itself.

In the whirlwind of activity that Qadhdhafi creates everywhere, public opinion outside Libya remembers only the support that he gives to the soldiers of Islam in the Philippines and in Mali, and not the religious reform that he pushes forward inside his country.

For a long time after his seizure of power on 1 September 1969, the young colonel Mu'ammar Qadhdhafi remained an enigma for all observers. Was he an Islamist or an Arab nationalist and follower of Nasser? In fact he was both at the same time. But if he has remained more than ever an Arab nationalist, this orientation has nonetheless marked him as a particularly unique Muslim reformer.

His way of going about his business is original. He is a practising Muslim, respects all the ritual injunctions, and refers himself to Islamic principles whenever possible. Still he chooses to ignore the *shari'a* rather than attacking problems head-on. His universal Islamism is an illusion. By helping all Islamist guerrilla movements, he gives the impression of following a traditionalist line. Now he scarcely makes reference to Islam in the elaboration of his doctrine of the 'third theory' between Marxism and capitalism sketched out in his *Green Book*. And by founding the Jamahiriyya, that 'massocracy' structured on peoples' committees, he launched a movement that nevertheless led astray both politologues and theologians.

In three stages – 1973, 1975, and 1977 – he moved from the organisation of peoples' committees to the dissolution of the classical state. Women made a spectacular return to the scene. In addition to education and the professions open to young women, they had henceforth the possibility, unique in a Muslim country, of entering the military services and being initiated into the use of arms. Moreover, the personal guard of the Libyan leader is composed in part of women. The size of property holdings was reduced, rents were suppressed, land belonged to those who worked it, individual freedom was henceforth tied to the satisfaction of basic needs, the liquidation of the bureaucracy resulted in a form of administration by the workers, and the general militarisation of society promoted a barracks mentality. But it was not until 1978 that he struck his greatest blow by declaring twice, in February and in March, that in order to regenerate the Muslim world, one must refer only to the Holy Book – the Quran. Qadhdhafi rejected the *sunna* – the Tradition, including that of the Prophet. Al-Afghani and Abduh had demanded, not without a certain ambiguity, a return 'to the Quran and to what is sure in the Tradition', and deliberately used the generic word *athar* (religious vestiges) rather than the classical expression *sunna* (tradition). Ibn Badis had limited the *sunna* to the Four Rightly Guided Caliphs 'before the appearance of schism'. Qadhdhafi has declared that he holds to the Book alone, considering that all the rest is nothing more than a commentary on the text linked necessarily to temporal conditions. This position, revolutionary as it is, has caused violent reactions among the *ulama* and some Islamists.

Qadhdhafi might have been able to pass himself off as the greatest Islamic reformer if he had concentrated his considerable efforts and means on that objective by organising true councils. He might have found throughout the Muslim world a large number of intellectuals and even *ulama* to further that goal. Publications throughout the Muslim world testify that these men and women exist and they have an expressed need to meet each other and to benefit from a real support so that they may act effectively. The multitude of the Libyan leader's initiatives, the bellicosity of his politics with respect to a large number of Arab, Muslim, and African countries, the nature of the regime that he has established and that does not distinguish itself by its tolerance towards its own dissidents have produced a reformism that has led only to the creation of new enemies when it ought to have assured him new sympathisers.

If al-Afghani, Abduh, and Ibn Badis were *ulama* without power, Qadhdhafi is himself a man of power without theological baggage. Habib Bourguiba, former President of the Tunisian Republic, did not have a theologian's or a *faqih's* education either. He was first and foremost a statesman and political thinker.

Bourguiba's basic values were marked by the pre-First World War liberalism that had its heyday in Europe at that time. His long struggle for the independence of his country had considerable influence on the direction of his thought. Although he was trained as a lawyer, he always had a great passion for history. His religious sensitivities were extremely limited, to say the least, but this did not prevent him from reenacting in his public speeches the historical drama of the Muslim world as a family tragedy. He knew Shakib Arslan and in the course of his many voyages met men who, in their first youth, had heard Abduh speak. He followed passionately the great adventure of Mustafa Kemal Ataturk. He launched his own political movement in reaction, among other things, to a pseudo-crusade organised in 1930 in Tunisia by the Catholic Church in the form of a eucharistic congress. He solicited for his country the aid of numerous Arab and Muslim organisations. And he probed with much bitterness the limits of solidarity in the *umma* and the Arab nation.

Having attained power in 1956 at the age of 53, it was as a man matured by experience that he applied his energies to the problems of his country. His goals can be summed up in this way: a modern state, free from all constraints. A state meant both independence (hence the renunciation of all pan-isms) and a strong government, therefore without a competing governing class. Modern implied the development of the country, industrialisation, universal education, and – Bourguiba never hesitated to use the words – 'the adaptation to Western ways'. Free from all constraints this presupposes a rupture of ties with superannuated customs, archaic traditions, structures of the past however religious, and even with certain forms of religious practice.

In five years, from 1957 to 1961, he put into action a radical reform: female suffrage; the promulgation of a personal statute outlawing polygamy and repudiation (replaced by divorce before a judge); the suppression of religious courts and the extension of the jurisdiction of civil courts henceforth in all aspects of the law; the promulgation of a series of codes of positive law; the limitation of the number of persons permitted to go on pilgrimage; and finally –

and this was the last step – the call in 1961 for the nonobservance of the Ramadan fast so as 'better to lead the struggle against underdevelopment'. Accompanying the suppression of the traditional religious hierarchy were the following measures: the dissolution of the classical Zaytuna University and its reduction to a faculty of theology integrated into the modern university; the abolition of the veil for women; the institutionalisation as a national holiday of a 'Women's Day'; the starting up in 1958 of a program for the spread of modern education; and finally the licensing of all mosque preachers, who were required to deliver every Friday a standard sermon prepared by a governmental department entrusted with religious affairs, which gave Bourguiba's programs the allure of a war against religious traditionalism.

In truth Bourguiba had learned from the practical experience, thirty years previously, of Kemal Ataturk. He never fought religion itself. Islam is the official religion of the Tunisian Republic. The candidates for the presidency must be Muslim. Without claiming to be the 'Commander of the Faithful', Bourguiba underlined the necessity for the chief executive of the state to be a Muslim and to be both a temporal and spiritual leader by presiding himself (in native dress) at the ceremonies of the twenty-seventh day of Ramadan and those of Mawlid (the birth of the Prophet). It was as such that he transformed the religious hierarchy by suppressing it and named a single dignitary to be the mufti of Tunisia, all the while taking as the prerogative of the state the construction and maintenance of mosques as well as the nomination and remuneration of imams, sextons, and caretakers of these places of worship. The other aspect of Bourguibism was neatly put foward at the end of the 1970s when the government, attacked by the Islamists, responded that the republic had constructed in twenty years of independence more mosques than in the 1,350-year history of Islam in Tunisia. Finally, regarding the law, Bourguiba is more a legislator than a codifier. Nevertheless, he has always taken care to justify his judicial actions by quoting verses of the Quran, a *hadith* of the Prophet, or even the opinion of such and such a legalist, exegete, or doctrinary of centuries past.

In sum, it is clear from Bourguiba's doctrine that only the demands of the present and future count, a future that must be marked by industrialisation and the latest technology. To accomplish this, it was necessary to adapt Muslim society to these constraints, not, however, by tossing out the heritage of the past altogether, but by desacralising it and keeping only what would favour the march of the country into the twenty-first century. Bourguiba was more like an al-Afghani in power than like an Ataturk, as many have already observed.

To say that Bourguiba succeeded in his work would be to ignore the existence of relatively strong Islamist movements in Tunisia. With respect to the Ramadan fast it must be said that his government had to fight a rearguard action. Tunisia is a land of tolerance. The coexistence between those who fast and those who do not observe the rule has been achieved with little friction. The mosques are full, even if their number has doubled. Islamism has gained ground among engineers and in the faculties of medicine more than elsewhere. The new militants attach no particular respect to the few living representatives of the former religious hierarchy. They have new idols. They swear only by

Mawdudi and Sayyid Qutb. Without it being necessary to elaborate on the question here, suffice it to say that the same conditions that were present at the birth or at the development of Islamism elsewhere are found in Tunisia. That the movement is led by the young and by the technocrats more than by the fossilised traditionalists is indication enough that the crisis of civilisation affecting the Muslim world has not spared Tunisia.

This discussion would be incomplete if we forgot to mention that Islamic reformism is not only the work of the principal figures whom we have just evoked in the preceding pages. In countries like Senegal, Mali or Niger, it is also at work in governmental circles without excess or radicalism. The conditions specific to each country – brotherhoods here, multiethnicity there – play a decisive role.

Can we forget Egypt, the country of Shaykh Abduh and the land that welcomed al-Afghani for ten years? A work of impressive legislation was accomplished there at the beginning of the century. Egypt was also the first Arab country to deal with the question of women's social emancipation. And for a long time it was the most bustling intellectual centre in the Muslim world. Alas! Egypt has not succeeded in resolving in a satisfactory manner any of the fundamental problems of economic underdevelopment. The six million inhabitants that al-Afghani talked about were already forty million in 1980. The state of war with Israel has literally rendered hypothetical the development of the country. Nasser's pan-Arabism was stopped dead in its tracks by the tragedy of 1967. Sadat's policy of peace did not gain the unanimous approval of his people. Put outside the pale of the Muslim and Arab world, the Egyptians have resented this ostracism as a humiliation. Now violent extremes can hardly coexist with serene and contemplative thought. The reformism of the state has come up against a political radicalism with an Islamist and a Marxist face.

In the final analysis one cannot ignore the specific approach of the Arab socialists who attempt to illuminate the Islamic roots of a non-Marxist socialism. It is not by chance that in Iraq, as well as in Algeria and in Egypt, the interesting figure of Abu Gharr al-Ghafari is often evoked, this companion of the Prophet who fought the rich and preached the distribution of wealth. Is Islam a religion of socialism? Yes, answer the Algerians, the Iraqis, the Sudanese, and the Egyptians. No, answer the Kuwaitis, the Saudis, the Pakistanis, and certain Egyptians. But all are in agreement that Islam is an egalitarian religion. All depends on the verse cited, on the principles one invokes, and on the personage one evokes. And all these ideas are at work in Muslim society while Islamic socialism still awaits its theoretical genius prepared to present a coherent, supporting view of the whole.

The Muslim world is, therefore, not the prisoner, as one might believe, of the Khomeinist movement to which it can only oppose the radicalism of Kemal Ataturk. The choice is not confined to the laity, on one hand, and the theocracy, on the other. We have already stated that from al-Afghani to Qadhdhafi many similar ideas appear among all the reformists: return to the Quran, nontraditional understanding of religion; a taking into consideration of actual contingencies, the necessity for development, the elaboration of principles of law and not their literal translation in frozen form for centuries, and, most of all, education and emancipation of women. The first reformists to our knowledge had not been very explicit on this subject even though Abduh preached the education of women and monogamy. But all the same it was an Egyptian disciple of Shaykh Abduh, Qasim Amin, and a Tunisian, Tahar al-Haddad, educated at the Zaytuna Mosque in a reformist atmosphere, who made two appeals in the 1920s for the emancipation of Muslim women.

Thus ideas move forward in rhythm with succeeding generations. And, if certain economic and political conditions as well as the problems of civilisations are about to favour a vast wave of anachronism, this must not obscure the competing force of reformist ideas. Certainly, reformist ideas did not succeed at the end of the century either in transforming the Islamic world or in serving as a program for the masses and their struggle for progress. The multiplicity of actors, the different national conditions, and the absence of communication have left many aspects of reformism in the shadows. We may wager that many Muslim readers will read this short chapter with the eyes of children who are just now discovering the world. These ideas correspond nonetheless to the ultimate conviction, sometimes clumsily formulated, of large segments of the Muslim population.

Paradoxically, it is because they did not lack political sense that these reformers wanted to adapt Islam to their times; and it is because they were politicians that their activity was blocked. From al-Afghani to Qadhdhafi, through Ibn Badis and Bourguiba, it was politics that put a brake on their reformism every time. Let us say, to be more precise, that it was in the name of religion that their ideas were condemned, not because these ideas were grounded in indisputable theological arguments but because their policies were everywhere contested, right or wrong. It is under these circumstances that we must ask ourselves if other approaches would not be better to relieve Islam of its torture, a torture that may lead to the destruction of a great civilisation.

Notes

1. On the reformists of India, see Edward Mortimer, *Faith and Power* (New York: Vintage Books, Random House, 1982).
2. The following quotes are drawn from the book that bears the same name as the journal written in Arabic. See *al-Urwa al-Wuthqa* (Beirut: Maison du Livre Arabe, 1980).
3. These quotations are taken from the work in Arabic of Muhammad al-Mili, *Ibn Badis wa 'Urubatu al-Djaza'ir* (Ibn Badis and the Arabness of Algeria) (Algiers: SNED, 1973). Also see: Ali Mrad, *Ibn Badis, commentateur du Coran* (Algiers: 1971); and Ammar Talibi, *Ibn Badis, Hayatuhu wa Atharuhu* (Ibn Badis, His Life and Work) (Algiers: Librairie de la société algérienne, 1968).

10.   The Cage and the Horizon

What meaning does Islam have today? To ask that question – and one anticipates it – is to make the believers uneasy. There is nothing sacrilegious in this. It is only to the extent that one agrees to question oneself about the taboos that one can best appreciate the role they play. All the disciples of all the religions shout on high the obvious truth of their faith. Believing Muslims, even when they are not practising, willingly use a traditional formula: Islam, they say, is valid for all time and all places. This claim is accepted with absolute confidence and credited with permanent value. So why should one bother to go beyond pure rhetoric?

Nevertheless, it is inconceivable that modern man can have the same vision of the universe as one who believes according to a well-known popular image that the world is assuredly flat, not round, and that it is balanced on one of the horns of a fabulous bull which every hundred years shifts it to the other. What meaning can be given to the 'six days' of Genesis when we 'know' that man appeared on earth only several billion years after the birth of the solar system? How, in sociology, can we understand the duty to preserve blood ties – the Arab says gut ties – while the 'family' at home is becoming smaller and smaller? In a situation in which women, who more frequently work outside the home than not, are less and less dependent on men, what effects can this evolution have on a question as thorny as that of inheritance? And the practice of religion itself cannot escape such questions. With two million pilgrims massed at Mecca, the obligatory passing of a day upon the hill of Arafat near the holy city – an event without which the pilgrimage cannot be in conformity with ritual – assumes more and more the aspect of a bivouac around a mountain. What is the furthest limit of the acceptable? For example, could ten million pilgrims fulfil this obligation, each one of them on the same day?

One could give other equally compelling examples by invoking the problem of the cosmonaut, the biologist, or the physician confronted with new definitions of death, the physicist engaged in research on the origins of the universe, and, even more prosaically, the judge called upon to pronounce on new kinds of economic offences or new psychological and social deviations.

To be content with saying that everything is in the Quran is not enough. It is too easy. Most Islamist movements refuse, for example, to elaborate on their programs. Their leaders almost everywhere give the same answer: 'The Quran is the message of God and also a way of life. Islam is our ideological base, our goal, and our means.'[1] At best, this is an evasion if not deliberate demagogy. Indeed, one must not forget that the persons who speak this language are the same who reproach a man like Qadhdhafi for wanting to rely only on the Quran!

The fundamental question posed here could be stated in this way: what is the best way to demonstrate the universal aspect of Islam while freeing it from the matrix of customs and tradition?

Muslims are never in doubt of the universal significance of their faith. Yet they do not all agree that there is a universal Islam distinct from an Arab, Malay or African Islam. In 1964, when Vincent Monteil published a book on Black Islam in Africa and the Americas,[2] a violent reaction took place: 'There is no White Islam or Black Islam,' his detractors declared. Yet it was never the intention of the author, who moreover later converted to Islam, to make a normative judgment on any people whatsoever. Islam is one, certainly, and we have defined what makes it one everywhere. To deny, nonetheless, for example, the Arab influence, at least with respect to certain juridical formulas integrated into the *shari'a*, is to ignore history or interpret it in a dogmatic way.

It has already been noted how in the eighth century, more than 100 years after the death of the Prophet, the great *faqih* Malik, in opposition to his senior Abu Hanifa, invoked the tradition of Medina in order to refute the free interpretation of juridical principles every time he was able to make reference to a *hadith*. 'This is the way of our community,' he said. Even the history of the revelation of Quranic verses shows how juridical pronouncements had the object either of resolving new problems, or of modifying customs that had turned out to be contrary to the preached faith. What did not challenge a dogma was not touched on by the maker of laws. Moreover, when it came to elaborating entire juridical systems, the problem was to know what point of reference to take. North Africa, for example, which remained outside the serious political and theological dissensions of the classical heartland, adopted very quickly under the influence of pilgrims returning from the Holy Places the system of Malik. On the other hand, in that veritable arena of controversy that the Middle East had become, several dozen juridical schools appeared before the four Sunnite models could impose themselves.

The heritage of its ancient civilisation is often invoked to explain the resistance of Persia to Arabisation despite its geographical proximity to the Arab world. The argument is not valid, however, for the Turkish tribes that entered the region in successive waves. They too resisted Arabisation. At the other extreme, North Africa, heir in large measure to Roman civilisation, active in all the quarrels of the Christian Church, participant in Latin literature through a number of her sons, converted to Arab culture. This occurred, naturally, in gradual stages, but it ended with an integration into the Arab family. Is it not possible to see in this evolution the effects of an Islamisation founded precisely on the teachings of Medina and Malik? Furthermore, can we not find in this the reason for the formidable resistance of North African traditionalism to the Kharijite schism that remained circumscribed in small geographical pockets, to the Shi'ism of the Fatimids who ended up by being rejected, and to the Sunni Hanifism introduced by the Ottomans?

To investigate the specific relationships of the Muslim peoples to their religion is to attempt to understand why the universal appeal to which their ancestors responded found itself relegated to a tradition strongly marked by national heritage or cultural identity. The question has lost none of importance today, since it is imperative that Muslims must adapt themselves to their times. Is not the crux of the problem expressed by the fact that when, in 1979, the Algerians organised a conference on socialism and Islam, a minister was upbraided by a Saudi shaykh who denied that Islam contains the seeds of socialism. The former was invoking manifestly the universal principles of his faith, the latter the traditional way of apprehending it.

The Islamist movements feel that they cannot escape the universalism–traditionalism dilemma. And so they find themselves like those they denounce confronted with an insurmountable contradiction. How can one postulate that 'Islam is valid for all time and all places' and yet want to practise according to the Tradition which carries necessarily the mark of time and place? One either refers to fundamental principles and deduces freely from them a mode of behaviour for the present or one prefers to maintain intact the whole of one's heritage and thereby withdraws into the sophisms of false justifications. One cannot be simultaneously on the side of Ibn Rushd and al-Ghazali when one realises that the former refuted the ideas of the latter. Neither can one glorify Ibn Taymiyya and the *ulama* of other schools who threw him into prison where he died.

Nor can we invoke any author at all in an irrational manner just to support the thesis that Islamisation is the prerequisite of power. That would be to forget that throughout the centuries there have been *ulama* for power and others in opposition to power. No reader of Islamic history can ignore that the theses of the Shi'ite scholars, for example, sought to justify, sometimes by debatable quotations from the Prophet or by a veritable scouring of the Quranic text, the necessity to maintain the imamate in the family of the Prophet through 'Ali and Fatima. The scholars of Sunnism did not take a backseat to them in this issue, and the line of their thinking tended without respite to legitimise established power, especially in Abbasid times. In a collection of essays on 'ideologies',[3] a North African scholar, Ahmad Hasnawi, showed in a convincing manner how a great master of Muslim civil law of the Shafa'i school (991–1031) wrote his book *al-Ahkam al-Sultaniyya* – the full title of which is 'Judgements Relative to Power in Matters of Civil Politics According to the Law' – so as to support the Abbasid caliphs threatened by both their own generals and the Fatimid competition. Hasnawi recalls also that the work of Abu Ya'la al-Farra, which carries the same title, had the same objective. Now, we can cite these two books and others to justify the founding of a modern theocracy while forgetting that they aim at legitimising a particular dynasty at a given moment.

The renewal of the faith that is evident in today's Muslim world poses a simple problem which in reality is complicated by ignorance and the lack of culture. Men and women, often very young, devour today, with great voracity and passion, any and all books provided that they speak to them of faith and of the past and of a glorious tradition. One is struck by the anomalous character of what Islamist militants read.

In Tunis a specialised bookseller recently published about a hundred titles and offered nearly two thousand works! Among them one found the writings of Hassan al-Banna and Sayyid Qutb side by side with those of Mawdudi and Iqbal.[4] Young Islamists cannot, at least not without a summary historical preparation, know what they have in their hands. Among many religious families violent conflicts flared up. An Algerian father, exasperated by what he called the fanaticism of his son who considered that the truth professed by his group was the only Islamic way, challenged him to demonstrate its validity. The son was incapable of distinguishing what was obligatory from what was local usage.

Without this ignorance, for which all those who contributed to the perpetuation or the founding of an educational system are responsible, the problem would have been posed differently since no one thinks of repudiating what is essential; to wit, that Muslims are challenged to give correct answers to questions that are asked of present-day society.

The history of Islam furnishes us with valuable information. Muslims subsume under the rubric *'ulum al-din* (religious sciences) several disciplines. The credo that deals with the unity of God gave birth to the *tawhid*, a nominal derivative of the verb 'to unify', that gives form to theology in the strictest sense. The Quran engendered the *tafsir* (exegesis) but also the subsidiary disciplines of *tanzil* (the conditions of the Revelation) and the *nasikh wa mansukh* (knowledge of which verses cancel others). Ethics were at the centre of written works concerning the *sira* (the life and behaviour of the Prophet) in which were emphasised the high moral values that he incarnated. The *sunna* stimulated the discipline of *hadith*, underpinned by the knowledge of the biographies of all the companions of the Prophet and the history of the Arabic language. The religion stimulated the development of the science of *ibadat*, literally the manifestation of the worship of God. The *shari'a* (the law) gave birth to *fiqh*, in its literal sense, 'intelligent knowledge'. Although it is more an asceticism than a science, the Islamic vision of the universe brought into being an extraordinary mystical movement, the *tasawwuf*.

An *'alim*, doctor of religion, and a member of the corps of *ulama*, cited so frequently in this work, is normally knowledgeable in all these disciplines and is a linguist besides, since all these sciences require a high degree of familiarity with the Arabic language. He is more than a *faqih* who, properly speaking, is a legalist. Now what does Islamic history teach us? Very quickly *'alim* and *faqih* become synonymous because theology, Quranic research, and the primacy of ethics were displaced by and merged into juridical speculation and the rules of ritual. Even *tasawwuf*, which lasted a long time, ended up a frozen form, that of the brotherhoods, some of which – not all and not always – have been a veritable calamity for the countries in which they appeared.

Where is the theology – the *tawhid* – of the twentieth century? How many high school students have become religious zealots because of the antiquated and stupid explanations of their theology teachers? Muhammad Iqbal (1877–1938), whose work certain Islamists read, used to say:

> Einstein's theory produced a new vision of the universe and suggests new ways to see problems common to both religion and philosophy. It is not surprising that the new Muslim generation of Asia and Africa demands a new direction for its faith. With the renaissance of Islam, it is necessary to examine without any preconceptions European ideas and the degree to which the conclusions Europe has arrived at can help us to rethink and, if necessary, reconstruct the theological concepts of Islam.[5]

Iqbal was evoking Einstein. He died before the theory of the Big Bang, that great cosmic explosion which might have created the universe, and before the work of the physicist Abd al-Salam on the unity of cosmic forces. Yet his point of view has more than ever implications for the present.

Now is it not possible to notice that once theology becomes for all intents and purposes frozen, only the great mystics continue to pursue its study? The *ulama*, whose task it is to illuminate theology in all its diverse aspects, neglect it. What kind of books do they suggest we read concerning the life of the Prophet? Collections of events in which battles occupy the greatest number of pages. Now the Muslim ethos cannot be reduced to a collection of moral precepts. It concerns an entire way of life that touches on questions of work, socio-economic relations, the seeking of knowledge, and even the study of languages. Muhammad once asked one of his scribes to learn Hebrew so as to understand better what the Jews of Medina were writing. It should be noted that that ethic is totally absent from education today. Certain Islamist movements try to restore it to pride of place, but without any forethought and without recapturing its essence. Pushed by an overweighty traditionalism, they are content with the good deeds of Boy Scouts.

And yet books proliferate that expose the point of view of the *shari'a* on economics, finances, banks, society, power, social organisation, prayer, pilgrimage, and so on. Always there is the supremacy of *fiqh* over all the other 'religious sciences'. Is it audacious to remark that because *fiqh* has power over the others and because it carries the promise of social advancement, it has always been the preference of the *ulama*? One can be a great theologian and still lead a humble life. One can become a sufi and live 'elsewhere'. Only *fiqh* allows one to become a judge, a jurisconsultant, *shaykh-al-islam*, or ayatollah. This is a social, not a religious, fact. As for religion, it has need of all these 'sciences'.

For the moment, those who agitate in the name of Islamist militancy believe still that they must promote their cause by preaching a hybrid and sectarian traditionalism. Hybrid because they do not disdain to appeal to the arguments of the reformists without daring however to follow the logic of reformism to its conclusions. Sectarian because they do not hesitate to cast anathema on others. Did not a leading Islamist once say categorically: 'Neither the people nor the government practise the true Islam, no more in Tunis than elsewhere?'[6]

Here again, history provides us with valuable information. It is not by chance that the mass of Muslims in all ages has rejected extremisms and whatever is by nature bound to set the religion suddenly tottering. Despite their indisputable puritanism, the Kharijites were never more than a minority. The Shi'ites also, like all Muslims, even non-Shi'ites, had as much as the Kharijites a particular veneration for the descendants of the Prophet whom they called *ahl al-bayt*, people of family, or *shurafa*, the nobility. Among the Shi'ites themselves, the majority took the side of the moderate Twelvers and not the side of the Ismailis, still less that of the Alawite sect. The Qarmathians[7] were the representatives of a certain Ismaili community. They were excessive in the eyes of the masses. They disappeared. Tunisia and Egypt were the capitals of the Fatimids. This is no longer the case for either of them today. Slowly, despite the efforts of the zealots, the pendulum has swung back to dead centre.

Islamists would do well to remember that, fundamentally, the Muslim is both peaceful and moderate. And we may quote Iqbal again on this point:

> The principal goal of the Quran is to awaken in man a higher awareness of his manifold relations with God and the universe. It was while contemplating the essential aspects of Quranic teaching that Goethe, a student of Islam principally as an educational force, said to Eckermann: 'You see, this teaching will always succeed; despite all our systems, we cannot, and in general neither can any individual, go further than this.'[8]

It is often said that Islam is a religion of the desert. That is true, providing that one understands this to mean the solitude of one before God. The uncultured, illiterate Muslim feels and lives his/her religion in confusion as a direct relationship between self and divinity. When a mother in Tunisia, for example, does not succeed in getting along with her son or daughter, she ends the discussion by declaring: 'Why should I bother about this? It's between you and your Creator.'

It is also in the name of a false 'theology' that violence is raised to a sacred commandment. The Islamists who twist the meaning of the words *jihad* (struggle) and *gisas* (retaliation) fall into the same error as those they fight: the governments that believe only in brute force to remain in power. If Islam has a meaning today, it is certainly not a meaning that justifies the cutting off of a thief's hand, the stoning of an adulterer, selective assassination, or summary executions. All the ills that can be combatted by radical treatment have deep causes – or even justifications – which defy the tradition. In the Middle Ages, in Europe, the sick of society were cut off from their fellows so as not to contaminate the rest of the social body which was healthy. Medicine did not advance until it strove to discover the origin and the cause of illness. To claim that society can be doctored with machine gun bullets is to expose a total poverty of thought; and to make sacred the repressive or subversive act by appealing to the Tradition is to prove the shortcoming of the law that is invoked. If Islam were able to act only in this way, it would not be 'valid for all time and all places'.

Sooner or later, the moderate mass of Muslims will reject barbarism.

Whether violence is a revolutionary fact or a fact of war between armed forces, its interpretation and its eventual legitimisation is a question for the social sciences. To sacralise it using religion is fanaticism and hypocrisy. The Filipino Moro Front and the Muslim Eritreans are fighting against governments that refuse them autonomy or independence. No doubt they are in revolt because of their religion or their national consciousness. But they are not fighting to make one Islamic doctrine prevail over another. Even in so-called wars of liberation the door is always left open for negotiation to find a peaceful settlement for conflict.

The history of Islam itself challenges its passionate defenders to establish a true renaissance of thought and action. The explosion of knowledge that, beginning with a single sacred book, has given birth to endless encyclopaedias before being frozen in summary abridgements, stands as an obstacle to a simple rehabilitation of the traditional. The problems which a society must face that is both pre- and post-industrial and still underdeveloped but already called upon to enter directly into the age of the computer and international communications cannot be resolved by recourse to superannuated formulas. Whether they wish to or not, the Islamists are condemned to give Islam a new start that will take it beyond its universal content.

Notes

1. See the article by Souhayr Belhassen, *Jeune Afrique*, Paris, no. 951, 28 March 1979, p. 89.
2. Vincent Monteil, *L'Islam noir* (Paris: Editions du Seuil, 1964).
3. See Ahmad Hasnawi, *L'Islam, la conquête et le pouvoir*, ed. François Chatelet (Paris: Editions Marabout, 1978).
4. Souhayr Belhassen, *Jeune Afrique*, Paris, no. 949, 14 March 1979, p. 84.
5. Muhammad Iqbal, *Reconstruire la pensée réligieuse de l'Islam* (Paris: Editions Adrien-Maisonneuve, 1955), p. 14.
6. See *Jeune Afrique*, Paris, no. 951, 28 March 1979, p. 90.
7. The Qarmathians were the disciples of a Shi'ite sect close to the Ismailis. They had denied the legitimacy of power in Baghdad and launched a bloody revolt in the ninth and tenth centuries. They ravaged Mecca where they stole the sacred Black Stone fixed in the house of the Kaaba, took Damascus, and threatened Fatimid Egypt. Defeated by the Caliph of Cairo in 972, they retreated to the shores of Arabia in the region of Bahrain where their influence held sway until 1027. Their ideology is little known because they were annihilated. The Fatimids, of Ismaili Shi'ite persuasion, considered them from the beginning as their followers. They were disappointed, as has been noted elsewhere in this work (Chapter 6). It seems that the Qarmathians preached a kind of primitive 'communism'.
8. Iqbal, *op. cit.*, p. 15.

11. The Call of Life

The Prophet said: 'Behave in your earthly life as if you were to live eternally; and in your life in the Hereafter as if you were to die tomorrow.' An exhortation to action in two instances but also an appeal to the individual: *your* earthly life and *your* life in the hereafter. One could write a thesis on this exaltation of humankind! And one can already infer from this the necessity for action in this world, our world.

Supposing the problems of the most aggressive Islamists were resolved if they succeeded in establishing everywhere a theocratic power such as Khomeini's, which Mawdudi and Qutb dreamed of, the society for which they would be responsible will not be able to function by prayer alone nor be capable either of cutting itself off totally from the world. All Muslim countries without exception, including those of the Soviet confederation, belong to what we call the Third World. The problems they must solve are those that affect Chile and Angola, gigantic Brazil and tiny Burundi: develop their resources, especially their intellectual resources, in order to act upon the material environment with a view to assuring man the satisfaction of his needs within a certain social equilibrium, the only guarantee of universal peace.

The difficulty lies in the necessity to maintain the initiative for this objective without losing sight of any of its constituent elements. Since the Second World War, and specifically since 1980, we have begun to recognise the multidimensional character of development without knowing, however, how to account for it. It is just that the road to recovery has been long.

Evidently, it is not a question of retracing here the historical steps in the evolution of the modern world. Let us remember all the same to what extent certain 'great ideas' have, at a given moment, oriented human thought and activity in different directions. The industrial revolution, economism, technology and class struggle have occupied, each in its turn, and sometimes at the same time in various countries, dominant positions as regards the determination of human behaviour. Each period had its corresponding deviation. On closer examination, one may even state that imperialism, colonisation, fascism and war are the fruits of different tropisms. Every time we believe we must favour a certain aspect of social life, we have created a dangerous disequilibrium that cannot leave indifferent the thinkers, sociologists and politicians who have a sensitivity to the world. And so man has regularly tried to react through violence or consensus, by straightening out the crooked path. Thus the League of Nations was created, then the United Nations and the bodies that depend on it; the proclamation of the Rights of Man; the emancipation of women; the idealisation of liberal and pluralist democracy; the development of international law; the condemnation of Nazism, fascism, and racism; the proclamation of self-determination and its consequences; decolonisation, the denunciation of a consumer society; the importance of ecology and the defence of the human environment; and now, the struggle for a new order in economics, communication, exploitation of the seabed and exploration of space. No one can turn up their nose at such struggles because there are answers there, good or bad, but answers, nevertheless, to concrete problems. 'Behave in your earthly life' means also that we understand what that phrase implies.

The Christian church, after the separation of church and state, has most often kept itself apart from earthly troubles and has not confused what ought to be rendered unto Caesar and what ought to be rendered unto God. Then the Christian Socialists and Christian Democrats appeared as did the worker-priests and the committees against hunger. As for the clergy of Brazil, Argentina and elsewhere, they even ended up by championing the claims of their flocks against the advice of the Curia. On another level, a man like Teilhard de Chardin devoted his efforts to the development of thought with a view toward the integration of the new vision of the universe into a modern theology. Still more important was the effort of the Vatican to enlighten, through encyclicals, Christians involved in a daily social struggle.

Today, Islamism militates for the entry of religion into the social arena. How could Islamism bring its enterprise to a successful conclusion while neglecting what we have just noted concerning the multidimensional character of society?

What remains to be said? Well, first – and this is pertinent – we must not cut off from society one of its constituent elements: woman. The actual supremacy of man is not natural to Islam. It is the translation of economic and social relations which we have regularly sought to mask and, of course, justify by the religious explanations of those who seek to demonstrate the Islamicness of male superiority. 'Men are responsible for women' says the Quran. What could be more normal in a patriarchal society? All structure requires someone to be responsible and in the family structure it is the head of the family who assumes this burden. Does that mean that the other members of the family can be declared inferior, incapable or simply less intelligent? Woman has a different physiology; she carries children and brings them into the world. And so, because a human being has additional burdens, that creature must be diminished by them! It follows that woman ought to stay home and bring up children. Very well! But how can we explain that in general it is the man who takes the responsibility for the education of boys? And furthermore, how can we justify that a division of labour becomes a standard of evaluation?

Moreover, the Quran does not make the same distinction as the Bible between the two sexes and does not hold Eve to blame for original sin, but only Adam; and Satan, in Arabic also, is male! From earliest Islamic times no discrimination was made between men and women, even inside the mosque at Medina! Later on, the traditionalists were quite happy to find in Aisha, the youngest wife of the Prophet, a marvellous source for the *hadith*. How curious that, on one hand, men found woman inferior and, on the other hand, referred to a member of the weaker sex as the most solid base for an authentic Tradition! One could cite innumerable examples of women who have played a decisive role in the history of Islam, beginning with Khadija, the first wife of the Prophet, who financed the caravans that he managed, who was the first to believe in his message, and who supported him in adversity. Until her dying breath, she demanded that people respect him and he returned that respect by not taking another wife while she lived.

It is certain that the problem of women is not specifically Muslim and that, to resolve it, it is indispensable to distinguish its economic, social, national, and traditional givens from those that relate directly to the faith. But in any case, no society engaged in the process of development can attain the desired objective by beginning to render inactive half of its effective force.

Multidimensional implies that development must favour teaching, vocational instruction, apprenticeship, education and the struggle against ignorance and obscurantism. Islamists take a deeply religious education as the basis of their approach – deeply religious but not only religious, since they recognise the need to acquire knowledge in other fields. Still, one can propagate knowledge and obscurantism at the same time; it all depends on the kind of education chosen. A recent example illustrates and explains this paradox. In some Arab countries, out of a solicitude for authenticity, there has been a sharp reaction against the dethronement of Islamic thought in the teaching of philosophy. The arabisation of this discipline has been decreed. This is only right. In fact, it is inadmissible that in Muslim countries they study Spinoza, Kant and Nietzsche but ignore al-Kinda, al-Farabi and Ibn Rushd. Moreover, philosophy was taught only in European languages as if Arabic had not served for centuries to express the nuances of human thought. Only in certain countries has teaching been arabised while at the same time the former programs have been maintained with the result that we have fallen between Scylla and Charybdis: the student is introduced to the thought of the very same European philosophers, but as this teaching is given to him in Arabic without the aid of books developed for this purpose, in the end he learns very little, to say nothing of the fact that he studies Muslim thinkers not at all. What has been said in the preceding pages shows sufficiently the traps and the impasses toward which the choices of unreasoning traditionalists lead.

To define an educational policy, one must also make choices in the field of science and technology. Everywhere Islamist movements denounce imported ideas and doctrines. Iran no longer knows what to do with its universities. But the movement that, from the middle of the ninth century and thanks to the translation of Hindu, Persian, Greek and even Latin works, gave a decisive push to Islamic civilisation – what was it nourished on if not the considerable flow of imported ideas? One must not confuse the materials and the use made of them. If imitation impoverishes and degrades, the hybridisation of cultures is a source of progress. 'Seek knowledge even in China,' the Prophet said. What does this mean if not that there is everywhere something to learn?

It is because Muslims of the Golden Age had internalised external contributions that the civilisation to which their labour gave birth was authentically Islamic and not Greek or Hindu. It is precisely this response, moreover, that Islamists of all persuasions make to the tendentious affirmation which at a certain time had currency in the West and which portrayed the Arabs as simple transmitters. By what perversion of logic have we reached the point of wanting to suppress today the importation of all ideas? And what makes us believe that a theocratic government would allow, for example, a physicist or a biologist to conduct research freely on the origins of life? Malik, the great jurist, founder of the *fiqh* that carries his name, was whipped in public at the age of fifty despite his great fame, and never fully recovered from it, simply because he dared to give a *fatwa* (opinion) that the authorities judged contrary to orthodoxy.[1]

The physicist Abd al-Salam declared that there is no possibility of development without the spending of at least 1 to 2 per cent of national revenue on scientific research. We would like to cite him at length, but several quotations will suffice to show clearly the direction he has chosen to take:[2]

> In the light of the last several centuries of Islamic experience, in the light of others' experience, and in conformity to the obligations imposed upon us by the Holy Book and the Prophet, our society as a whole and our youth in particular have the duty to engage in the passionate struggle to create a scientific renaissance.

Evoking the freedom of research he declared: 'I have spoken of protection and of encouragement. It is absolutely necessary for a man of science to have in his work a feeling of security and permanence.' And as a realist he makes clear that 'we need a global assurance of immunity for at least twenty-five years, for example, during which members of this scientific community, of this *Ummat al-Ilm*, will not risk discrimination based on nationality or other factors.' What are these other factors? Abd al-Salam tells us by enumerating

> the five *sine qua non* conditions of a scientific renaissance in the Islamic world: an enthusiastic involvement, generous encouragement, guaranteed security, the absence of all discrimination based on doctrine or nationality, control of administration and finance, and the internationalisation of our scientific effort.

Who better than a Nobel Laureate, and a believing Muslim, who bases his research on the proper understanding of the Quran, could thus describe the precarious position of the Islamic researcher?

Asking himself the question why Muslim countries have not yet reached the first ranks of technology, Abd al-Salam declared:

Experience shows that in the long run the acquisition of technology depends on a strict collaboration between the scientist, the technological specialist and those responsible for national development, each having full confidence in the other's ability in his field. And the same rule extends to the entire spectrum of the possible applications of science to agriculture, public health, production of energy, and national defence.

By insisting on the internationalism of the effort, Abd al-Salam has evoked at the same time the first steps, the exchanges, and the application of the individual's contribution to the planetary advance of science. No country today can advance in isolation. The rapidity of discoveries, the invention of new technologies or new uses for those already in existence, and the cost of research are such that progress is possible only within the international scientific community. The members of this community, having established among themselves the rules of exchange, exclude those who make no contribution to the process. Like it or not, and despite its many components, the world participates in a certain universal culture.

This participation ought not to exclude the development and expansion of the individual. The Moroccan scholar Mahdi al-Mandjara remarked, during an international colloquium at Dakar in January 1980, that man today is pulled between the infinitely small and the infinitely large. 'On one hand progress in space, on the other progress in molecular biology; on one hand grouping together of nations, on the other the exhaltation of a veritable cultural provincialism, etc.' Difficulty arises when we propose to find the point of balance between standard behaviour on a planetary scale and what they call in Muslim countries – but also in Zaire – authenticity. How can one remain true to oneself and at the same time be a full member in an international community? The evolution of the world has proved the necessity to respect the two terms of the equation. In addition, the same evolution has demonstrated that it is difficult to escape the norms that a way of life and of international thought impose which can only gain more ground due to the fact that, thanks to satellites, information is universalised. The other side of the coin is that all Third World experience of development has led to dangerous social, cultural, and political ruptures whenever such experience causes an uprooting of people, a loss of personality, and a disappearance of 'authenticity', so that all societies not prepared to play a role in a functioning international community find themselves faced with an alternative whose two options represent a mortal danger: step aside and yield to cosmopolitanism or fall back on one's resources in the name of protecting one's identity.

The search for a solution to obviate this alternative seems to be the great task of the years to come. It presupposes the acceptance of the inevitability of participation by each region of the world in the development of the international community. Whoever says participation says contribution; and it is the nature of this contribution that must be made precise. The other dimension to take into consideration – authenticity – constitutes nothing more in fact than a slogan.

The Tunisian scholar Hishem Djaït has made an examination in depth of the question of identity in his work *La Personnalité et le devenir arabo-islamiques*.[3] He reveals the complexity of its constituent parts and the hesitations of the Arab and Muslim individual to give importance to one element over the other. He analyses, systematically, the pernicious effects that have provoked the breaking up of the Arabo-Islamic personality. The Moroccan historian Abdallah Laroui attempted, for his part, to analyse Arab ideology and favours the political dimension without neglecting, however, the role of religion. This is the kind of intellectual effort that should be pursued since it is not enough to say that the national or cultural identity must be safeguarded when what one really is still remains unknown. Identity is not folklore and its preservation does not consist of dressing in a certain way, adding domes to buildings, or resurrecting the ancient ceremonies of religious brotherhoods. To know what one is and what one wants to be are the *sine qua non* conditions of a real participation in the life of a perpetually changing world.

In the tenth century the Arab Muslims who wrote treatises on mathematics felt no irritation in calling *arithmatiqi* that discipline which is named today *ilm al-'adad*, or 'science of numbers'. They learned it from the Greeks and did not hesitate to give it its original name because they knew that it was their turn to add something new to human knowledge. They had developed another discipline and they gave it an Arabic name by which it is known in all languages: algebra. And still today no man of science throughout the world feels lessened because he uses the word *logarithm*, which is the Latinisation of the name of the Muslim mathematician al-Khuwarizmi. Everything happens today as if the defence of authenticity consists in translating obligatorily words such as radar, sonar, computer, and so on, and not in creating microprocessors or in making discoveries in the field of medicine.

It is to the extent that the individual work, the necessary fruit of a personal vision, tends towards the universal that it expresses both a defined identity and what characterises the human in the absolute. There is in this new Western vogue for the Muslim mystics of past centuries a grand meditative theme for the defenders of authenticity. What the modern public is seeking in Rumi, Ibn Arabi, Attar and al-Hallaj is neither the stoning of the adulterer nor the veiling of women but rather a vision of the Supreme Being and the Universe that responds to the need for a renewal of spirituality. It was the Englishman Fitzgerald who gave international recognition to the poems of Omar Khayyam, the famous 'Quatrains'. It was the Frenchman Massignon who made known the works of al-Hallaj. It was the Spaniard Palacios who uncovered the mystical texts of Ibn al-Arif. All these Westerners were inspired by these specifically Muslim writers who, in touching upon the human in the realm of the absolute, made a connection to the universal, the permanent.

But let us return to earth and state that development also requires us to move toward a balance of social classes, between provinces of the same country and regions of the globe. There, too, all inclination to favour one class, one category of the population, at the expense of others, provokes conflict and schism. Islam does not propose a socio-economic construct that one can paste on to systems already in vogue. It established the principles of equality, fraternity, solidarity, charity (in the sense of doing good, *ihsan*), and it encourages activities such as commerce, agriculture, the reclaiming of dead land, manual labour, the mastery of the elements (*taskhir*), animal husbandry, and so on. It imposes neither capitalism nor socialism, as we understand these words today. The building of a coherent system also implies choice and effort. The elaboration of an economic and social policy is neither contrary to Islam nor determined automatically by Quranic verses. It is simply there to be done!

Many people the world over are convinced that the difficulty in following development schemes conceived in the West lies in the necessity to explore new paths. This is not only an Islamic reaction. That Islam could point the way towards which all effort might be directed is so much the better if it comes as a response to a universal need. Only this response does not consist in saying that it is enough to return to the Quran. There is still more to be accomplished. Class antagonism, regional imbalance, national egoisms, the conflict between haves and have-nots, between North and South, but also inside the nation are concrete facts. Invoking tradition amounts to the idealisation of an economic system that has not prevented an abyss from being opened and a breach from enlarging between Muslim countries and the West. By what miracle might this tradition become suddenly a source of energy for an accelerated development in all areas?

In the last analysis development implies that man does not live by prayers and bread alone. The dimension of play, the dimension of art are essential in a living society. At their height Islamic societies gave birth to sports, to *belles-lettres* and to art, and sometimes attained an incomparable splendour, to say nothing of the horsemanship which in the popular imagination everywhere is associated with the Arab purebred. Let it also be noted that the English discovered hockey in Muslim India and that its cousin, golf, was known in North Africa under the name *agfa*. In addition the word 'racquet', designating an instrument used in tennis and other hand sports, comes – as the Littré Dictionary tells us – from the Arabic *raha* which means precisely palm of the hand or foot, and arrived in Europe during the Middle Ages through Muslim Spain.

This is not the place to enumerate the literary riches produced in the Islamic world in the Arabic language for the most part but also in Persian and in Urdu; nor to extol the plastic arts for which – because they consider such art sinful – the Islamists, curiously silent, wish to substitute among today's Muslims a world of incommensurable sadness, a world mute and expressionless. And yet what would Islamic civilisation be without the Alhambra of Granada, the Taj Mahal of Agra, the Gardens of Shalimar in Lahore, without Persian miniatures and the Hispano–Mauresque sculpture in stucco, without the Ziryab musicians and singers, the two al-Mawsilis and their teacher, Sujat al-Makki, without the musicology of the philosopher al-Farabi, and without the incomparable encyclopaedia of al-Isfahani whose title is precisely *al-Aghani* (The Songs), and which furnished the best information about Islamic art up to the tenth century?

On this question and many others the lessons of history are quite clear. Artistic flowering has always accompanied the growth of Islamic civilisation. The flowering stopped when Islamic civilisation entered a period of torpor and retreat. If logic seems unconvincing to certain dogmatists, history presents, one may say, some counterexamples. What art have the centuries of apathy given rise to if not the nostalgic expression of a tortured soul? The great twentieth-century Egyptian writer, Taha Hussayn, remarked thirty years ago that the lament which often begins Arab songs – *ya lil, ya 'ayn*: O night, O eye! – takes up the litany of blind beggars who sought to inspire pity in the hearts of believers at the doors of the mosques. What was in fact the art of the great singer Umm Kalthum, who died in February 1974, if not a long repetitive lamentation for a lost or unattainable happiness? The music, the songs, the poetry, and the dance that express a voluntary renewal appear in this century only with liberation movements. And if they founder under the weight of an often naive politicisation, it is because politics dominates, despite its shortcomings, a handicapped society.

Development supposes structures to support it and to assure equilibrium. These structures are economic, industrial, scientific, technological, and social. They are familiar and educational. They pertain to public health, to culture and to politics. Whatever the references for theocratic justification may be, the evidence today is such that there is no cause to wait for a balanced development within a system where humankind is not free, does not voluntarily accept the choice of action to take, and does not profit from the respect due to the physical person, independence of spirit and to his/her own conscience. It is not a question of sweeping away with a word the Western economic model of democracy by calling them imported and therefore unadaptable products. Whatever the model one chooses, the question is to respond to the demands of true development. If the universal principles of Islam can give birth to an original model, why exclude it? But this necessary work is still awaiting, as we have already said, its thinkers to consecrate themselves to the task so as to be able to propose to their coreligionists something other than mummies to worship.

The history of the past fifty years shows that in Muslim countries we can answer the challenges of modern times. Witness the progress realised during this period. On the other hand, the answers offered have not always given the proper value to each factor that must be taken into account: spirituality, rationality, modernisation and humanisation. Modernisation alone (and only in its material aspect) has received pride of place. In the face of crises, temporary setbacks and sometimes failures, certain people have preached rationalisation and others have called for a return to religion. The answers still remain inadequate. More and more the need is felt for global action in which all the citizens of developing countries are called to participate, out of conviction and free association, and for the success of which all sectors of society are invited to apply the fruit of their thinking. This means that within a nation there is democracy to be reinvented and, with respect to the outside, this implies a willingness to participate actively in the progress of the international community. This is the meaning of the development plan adopted in Lagos, in Nigeria, in

April 1980, by the representatives of all the countries of that Africa of which half the population – let us not forget – is Muslim.

Notes

1. See Ahmad Bakir, *Histoire de l'école malekite en Orient*, printed privately in Tunis, 1962, p. 33.
2. See Muhammad Abd al-Salam, in the *UNESCO Newsletter*, August–September 1981, pp. 51–5. All the cited quotations of the physicist were taken from this text.
3. Hishem Djaït, *La Personnalité et le devenir arabo–islamiques* (Paris: Editions du Seuil, 1974).

12.   The Will to Respond

> Ye assembly of Jinns and men! If it be ye can pass beyond the zones of the heavens and the earth, pass ye! Not without authority shall ye be able to pass! Then which of the favours of your Lord will ye deny?
>
> Quran 55:33-4

Muslim society cannot resign itself to living in a state bordering on schizophrenia without running mortal risks. It cannot at the same time impose on social life the requirements of the traditional and submit material development to the demands of the rational. Above all, progress is man's and not that of an 'objective' external world, independent of consciousness. Moreover, history teaches us that whenever social thought took hold, material development in Muslim civilisation followed. It would be beyond the scope of this essay to comment upon causes and effects. It behoves us to say only that the period of a slowdown in development corresponded in that past to one of social immobilism and intellectual stagnation. Muhammad Iqbal wrote:

> Out of a fear of greater disintegration, a fear that was only natural at such a period of political decline, conservative Muslim thinkers concentrated their energies on a single point: the maintaining of a uniform social life for the people and the jealous exclusion of all innovation from the law (*shari'a*) as it was propounded by the first theologians of Islam. The idea that guided them was that of social order and there could be no doubt that they were right in part, because organisation counterbalanced to a certain degree the forces of decadence. But they did not realise, as our modern *ulama* do not realise, that the ultimate destiny of a people depends not so much on organisation but on the value and the capability of individuals.[1]

The analysis of the evolution of societies, of the birth, decline and rebirth of civilisations, shows that there operates here neither determinism nor fatalism, but a mechanism that is animated by challenges and responses to these challenges. Every effective response presupposes solutions adapted both to the original social environment and to the envisioned goal. One does not appear without the other. It is because the modernisers had not taken into consideration the necessity for these two conditions that their methods have produced discrepancies between the 'plan' and the environment it was supposed to create. On the other hand, those who respect the environment as an end in itself condemn their society to stagnation and backwardness. Furthermore, every effective response also presupposes structures in which the solutions adapted or adopted can begin to grow and mature.

It is necessary at this point to add a small correction to Iqbal's statement that 'the vigour of nations does not depend so much on organisation.' If it is true that the power and value of the individual are essential, the environment in which the individual develops is even more so. And Abd al-Salam is quite right to insist on the *conditions* in which the Muslim man or woman of science can work. The same is true for the thinker, the philosopher, the researcher, the politician and the citizen. Al-Ghazali, the sad Muslim thinker of the eleventh century, had already cast doubt on 'the key to certitude'. The use of this key supposes the right to doubt, as the right to doubt supposes the right to differences and the oppositions that flow from it. Only a frank and open debate permits us to measure the weight of the arguments. And only a context that protects liberty offers possibilities for the evolution of ideas, programs and solutions.

From the beginning there has also been a contradiction in the plan of the Islamists. From a religious point of view, the declared goal was to return to a pure Islam that ought to penetrate state and society and be assimilated by the Muslim masses. From a structural point of view, the objective was elitist since to guarantee the purity of this Islam, state and society are placed under the direction of the *ulama*, who above all are the depositories of an encyclopaedic knowledge that allows for a correct interpretation of religion in all its aspects. This *wilayat al-faqih* – rule of the clergy – that Mawdudi foresaw and which Khomeini has seen fit to inscribe in the Iranian constitution blocks definitively all possibility of the intervention of believers in religious affairs. This would no longer be 'the religion assumed' that Ibn Badis evoked but a religion imposed.

The cavilling of the most politicised among the Islamists has changed nothing in this regard. Muslims are asked to become more fervent believers and adhere more solidly to ritual, and yet all initiative is taken away from them, all right to discuss, and, what is more, to doubt, 'the key of certitude'. With an admirable lucidity Iqbal, who died in 1936, had foreseen this evolution. He had declared himself categorically opposed to it in the aforementioned passage of his book in which he commented on the 1906 Iranian Constitution that had already anticipated a 'committee of *ulama* arrogating to itself the power to oversee parliamentary activity'. 'This arrangement is dangerous,' Iqbal wrote. And he went on:

> The *ulama* as representatives of the Imam consider themselves as having the right to oversee every aspect of communal life, although I am not able to understand how, in the absence of an apostolic succession, they can establish their claim to represent the Imam.[2]

The only path that will not end in disaster is for Muslims to readapt their religion to present circumstances. It has often been remarked in the West that entrepreneurial spirit manifests itself more among Protestants than among Catholics. One of the reasons that could explain this difference is the fact that Protestantism has liberated believers from the guardianship of the Church. According to Weber, Protestantism has laid responsibility on the shoulders of believers by calling each Christian to a direct familiarity with the Bible and by transforming each communicant into a pastor. In doing this, Protestantism is applying principles that are already inherent in Islam. The Prophet said, 'You are all shepherds and every shepherd is responsible for his flock.' An authentic tradition has the Prophet say in the presence of 'Umar just before the Prophet's death: 'God's Book will suffice for you.' The man who was to become the second of the Rightly Guided Caliphs therefore did not allow the Prophet to make a religious will.

Only a society that gives man responsibility can lay claim to a kind of life insurance. Mawdudi's argument according to which men are weak and tend to obey their passions more than divine prescriptions is inadmissible when, at the top of the social hierarchy, 'Guardians of the Faith' are installed. For Muslims, divine prescriptions are contained in the Quran. The 'guardians' are only men and no one holds the power of divine right permitting him to decree that the letter, but not the spirit, of the Quran must be respected. Nobody can seriously claim that the doctors of the law ten centuries ago were more intelligent or better equipped to render interpretations that are today forbidden to simple men. The *sine qua non* condition for a true return to the sources that is not at the same time a step backwards is to give each Muslim responsibility. Otherwise, Muslim societies are heading toward a rupture between modernists and traditionalists.

In the West thinkers had already answered Weber's theory by invoking the development of English and French Catholic societies. It was forgotten that these societies were also the birthplace of atheistic, social and economic doctrines that were no less anticlerical. Secularism was born in Europe and a French head of state would be held up to ridicule if he took the oath of office, hand on the Bible, as do American presidents. The choice is simple: either society remains marked by religion thanks to its reappropriation by individuals outside of all canonical context, or society sets out on new, independent paths. Islamists and Muslims in general should give this well-established social phenomenon the attention it rightly deserves.

Is it necessary to point out that in societies where religion is accepted positively by the individual, beginning with the early Islamic society, ethics has a particular importance even greater than that of ritual practices? In 615, when a first group of Muslims was persecuted and sought refuge in Abyssinia, the Quraysh of Mecca sent a delegation to the Negus to ask for the extradition of the fugitives. The speech that their spokesman Ja'afar made was on so high a moral plane that the Negus, as history tells us, openly wept with emotion and rejected the demand for their extradition.

In Muslim countries today, it was not so much the law which compelled the native population to convert but rather the example of their conquerors. One might say the same with respect to Protestant societies in which 'churches' proliferate and vie with each other in a true moral competition. It was an observation of this kind that Ibn Badis made when he distinguished between the Islam of the heart and a hereditary Islam: the former attaches importance to the conformity between a deep faith and daily behaviour, whereas the latter is content with the visible cultural compliance. And it is in the Quran that we find a perfectly clear verse on this subject:

> It is not righteousness that ye turn your faces towards East or West; but it is righteousness to believe in God and the Last Day, and the Angels, and the Book and the Messengers; to spend of your substance out of love for Him, for your kin, for orphans, for the needy, for the wayfarer, for those who ask and for the ransom of slaves; to be steadfast in prayer and practise regular charity; to fulfil the contracts which ye have made; and to be firm and patient in pain (or suffering) and adversity, and throughout all periods of panic. Such are the people of truth, the God-fearing. (2:177)

Since this ethic has been forgotten, since theology has been frozen for centuries, since its vision of the world has been undermined by new knowledge, how can we speak of a renewal of Islam by limiting ourselves only to a rehabilitation of the Law?[3] In general the Islamists answer that the return to the original morality is one of their primary objectives. This is perfectly accurate on the level of professions of faith, but this view only begs the question because, by definition, the Muslim ethic calls man to responsibility for his personal actions. We can decree that at the hour of prayer everyone must come to the mosque. We cannot make a law obliging men to be good if they do not freely subscribe to a morality. The renewal of Islam requires a rebalancing of the constituent elements of religion. On one hand, faith, morality, the world view, and, on the other hand, ritual and the principles of law. Without such a balance which, to my mind and at the risk of repeating myself, passes through a stage of promoting responsibility as a condition of liberty, renewal can only end in a violent clash between conformists and rebels.

Yet a new theology, reconciling science and conscience, and a new ethic can result in a renewal of Islamic values. Every system of values is rooted in a concrete reality and describes a human ideal that assures the continuity and balance of this reality. The values of a society founded on a subsistence economy or agriculture are not – at least not all – those of a complex industrial society. Similarly, moving from a life of dispersion in the environment to a life of organised towns, man has changed systems: the town breathes urbanity; cohabitation and proximity impose their rules. A tribe that, in a climate of permanent insecurity, can survive only by counting on people ready to fight, sabre in hand, makes a value of maleness and virility.

The Arabs have invented a word so charged with meaning that its meaning is almost impossible to translate: *muruwwa*. The word derives from a root that suggests the good and the healthy. It gave birth to the word *mar*: man, and *mar'a*: woman. *Muruwwa* ought to mean then, in this hierarchy of ideas, a healthy and sound humanity, full of goodness. In tribal society it signifies all the virile qualities that are idealised by the nomadic life. One must read the very beautiful pre-Islamic poems – the famous *Mu'allaqat* – to imagine what a life of violence, war, repeated vendettas, fantastic exploits on horseback, endurance, bravura, pride and esprit de corps might have been like, a life also of lovemaking and of pleasure never gained without risk.[4] To seize another's property is never theft during a raid: it is the booty of war. To take the enemy's women is not a kidnapping that requires retaliation but a prize of war that can be compensated for by a ransom. On the other hand, outside the collective raid, such an act becomes a crime that demands reparation, often blood. The honour of the individual is indissoluable from that of the tribe. To lead such a life, man must always be on guard with only his horse, his bounding camel, and his sabre, preferably forged in India, for his companions. How many qualities are necessary, then, to live up to the ideal of one's ancestors?

Without doing away with *muruwwa*, Islam proposes another ideal, that of *birr*, probity, in the sense of the Latin word *pietas*: recognition and fulfilment of all one's duties toward divinity, relatives and the community with love, respect, tenderness, affection, equity, kindness and good-will. This word was not a neologism but it was so little heard by those rude desert riders that many Companions of the Prophet asked what it meant when they encountered it in Quranic verse. Not only was the word susceptible to many definitions, but it experienced the same fate as its Latin counterpart *pietas*: it became synonymous with a living faith and with devotion. Its appearance was logical according to the norms of Islam which proposed that the Arabs substitute for blood ties those of faith and overturn their system of values. The law of the desert, that of the strongest, was thus supplanted by the law of civilisation, that of God. But how should we interpret *birr* in a society of great urban centres, of concrete, of interplanetary voyages and of satellite communications? What ought the values of humanity be when, more and more, everything is played out on the global level? The solid base of a value system is being changed under our very noses despite us.

The Eskimos, who lead a life of total isolation at the North Pole, are reported to have the habit of letting the old, who have become a burden to society, die apart from their fellows. For us, this is a barbaric practice that our system of values condemns. For the Eskimos, youth is a value, because it is the promise of action; age is a non-value because it is a heavy burden. The Muslims, brought up to respect age, react badly when confronted with such practices. They would answer that respect for life must be absolute. Without a doubt! But does this absolute respect for life apply to those who do not share the same faith, those of one's coreligionists who deny their religion? There is the rub, even if arguments are not lacking that may be supported with Quranic verses. It is these arguments that have justified the executions of Baha'is in Iran. These are some precise cases where the value that one can give to a human ideal – the respect for life – may cause a problem and is worth the undivided attention of all Muslims.

The Iranians like to cite verse 32 of the chapter entitled 'The Table' in which there is made mention the crime of 'mischief in the land'. The verse from which the lesson of the murder of Abel by Cain is drawn goes thus:

> On this account: We ordained for the children of Israel that if any one slew a person – unless it be for murder or for spreading mischief in the land – it would be as if he slew the whole people. And if anyone saved a life, it would be as if he saved the life of the whole people.

What does 'mischief in the land' mean in the twentieth century? That is a subject of debate for theologians but also for sociologists, philosophers, jurists and those who rule a state. One cannot avoid the question by contenting oneself with an archaic answer that ignores the concrete context of 'mischief'. Why could this crime not be imputed to those who allow the development of nuclear or biological arms against humankind? What do these new threats of univeral devastation bring by way of modification to the system of human values? Could not the solidarity preached by Islam between coreligionists be extended to all brothers in humanity, especially when the same fate is reserved for everybody? The Iranian regime and all Islamists declare their solidarity with the Palestinians, among whom are counted many Christians, authentic Arabs. Is this a question of Islamic or political solidarity?

When we examine all the values that profess to be moral, we will find that their meaning changes with the transformation of society. I would like to cite only one more before finishing with this point: that of the justice that Islam, all religion and most ideologies are bound to respect. To be just, to live in a just society, represents an ideal to which men everywhere are invited to adhere. But how do we define this ideal, how do we give it a content without reference to everyday life, to the sociopolitical system, to economic relationships, and to the structures that condition everyday experience?

Here we have brought together all the elements of a formidable transformation, desired by some and feared by others. This is a major problem. Whether we approach it from the viewpoint of the requirements of development or from the viewpoint of power, we are obliged to recognise the existence of an organic link between all the gears of this gigantic piece of social machinery. The idea that we have of it can vary. The Islamist program is so far removed from the requirements of life today that it cannot help but encourage rupture and breakdown.

No one can deny that the Islamist movement is political; certainly not any of its advocates who propose to organise the *polis* according to divine ordinance. The complexity of the problems posed has posited diversity within an apparent unity: unity in the will to Islamicise, diversity in methods, doctrines and programs if they exist at all. Violence is the handmaiden of an impatient minority and the disease of the age. The recourse to religion is seen as a panacea. Illusion is perpetuated by the sacralisation of action, the affirmation of identity, the totalism of the religious idea, and so on. Nevertheless, since reformism has not succeeded in giving the appearance that the total program is coherent, then the proposed theocracy can only impel society on a course without any direction or end in sight.

From this perspective, we can only end up with an institutionalised duplication of personality, the rational governing the material aspects and the divine holding sway over the existential aspects. The former will control the actions which apply to matter and the latter will control the relations between men. Every individual in this two-tiered system is called upon, by his own professed absolutism, to believe in two different ways at the same time. It is not possible to shift from one side or to the other. But this program is only an option. There is nothing predetermined about it. Religion, which is first and foremost a vision and a morality, conceals in itself immense possibilities for adaptation to the times and this opens the field to a veritable renaissance.

Can one envisage a world in which Islam can overcome its problems? Nothing survives in isolation. What, then, can Islam still bring to the world and under what conditions? Ought the world fear Islam? What would a totally Islamicised world resemble? These are the questions we need to ask ourselves at the end of the essay.

To the first of these questions, there can only be personal answers. We may note, nevertheless, the incomparable faculty of Islamic adaptation which permitted it to survive sixty years of Soviet communism and, even before, the Crusades and the Mongol hordes. We may note also that the most intransigent Islamists have not succeeded in attracting to their program the attention of the majority of Muslims who remain quite moderate, a moderation that is neither cowardice nor indifference. It is this balance that has kept the majority of Muslims within the Sunnite fold; even, among the Shi'ites, the loyalty of the largest number belongs to the Twelver tradition and not to the other extremist branches. We cannot praise this balance for having saved Islam from past excesses while at the same time we condemn it whenever it is opposed today to adventurism. Finally, we may note the will of statesmen, scientists, scholars and, in general, public personages in proposing answers to the challenges of this new time. Stammering follows hesitation. Many errors have not been avoided and problems pile up. But, as we have seen in the chapter on reformism, from one generation to another, despite the differences of culture and environment, ideas in this respect remain the same, and they are enriched by continual contributions.

These are the ideas that today's actors – political rulers, party leaders, free intellectuals, men and women – are expected to promote. The call to a return to the Quran is heard like a refrain in the work of the reformists. Those who grapple with the difficulties faced by the Muslim world cannot allow the appeal to be stifled, for what does the word 'return' mean since it is evident that the Quran has never been abandoned or forgotten? The word suggests a new departure. It incites us to act as if Muslims had only the Quran at their disposal; as if, should the Holy Book be revealed today, they would be thus called to understand it with the knowledge and the mentality of twentieth-century men and women. Muslims, all Muslims, provided that they know how to read, can have access to the Quran. In Arabic there are editions of the Quran in which all the difficult words are explained and which are published in one volume such as that of Muhammad Farid Wajdi in Cairo in 1957. In other languages there are translations whose value is recognised by the highest religious authorities. No need, when the objective is not specialisation in Quranic matters, to have recourse to the standard books of exegesis, each work of which covers dozens of volumes.

It is against this claim which consists in permitting Muslims individual access to the Quran and to its interpretation without the benefit of traditionalism that the conservatives rise in righteous indignation. Whereas it is in defence of the right to free interpretation that the reformist movement never ceased to call for a 'return' to the Quran.

Is it necessary to recall that this question has been obsessing the minds of Muslims for more than twelve centuries? Scarcely thirty years ago Ahmad Amin, the Egyptian specialist in the cultural history of Islam, cited in the second volume of his *Dhuha al-Islam* the Imam Shafa'i, who evoked – at the end of the second century Hijra – the opposition shown by Muslims of the time to the codification of the Prophetic tradition. Shafa'i said, according to Amin's account:

> Some people declare: You report to us a *hadith* that a man says he learned from another to whom it was transmitted by a third who heard it from a fourth, etc. Now each of these transmitters is under an illusion. We accept only the Book of God, the words of which no one may doubt.[5]

These men acted just like the generations preceding them before the Tradition was elaborated. Their voice had been stifled as was that of the reformists, little by little, for more than a century.

Islam can make a new start, thanks to a return to the Quran that should go hand in hand with an understanding of the text according to the needs of the present century. Curiously, the argument against the supporters of this thesis is found among both Muslim conservatives and the detractors of Islam. What do you do with the *shari'a*? was asked of al-Afghani, Abduh, Ibn Badis, and many others. The Quran states that it is obligatory to cut off the hand of the thief! Certainly, but what is not stated is that a man like 'Umar Ibn al-Khattab, the second caliph, whose thought and deed was so close to that of the Prophet, refused to cut off the hand of thieves during a year of famine. He had adapted his understanding of the Quran to the needs of his time. Closer to us, Mawdudi, whose intransigence is plain to see, supported the candidacy of a woman – what heresy! – for the presidency of the Pakistani republic. Despite the fact that he believed women could not direct the Muslim community, he gave his wholehearted approval in 1964 to Fatima Jinnah in opposition to Marshal Ayub Khan, whom he abhorred. He had adapted his understanding of Islam, however fundamentalist, to the politics of the time.

At every stage of the history of Islam we have sought to enclose Muslims in a tight little box. It is not useless, in conclusion, to recall some previously mentioned facts. The Prophet Muhammad did not compile the Quran. He ordered it to be recorded in written form but did not require it to be recited in a certain order with a beginning and an end. He might even have formally counselled against taking down what he said outside the verses of the Quran.

His companions, after his death, did not write down his words, nor his deeds, in other words the *hadith* and the *sunna*. The first great masters of *fiqh* did not all write books: Abu Hanifa did not codify his philosophy of the law, it was his students who did it; and Ibn Hanbal, who was very attached to the Prophetic tradition, wrote a book of *hadith* but refused to give his point of view when he could not refer himself directly to the acts of the Prophet. At the end of his life the reformist Shaykh Abduh gave courses in exegesis but his pupil Rashid Rida wrote them down. Clearly, all these masters, like the Prophet, wished to teach, not to put a yoke around the Muslim's neck.

A return to the Quran and the adaptation of its precepts to the needs of the times could help to show that 'Islam is valid for all time and all places;' it could allow for a return to the essentials: faith and morality.

It is there that Islam, with its universalist vision, its morality, its permanent appeal to human intelligence, can give today a meaning to Muslim actions. This is quite distinct from the call to violence and to the defence of tradition.

Is there any reason why the actions of a liberated Muslim ought to frighten the world? Let us be straightforward about this: the day Islam causes fear will be the day that the religion is finished. Islam would then not be what it is. It would be the religion of barbarians, of those *deaf* (in spirit), *mute* (in heart), *blind* (to light), *incapable of understanding*, whom the Quran denounces. It would no longer be the religion of *samaha*, of the magnanimity and generosity of the soul, but a program for domination by violence, steel and blood. That could only mean that between Averroes and Khalkhali, between the religious philosopher whom the Spanish still honour and the hanging judge of Teheran who no longer remembers how many he has condemned to death, Muslims would choose the second.

An Islam which, after the Arabs in the midst of whom it first appeared, won by its spirituality and its *samaha* the hearts of the Persians, the Berbers, the Turks of Central Asia, the Hindu, the Malays, the blacks of Africa and America, the Slavs, the Mongols, the inhabitants of the Balkans, and which still attracts today Europeans, Americans and Africans – this Islam has a meaning. It is universal precisely because these men have never understood it to mean either women wrapped in veils or the bloody hand cut from the wrist of the miscreant, but, as the Quran says: 'The face of your Lord in His majesty and in His munificence'.

Notes

1. Muhammad Iqbal, *Reconstruire la pensée réligieuse de l'Islam* (Paris: Editions Adrien-Maisonneuve, 1955), p. 164.
2. *Ibid.*, p. 189.
3. In fact the study of ethics in the Islamic world was not abandoned quickly. Muhammad Arkoun, professor at the University of Paris VIII, has devoted a

number of studies to this question. He has called the attention of at least those who read French to the works of Miskawaih, al-Amari, Tawhidi, and Mawardi, and especially to the links between ethics and the works of Muslim thinkers, whether they be philosophers, theologians, or historians. Avicenna, al-Ghazali, Ibn Rushd, and Ibn Khaldun had treated ethics widely in their works. But this was still the 'age of enlightenment', even if it came at the end of the Islamic Golden Age. See Muhammad Arkoun, *Traité d'éthique de Miskawayh*, French translation (Paris: Editions Damas, 1969), and *Essais sur la pensée islamique* (Paris: Editions G. P. Maisonneuve et Larose, 1977).

4. See the French translation by Jacques Berque, *Les dix grandes odes arabes de l'anté-Islam* (Paris: Editions Sindbad, 1979).

5. See *Dhuha al-Islam*, vol. 2., p. 241, which cites vol. 7 of *Kitab al-Umm* by the Imam Shafa'i.

Index

Abbas, caliph, 52
Abbasids, 52, 55, 65, 85, 86, 115
Abdallah, Muhammad, 68
Abduh, Shaykh Muhammad, 69, 74, 98-104, 105, 108, 109, 111, 112, 136, 137
Abu Bakr, caliph, 50-2, 65
al-Afghani, Jamal al-Din, 69, 95, 97, 98-104, 105, 108, 109, 110, 111, 112, 136
Afghanistan, x, 8, 9, 17, 18, 27, 28
Aga Khan, 26, 64
Ahmad I, bey, 97
Aisha, 52
al-Aqsa Mosque, 40
al-Arif, Ibn, 125
al-Assad, Hafiz, 2, 17, 73
al-Attar, Issam, 17
al-Azhar university, 14, 16, 63, 66, 72, 74, 98, 99, 102
al-Azraq, Ibn, 65
Alawites, 9, 27, 52, 53, 118
Albania, 88
Aleppo, killings in, 2
Algeria, 1, 4, 9, 19, 26, 30, 31, 52, 92, 97, 103-6
Ali, caliph, 10, 51-3, 59, 63, 64, 115
Ali, Mir Sayyid, 39
Ali, Muhammad, 71, 97
Ali, Qasim, 39
'alim, position of, 116
anti-Americanism, 27
Amin, Qasim, 69, 112
amr, 78
Arab culture, 72, 95, 104, 114, 122, 125
Arab League, 8
Arafat, Yassir, 1
al-Arif, Ibn, 125
Armenians, 87
Arslan, Shakib, 102, 109
asala, concept of, 21, 93, 106

Assiut, uprising in, 4
Association of Ulama (Algeria), 31
Association of Young Muslims (Tunisia), 31
Ataturk, Mustafa Kemal, 14, 86, 88, 93, 105, 109, 110, 111
Attar, Farid al-Din, 38, 125
ayatollah, position of, 63

Babi movement, 97, 101
Baha'is, 97; execution of, in Iran, 133
Bahrain, 4, 8, 17
al-Banna, Hassan, 14, 63, 80, 103, 116
Baraq Khan, 90
al-Barudi, Sami, 97
Al-Basa'ir journal, 103
Bayanuni, Muhammad, 17
Baybars, sultan, 86
Béjart, Maurice, ix
Bennabi, Malek, 69
Bin Ashur, Shaykh Tahar, 74
birr, concept of, 133
Bitrugi (Al Petragius), 39
Black Muslims, 8, 71, 114
Bouhajib, Salim, 103
Bourguiba, Habib, 23, 26, 40, 66, 93, 109-10, 112
British empire, 98, 99
brotherhoods in Islam, 91
Bukhari, Muhammad, 59, 63, 75
Bulgaria, 87

caliphate, 14, 53, 77, 102; disestablishment of, 86; suppression of, 105
Camp David Accords, 16
Canada, 8
Catholic church, 109, 121
charity, 59
Chelbi, Hind, 23
China, 8, 28, 31; Muslims in, 28-9

Indonesia, 8, 31, 91-3
industrialisation, 18, 89; in Iran, 13
inheritance, 113
Iqbal, Muhammad, 56, 116, 117, 118, 130
Iran, ix, x, 3, 8, 12, 17, 26, 28, 35, 37, 53,
    56, 63, 72, 73, 79, 82, 90, 133-4
Iran-Iraq war, 12
Iraq, 26, 27, 35, 37, 53, 72-3, 81
al-Isfahani, 126
Islah movement, 95
Islam: and socialism, 26; hierarchies in, 61
Islamic Council, 10
Islamic Declaration of the Rights of Man,
    11, 32
Islamic Liberation Party (Egypt), 15
Islamic Republican Party (IRP) (Iran), 82
Islamic Revolutionary Movement (Syria),
    17
Islamic Revolutionary Movement of the
    Arabian Peninsula, 3
Ismail, imam, 64
Ismailis, 26, 32, 64, 118
Israel, 14, 15, 16, 17, 25, 30, 37
istihsan, concept of, 57

Ja'afar, of Mecca, 131
Jabriyya group, 67
Jahmiyya group, 67
al-Jawziyya, Ibn Qayim, 56
jihad, 6, 35-7, 55, 91, 105, 118
Jihad group, 15
Jinnah, Fatima, 136
Jordan, 16, 18, 27
Jumbaz, Hisham, 17
Justice Party (Turkey), 89
al-Juwaini, 63

Kalthum, Umm, 127
Kashfi, Hussain, 97
al-Kazim, Musa, 54
Kemal, Mustafa, *see* Ataturk
Kenya, 8
Khadija, 122
Khalil, Shaykh, 74
Khalkhali, judge, 137
Khan, Ahmad, 97
Khan, Ayub, 136
Kharijites, 27, 32, 34, 41-2, 52, 54-5, 64,
    78, 114, 118
al-Kharqi, 74
Khomeini, Ayatollah Ruhollah
    Moussavi, xi, 3, 9, 10, 13, 27, 64, 75,
    87, 120, 130
khuluq, concept of, 47
al-Khuwarizmi, 38
al-Kinda, 122
Kissinger, Henry, 15

Kravetz, Marc, 34
Kurds, 73, 81, 87
Kuwait, 76

Laroui, Abdallah, 125
law, Islamic, ix, 26, 82
Lebanon, 16
lex talionis, 29, 58-9
Liberia, 8
Libya, 1, 31, 68; union with Tunisia, 30

al-Madani, Tawfiq, 104
Madarasah Mir Arab, 90
madhhab, era of, 55
Maitatsine, al-Hadj Maroua, 4
al-Majid, Abd, 85
al-Makki, Sujat, 126
Mali, 108, 111
Malik Ibn Anas, 57, 63, 69, 114, 123
Mamluks, 86
al-Ma'mun, caliph, 52, 66, 67
al-Mandjara, Mahdi, 124
marabout, 63
Marjani, Shihab al-Din, 96
Marxism, 15, 17, 19, 24, 89, 108, 111
Masakom, 92
Masjumi movement (Sumatra), 93
Mauritania, 26, 29
Mawdudi, Abu Ala, xi, 9, 75, 76-9, 103,
    111, 116, 120, 130, 131, 136
Mecca, 2-3, 5, 6, 7, 9, 44, 48, 49, 50;
    pilgrimage to, 91, 113
medical students, 20
Medina, 5, 6, 47-8, 51, 52, 53, 57, 64, 114,
    117, 122
Menderes, Adnan, 89
al-Mirghani, Shaykh, 96
modernisation, 127
Moneiminaati, Wali, 39
monotheism, 5
Monteil, Vincent, 114
morality, concepts of, 47
Moro insurgency, 8
Morocco, 3-4, 66
Movement of Islamic Tendencies (MIT)
    (Tunisia), 4, 80
Mu'allaqat poems, 133
muaddib, position of, 62
Mu'awiya, caliph, 64
mudarris, position of, 62
mufti, position of, 62, 65, 66
Muhammad VI Wahid al-Din, 85
Muhammad Youth (Syria), 16
Muhammad, Elijah, 71
Muhammad, Prophet, 2, 5, 6, 48, 50, 51,
    75, 117, 120, 122, 136
Muhammadiyyah association, 92-3

muhtasib, 62, 65
Mujahidin (Syria), 16, 17
Mujahidin-i Khalq, 31, 81
mujtahid, position of, 63
al-Mukhtafi, Muhammad al-Mahdi, 63
mullah, position of, 63
Al-Muntaqid journal, 103
Muridiyya brotherhood, 18, 31
muruwwa, concept of, 132-3
Muslim Brethren, 2, 9, 14-15, 16, 18, 27, 63, 65, 69, 73, 79, 80, 86, 103, 105
Mustafa, Shukri Ahmad, 15
al-Mutawakkal, caliph, 68
Mu'tazilites, 67, 68
muwahhidun, 52

Nahda movement, 56, 95
Nahdhatul-Ulama (NU), 92
al-Naifar, Shaykh Muhammad Salah, 31
Najjar, Muhammad, 102
Nakhli, Muhammad, 101, 103
Al-Naqd al-Dhati, 106
Naqshabandiyya, 91
Nasser, Abdel Gamal, 14, 15, 27, 30, 75, 111
National Salvation Party (Turkey), 89
National Union of Popular Forces (Morocco), 106
nationalism, 72, 89, 92
Niger, 111
Nigeria, 4, 8
Nizari sect, 65

Obaidallah, caliph, 54
oil crisis, 13
Oman, 27, 31, 52
Operation Peace for Galilee, 37
al-Oqbi, Shaykh Tayeb, 104
Oqla, Adnan, 17
Organisation of Islamic States, 8
al-Otaiba, Juhaiman, 3
Ottoman empire, 7, 72, 85, 86, 97, 101

Pahlavi, Muhammad Reza, 1
Pakistan, 8, 19, 26, 31, 72-3, 76
Palestine, 14, 16
Palestine Liberation Organisation (PLO), 1
Palestinians, 134
Pan-Arabism, 107, 111
panjasila, 92
Pasha, Nuqrashi, 14
Phalange of Muhammad (Syria), 16
Philippines, x, 8, 18, 72, 108
pilgrimage to Mecca, 44, 49, 113
polygamy, 30, 109
prayer, 48; preparation for, 48

proletarianisation, 89
protestantism, 131

Qabadu, Shaykh Mahmud, 97, 103
Qadhdhafi, Mu'ammar, 9, 15, 24, 26, 27, 108-9, 112, 114
qadi, position of, 62, 65
al-Qadir, Amir Abd, 68, 97
Qadiriyya, brotherhood, 91
al-Qahtani, Muhammad Ibn Abdallah, 2
al-Qarawiyyin university, 63
Qarmathians, 42, 65, 118
Qassim, Colonel, 27
Qum, university of, 74
Quraish tribe, 5
Quran, 6, 10, 29, 33, 34, 45, 46, 50, 53, 55, 58-60, 62, 64, 74, 77-9, 88, 90, 96, 101, 110, 112-13, 118, 121, 126, 132, 135, 136
al-Qutb, Sayyid, xi, 14, 16, 75, 79-80, 111, 116, 120

Raja'i, Masa'ud, 81, 82, 84
Ramadan, 23, 35, 44, 48, 75; fasting at, 87, 91, 110
Ramadhan, Said, 15
al-Razzaq, Ali Abd, 102
Republican People's Party (RPP) (Turkey), 89
repudiation, 109
revolution, 71
Rida, Muhammad Rashid, 52, 74, 101, 102, 103, 137
Rohan, Michael, 40
al-Rumi, Jamal al-Din, 38, 125

Saadeddine, Adnan, 17
Sabri, Ali, 14
Sadat, Anwar, 4, 14, 15, 17, 24, 26, 30, 35, 66, 111
al-Sadiq, Ja'afar, 64
Sadr, Bani, 82, 84
Sahara, Western, 12
Salafist doctrine, 102-3, 106
al-Salam, Muhammad Abd, 20, 38, 39, 40, 117, 123-4, 130
salat, 48
Salim I, sultan, 86
al-Samad, Abd, 39
al-Sanussi, Muhammad, 68, 96
Sanussis, 68
Sarekat Islam (Indonesia), 92
Sarton, George, 38
Saudi Arabia, 12, 17, 26, 27, 31
Sauvageot, Claude, 28
SAVAK, 1, 82, 83
SAVAM, 82, 83

science, 123, 130; relation of Islam to, 104
secret societies in Islam, 89
secularism, 85-93
Seljuks, 55
Senegal, 18, 30, 31, 111
Seveners, 64
shafa'a, concept of, 46
Shafa'i, Imam, 54, 57
Shafa'ites, 74, 115
Shah of Iran, 13, 81
shahada, concept of, 45, 48
Al-Sharia (The Law), 15
shari'a, 6, 49, 54, 58, 66, 79, 83, 84, 93, 103, 105, 107, 108, 114, 116, 117, 129, 136
shaykh al-Islam, position of, 62, 98, 117
Shi'ism, 8, 32, 41, 54-5, 63, 64
Shi'ites, 10, 17, 26, 52, 53, 78, 90, 115, 118, 135
Shibad journal, 103
Shidyaq, Ahmad Faris, 97
al-Sibai, Mustafa, 16
slavery, 60
socialism, 27, 30, 31, 42, 111, 121; and Islam, 26, 115
Socialist Union of Popular Forces (Morocco), 106
stoning, 26
Sudan, 9, 68
Sufi brotherhoods, 87
Sufyan, Mu'awiya Ibn Abi, 51-2
Sukarno, Ahmad, 91-3
sultanate, 85-6; abolition of, 85, 86
sunna, 6, 10, 34, 50, 53, 54; Qadhdhafi's rejection of, 108
Sunnism, 41, 54-7, 63
Sunnites, 9, 10, 17, 64, 68, 73, 78, 83, 86, 90, 114, 135
Syria, 1, 2, 3, 9, 16-17, 23, 27, 28, 30, 65, 73, 81
Syrian Islamic Front, 17

Tabari, Abu Ja'afar, 54
Tabataba'i, Ali, 97
Tabrizi, 39
Tahawi, 74
Takfir wa Hijra (Egypt), 6, 9, 15, 20
Talamsani, Shaykh Umar, 15, 16
Taleghani, Ayatollah, 81
Tall, al-Hajj 'Umar, 68
Tamerlane, 7, 83
taqlid, concept of, 84, 96, 100, 104
Tariq, Ahmad, 15
Tebessi, Shaykh, 105
The Islamic Point of View, 76
theocracy, democratic, 77, 79
Tijan, Ahmad, 96

Tijaniyya brotherhood, 18, 31
Tijaniyya, al-Hadj Umar, 18
Tirmidhi, Abu Isa, 54, 63
Toynbee, Arnold, 21
traditionalism, 91, 115
traditionism, 53
Tudeh party (Iran), 27
Tunisia, ix, 4, 9, 13-14, 17, 19, 20, 22-3, 26, 30, 31, 35, 53, 56, 64, 65, 68, 76, 92, 93, 97, 109-11, 117, 118; union with Libya, 30
Turkey, 8, 23, 30, 85
Tusi, Nasir al-Din, 38, 39
Twelvers, 63, 118, 135

Uhud, battle of, 78
ulama, 27, 42, 56, 57, 79, 92, 96, 97, 99, 101, 103, 105, 115, 116, 117, 130; conservatism of, 68; power of, 61-70
'Umar, al-Hadj, 96
'Umar, caliph, 37, 60
Umayyads, 52, 78
umma, 6, 28, 71, 72, 86, 109
Union of Religious Associations, 14
Union of Soviet Socialist Republics (USSR), 7, 8, 17, 27, 28, 30, 32, 90-1, 107
United Arab Republic, 73
United Kingdom (UK), 14, 66, 68, 85, 97
United Nations (UN), 121
United States of America (USA), 1, 8, 30
Al Urwa al-Wuthqa journal, 98, 100
Usul-i Jadid movement (Russia), 96
'Uthman, caliph, 37, 50-2
'Uthman Codex, 50

Vanguard of the Phalange of Muhammad (Syria), 17
veil, 125; abolition of, 110; wearing of, 40
violence, use of, 82, 134

al-Wahhab, Muhammad Ibn Abd, 56, 95-6, 101
Wahhabism, 3, 9, 10, 27, 32, 68, 69, 97
Wajdi, Muhammad Farid, 136
Waliullah, Shaykh, 95-7
Weber, Max, 131
White Revolution, Iran, 13
wilayat al-faqih, concept of, 130
Women's Day, in Tunisia, 110
women: emancipation of, 29, 30, 40, 69, 111; in Libya, 108; position of, under Islam, 19, 23, 104, 107, 113, 121-2, 136

Yemen, 27, 64; North, 1; South, 30
Yugoslavia, 8